Iowa

A Bicentennial History

Joseph Frazier Wall

W. W. Norton & Company, Inc.
New York

American Association for State and Local History
Nashville

Author and publishers make grateful acknowledgment to the following for permission to quote from their materials: Holt, Rinehart and Winston for lines from Robert Frost's poem ''The Gift Outright,'' from *The Poetry of Robert Frost,* edited by Edward Connery Lathem. Copyright 1942 by Robert Frost. Copyright © 1969 by Holt, Rinehart and Winston. Copyright © 1970 by Lesley Frost Ballantine.

Paul Engle for two lines from his poem ''To the Iowa Dead.''

Edmund G. Kelley for excerpts from *Civil War Experiences: The Journal of William H. Kelley 1864–1865.*

Grinnell College Library for quotes from Truman O. Douglass's unpublished manuscript ''Builders of a Commonwealth.''

Published and distributed by
W. W. Norton & Company, Inc.
500 Fifth Avenue
New York, New York 10036

Library of Congress Cataloging in Publication Data

Wall, Joseph Frazier.
Iowa: a Bicentennial history.

(The States and the Nation series)
Bibliography: p.
Includes index.
1. Iowa—History. I. Title. II. Series.
F621.W17   977.7   77–17546
ISBN 0–393–05671–6

Printed in the United States of America
3 4 5 6 7 8 9 0

For
my four Iowa grandparents,
who taught me to love the land

Contents

Illustrations

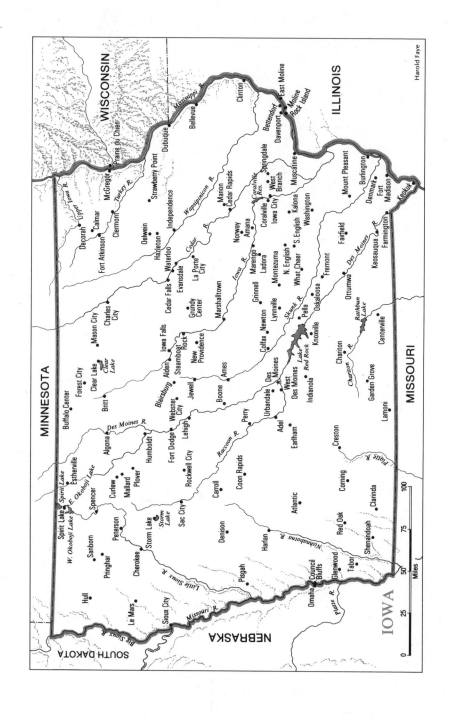

Invitation to the Reader

IN 1807, former President John Adams argued that a complete history of the American Revolution could not be written until the history of change in each state was known, because the principles of the Revolution were as various as the states that went through it. Two hundred years after the Declaration of Independence, the American nation has spread over a continent and beyond. The states have grown in number from thirteen to fifty. And democratic principles have been interpreted differently in every one of them.

We therefore invite you to consider that the history of your state may have more to do with the bicentennial review of the American Revolution than does the story of Bunker Hill or Valley Forge. The Revolution has continued as Americans extended liberty and democracy over a vast territory. John Adams was right: the states are part of that story, and the story is incomplete without an account of their diversity.

The Declaration of Independence stressed life, liberty, and the pursuit of happiness; accordingly, it shattered the notion of holding new territories in the subordinate status of colonies. The Northwest Ordinance of 1787 set forth a procedure for new states to enter the Union on an equal footing with the old. The Federal Constitution shortly confirmed this novel means of building a nation out of equal states. The step-by-step process through which territories have achieved self-government and national representation is among the most important of the Founding Fathers' legacies.

The method of state-making reconciled the ancient conflict between liberty and empire, resulting in what Thomas Jefferson called an empire for liberty. The system has worked and remains unaltered, despite enormous changes that have taken place in the nation. The country's extent and variety now surpass anything the patriots of '76 could likely have imagined. The United States has changed from an agrarian republic into a highly industrial and urban democracy, from a fledgling nation into a major world power. As Oliver Wendell Holmes remarked in 1920, the creators of the nation could not have seen completely how it and its constitution and its states would develop. Any meaningful review in the bicentennial era must consider what the country has become, as well as what it was.

The new nation of equal states took as its motto *E Pluribus Unum*—"out of many, one." But just as many peoples have become Americans without complete loss of ethnic and cultural identities, so have the states retained differences of character. Some have been superficial, expressed in stereotyped images—big, boastful Texas, "sophisticated" New York, "hillbilly" Arkansas. Other differences have been more real, sometimes instructively, sometimes amusingly; democracy has embraced Huey Long's Louisiana, bilingual New Mexico, unicameral Nebraska, and a Texas that once taxed fortunetellers and spawned politicians called "Woodpecker Republicans" and "Skunk Democrats." Some differences have been profound, as when South Carolina secessionists led other states out of the Union in opposition to abolitionists in Massachusetts and Ohio. The result was a bitter Civil War.

The Revolution's first shots may have sounded in Lexington and Concord; but fights over what democracy should mean and who should have independence have erupted from Pennsylvania's Gettysburg to the "Bleeding Kansas" of John Brown, from the Alamo in Texas to the Indian battles at Montana's Little Bighorn. Utah Mormons have known the strain of isolation; Hawaiians at Pearl Harbor, the terror of attack; Georgians during Sherman's march, the sadness of defeat and devastation. Each state's experience differs instructively; each adds understanding to the whole.

The purpose of this series of books is to make that kind of understanding accessible, in a way that will last in value far beyond the bicentennial fireworks. The series offers a volume on every state, plus the District of Columbia—fifty-one, in all.

Each book contains, besides the text, a view of the state through eyes other than the author's—a "photographer's essay," in which a skilled photographer presents his own personal perceptions of the state's contemporary flavor.

We have asked authors not for comprehensive chronicles, nor for research monographs or new data for scholars. Bibliographies and footnotes are minimal. We have asked each author for a summing up—interpretive, sensitive, thoughtful, individual, even personal—of what seems significant about his or her state's history. What distinguishes it? What has mattered about it, to its own people and to the rest of the nation? What has it come to now?

To interpret the states in all their variety, we have sought a variety of backgrounds in authors themselves and have encouraged variety in the approaches they take. They have in common only these things: historical knowledge, writing skill, and strong personal feelings about a particular state. Each has wide latitude for the use of the short space. And if each succeeds, it will be by offering you, in your capacity as a *citizen* of a state *and* of a nation, stimulating insights to test against your own.

James Morton Smith
General Editor

ACKNOWLEDGMENTS

Each author in the series has faced the same basic problem, how best to fashion a story of a particular state and its people so that it will fit into a Procrustean bed of little more than two hundred pages. Each of us will be criticized for what has been included, and even more for what has been omitted. In writing this, my own personal interpretation of Iowa as one state within our nation, I have been aided immensely by many people: Peter Harstad and Edward Purcell of the State Historical Society of Iowa; Gerald George and his editorial staff of the American Association for State and Local History; Robert Dykstra of the University of Iowa; Keach Johnson of Drake University; my Grinnell College colleagues Alan Jones, Jonathan Andelson, and Christopher McKee, along with the Burling Library staff. Above all, I must acknowledge my indebtedness to the dean of the historians of Iowa, Leland Sage, my good mentor and friend, who has given me a real appreciation for Iowa's history. All of these, and many others, have done their best to keep me from straying into error. For those aberrant meanderings that in spite of their efforts are still apparent, I accept full responsibility, for I alone held the road map.

Iowa—A Personal Perspective

$\mathcal{R}$ OBERT FROST, in reading his poem "The Gift Outright" at John F. Kennedy's inauguration, told Americans that "The land was ours before we were the land's . . . . Possessing what we were still unpossessed by," and that only in surrendering ourselves to "our land of living" could we find salvation.[1] I have found in these much quoted lines the central theme for the story of one of the states of the nation. What follows is an account of how a people took possession of a particular piece of land and how those people became possessed by the land they claimed as their own. By tilling the soil, laying out towns, building churches and schools, by fighting on the battlefield and in the political arena to have and to hold, and by enhancing the land with story, song, and art, they were to surrender themselves to the land.

This theme could serve for every volume in this series. Yet within each state, the people have fashioned their own individual story of possessing and being possessed. Political boundaries, no matter how illogically or arbitrarily drawn, quickly fix social and political attitudes and determine a culture. Within the limits imposed by surveyors, treaty makers, and politicians, a people develops a society adapted to and reflective of the partic-

---

1. Robert Frost, "The Gift Outright," from *The Poetry of Robert Frost,* edited by Edward Connery Lathem (New York: Holt, Rinehart and Winston, 1969), p. 348.

ular piece of geography which is contained within those boundaries. Maine cannot be confused with New Hampshire, nor Iowa with Missouri.

The history of any state must, then, begin with the land itself. For Iowa, the land serves as more than an introduction. It is the major story line. Of the fifty-six thousand square miles contained within the state's boundaries, ninety-eight percent is under cultivation, the largest percentage of any state in the nation. Of Iowa's thirty-six million acres, twenty-six million are rated Grade A, one-quarter of all the premium land in the nation. The rich land was here, only men and machines were needed to turn it into a garden. It was the fertility of the soil that bedazzled every visitor, from the first riverman who crossed the Mississippi on a makeshift raft to Nikita Khrushchev, who flew in by jet from the steppes of Russia to see for himself this corn granary of the world. It was the black soil that brought the people into the territory and distributed them evenly across the broad valley that is Iowa. Agriculture has always been the omniculture of the state. It has been the leveler and homogenizer of our society. No great cities were to be built here, the land was too valuable for agricultural production to be wasted in sprawling metropolitan complexes. What we have done with the land has been our one real source of pride. Yet, paradoxically, the very success of Iowa's agriculture has given rise to a deprecating embarrassment on the part of those Iowans who felt that their state was socially deprived, a curious anachronism in America's twentieth-century, urban-oriented culture. Iowans would grow weary of hearing about "the little old lady from Dubuque," and "the country hick from Iowa who bought the Brooklyn bridge." They still patiently have to explain to New Yorkers and Bostonians that the correct pronunciation of their state is "Iowa," not "Ohio" or "Idaho."

Writing an article on Iowa for H. L. Mencken's sophisticatedly slick *American Mercury* in 1926, one of Iowa's finest novelists, Ruth Suckow, described her native state as being in the center of the big region called the Middle West.

It combines the qualities of half a dozen States; and perhaps that is the reason why it so often seems, and more to its own people

than to others, the most undistinguished place in the world. . . .
All these diffusing elements, however, are smoothed down with a
touch of gentleness into that lovely, open pastoral quality which is
peculiarly Iowan after all. . . . Iowa is proud—fairly proud—of its
land and corn and hogs. But like an old farmer—or rather, like a
timid farmer wife—it has taken for granted that other things are
really above it. . . . Thus has grown up a timid, fidgety, hesitant
state of mind. Iowa has never had the rampant boosterism of
Kansas and Minnesota. . . . It has always been far too deprecating
and self-doubting for that. . . . Of all the meek states, Iowa, which
is on the fence geographically, politically, religiously and
aesthetically, has been the meekest. A trifle more of even Babbitt
bumptiousness would have helped it long ago. It was far too deeply
imbued with a reverence for Puritan culture to attempt even a
youthful swagger. . . . Almost the only claim of Iowa among these
United States (aside from a little pride in the matter of corn and
hogs) has been for the place of the lowest. But yielding itself thus,
not only submissively but with ardor to the charge of provincialism,
it lost colonialism, by far the more insidious disease of the two.[2]

With poetic license Suckow somewhat overstated her case,
but there is considerable validity in all half-truths, and her de-
scription of Iowa is more than half true, not only for then but
for fifty years later. In the two-hundredth year of the nation's independence and in the one-hundred-thirtieth year of its own
statehood, Iowa was still peculiarly in the middle, still seeking
to assert its own identity, still hoping there may be virtue in the
average. Part of that middleness, to be sure, is simply an ines-
capable geographical fact of location. Iowa is the middle
ground, a Mesopotamia lying between the two great rivers that
drain the continent, bisected by the 42nd parallel, John Dos Pas-
sos's latitudinal line of middleness, the line that was roughly
followed by the first transcontinental railroad and then later by
the transcontinental highway, so that for over a hundred years
the constantly moving Americans have had to cross Iowa from
New York and Chicago to San Francisco. Partly that middleness
in the accident of history, of drawing boundary lines and of
carving the land up into the family-sized farms, so that today of
the fifty states in the Union, Iowa ranks twenty-fifth in area,

2. Ruth Suckow, "Iowa," *The American Mercury,* 9 (1926): 39, 40, 42.

twenty-fifth in population. It meets perfectly the Supreme Court's standard of political units conforming to the one-person–one-vote principle, the only state whose U.S. senatorial representation could not be questioned by any equal-representation test. Iowa occupies the middle ground partly out of desire, having an almost instinctive fear and distrust of the extreme, whether in politics, economics, or in social structure. Among fifty states, Iowa ranks twenty-sixth in personal income, and in politics, historically, Iowa's Republicanism has been moderately liberal, its Democracy, moderately conservative. It has no real center where the elite of either power, wealth, or culture may congregate. Iowa, in short, is middle America. Some, including many Iowans, as Suckow indicates, would call that the dull average. Others, who have now become increasingly more assertive in an America that is dominated by the extremism of California and Texas, would prefer to call it the blessed golden mean.

In attempting to tell the story of Iowa, I have used both a chronological and a topical approach. As will be apparent, the first part of this book is essentially arranged in chronological order: the opening of the land to white settlers and the dispersal of American Indians; the establishment of a government; the arrival of the people, with their hopes and ideals; and the great civil conflict in the mid-nineteenth century, in which Iowa fought for free land and open river to the Gulf of Mexico. If an inordinate amount of space seems to be given to the Civil War period, it is because this writer believes that that war with its consequences has remained the single most determinative factor in Iowa's history, politically, socially, and economically. The first six chapters, then, are concerned with the acts of possessing and holding the land, told in a time-order sequence.

The remaining four chapters deal with how the possessors became possessed by the land. Here a topical approach seemed more appropriate, for we gave ourselves to the land in many ways, as farmers, merchants, and manufacturers; as teachers and preachers; as politicians and artists. Each activity has its own time order and pattern, and needs to be considered separately in the telling of the story of the "gift outright."

Iowa

1

Iowa—The Land Unpossessed

*T*HE formal cession of the land to the United States took place on 2 May 1803, in far-distant Paris, when Napoleon signed over to Jefferson's emissaries the 828,000 square miles of the North American continent known as Louisiana. It was a vast empire, greater than that which Napoleon had won by battle on the continent of Europe. It was also a nearly empty and largely unexplored empire, stretching from the delta of the great river that emptied into the Gulf of Mexico to the far side of the Continental Divide, where the wide Missouri is but a small trickle of mountain snow and glacial ice—a half-billion acres of land. All of this the Corsican conqueror, with his eyes fixed on those maddeningly close but still untouchable white cliffs of Dover, waved away with imperial disdain but with a peasant's greed for fifteen million dollars.

His minister, the ever smiling Talleyrand, congratulated the astounded Americans Monroe and Livingston, who had come begging for a city, New Orleans, and found themselves the possessors of a new world. "You've made a noble bargain for yourselves," the French minister told President Jefferson's emissaries. So they had. Still they were nervous, and with good cause, for it was a dubious transaction at best. Napoleon had yet to claim formal possession of the land from Spain, and in selling what was not yet his, he was violating his own nation's constitution and the treaty with Spain. The Americans, in accepting, were quite likely—they thought—exceeding the limits of the United States Constitution, and most certainly they were exceeding their instructions in promising four times more in francs than they had any reason to expect Congress would furnish.

But the emperor had been impatient; Washington, D.C., was five weeks away; there was no time for consultation. If the deed was to be done, it was imperative that it be done quickly. So "the gift outright" was accepted. Let the strict constructionist Jefferson wrestle with his constitutional scruples, let the subservient Congress dare to refuse the purchase of a half-billion acres of land and the mighty Mississippi for four cents an acre. James Monroe and Robert Livingston fixed their signatures to the treaty and shook Talleyrand's hand. The land was ours, but it was "still unstoried, artless, unenhanced," [1] still unpossessed.

In the very heart of this vast new empire called Louisiana, bordered by the two great rivers of the continent, lay fifty-six thousand square miles of prairie grass, a new Mesopotamia, a middle earth, which was yet without a name. It was but a faceless, featureless part of the uncharted whole, unknown and as yet unwanted by the Ohio farmer and the Kentucky planter who sought the Mississippi River as an exit for their products, not as an entrance to new land that would compete with their own.

This nameless grassland between the Mississippi and the Missouri had been occupied first by various nomadic tribes of the Paleo-Indian period perhaps as long ago as 12,000 years. They had come to this middle land to hunt the large game animals, the mammoth and the bison, which roamed the area. They were succeeded by nomadic hunters of the archaic period of 8,500 years ago, who in turn gave way to the Woodland Indians. These inhabitants may have possessed the land for as long as four millennia before they vanished into mystery without ever becoming a part of the history of their descendants, if indeed the later Indian invaders into the grasslands were their descendants. These people, as evidence of their existence, left behind their dead, ornamented with shell necklaces and equipped with

---

1. Frost, "The Gift Outright," p. 348.

weapons to defend their spirits against whatever perils the next world might offer, covered over by mounds of earth shaped like the bear, the lizard, or the bird. They had possessed the land and had been possessed by it, but they had left no wills, named no beneficiaries. Their lands were inherited not by the living, but by the dead. Their meeting places turned to grass where the animals they had called sacred were to roam undisturbed over the very effigies that had been sculptured to honor them. Even the words by which these first settlers called themselves and their lands were lost with them. Today their cultures bear alien Anglo-Saxon names—Hopewell, Woodland, Glenwood, and Mill Creek—names given to them by archaeologists who dug into their graves more than a thousand years later.[2]

On 17 June 1673 a French explorer, Louis Jolliet, accompanied by five voyageurs and a Jesuit priest, Jacques Marquette, came down the Wisconsin River to the point where it joins the Mississippi; the men looked across the broad expanse of water to the high bluffs of the western bank, but they could not have discerned from their canoes the monumental evidences of this ancient culture, for heavy woodlands hid the mounds and effigies that crowned those river hills. These first Europeans of historical record to view the new Mesopotamia saw a land apparently as virginal and empty of man as it had been at the time of creation. Only after eight more days of travel down the Mississippi, on 25 June, near the mouth of a river that was to give these grasslands their name, did the French explorers see evidence that the land had inhabitants. Noting footprints in the soft mud of the riverbank, they went ashore and followed the trail until they came to a village of a people whose family name the visitors gallicized into "Peoria." This was a small avant-garde of a great tribe living across the river to the east, called the Illini.

The Peorias were fascinated by these first white visitors to their grasslands and entertained them with song and dance and food, and would have allowed them to stay all summer if they

2. *Educational Series 1-7,* published by the Office of the State Archaeologist, Iowa City, Iowa, 1976.

had wished, for food was abundant and the Indians' curiosity was great. But the bearded leader and his black-skirted friend were eager to push on, for they sought the mouth of this great river, not the grasslands that bordered it. Had they stayed and gone up the river, which they heard the Indians call Ayuvois (Iuwa), they would have found no gold, no northwest passage to the Orient, and very few other inhabitants. These grasslands were nearly empty of people. The Indian attitude toward this open middle land was not unlike that of many twentieth-century Americans who would regard Iowa as synonymous with the dullness of the mean, not far enough east for culture, not far enough west for grandeur. For the Indians of the woodlands and lakes to the east, there were not enough trees and water to attract them; for the Indians of the west, the grass was too high and not coarse enough to attract the great herds of grazing buffalo that sustained their culture. Except for some poor cousins of the western Sioux and a few outpost villages of the Illini along the rivers of the eastern grasslands, the area had been left to the grass and sky, to the small animals and birds, and to the graves of the mound builders who had worshiped them.

The Louisiana Purchase signaled the end of this emptiness. Now that the Mississippi and the vast, still unwanted lands to the west were ours, the forever land-hungry farmers of the east turned their thoughts and their Conestoga wagons to the west, past Ohio and Indiana, into the woodlands and prairies of Wisconsin and Illinois. No threat now of Spanish or French reprisals against those who would press too closely to the Mississippi border. Only the Woodland Indians—the Winnebagoes, the Sauk, and the Mesquakie, whom the French called Reynards, or Foxes, were there to block their way. And the white man had seldom let either Indian settlement or solemn treaty agreement deter him from his inexorable push west.

The Indians were driven ahead of the advancing farmers with the same efficient dispatch shown by the Indians when they drove the fish of their streams into reed weirs. Down the Wisconsin, Rock, and Illinois rivers the Indians were pushed, to the Mississippi and the lands to the west.

Now the grasslands between the two great rivers had people at last—unwilling inhabitants who wept over their lost rivers, forests, and lakes—prodded into the open prairies by the soldier's musket and the farmer's shotgun. The hostile Sioux to the west had acquired neighbors whom they did not want, the Sauk and the Fox, Indians of an alien culture who would build villages along their rivers and kill their advance scouts.

The white man's answer to these intertribal Indian hostilities, which were of little concern to him, was to divide the grasslands: the southern half to be forever for the Sauk and the Fox, the northern half for the Sioux and the Chippewas. In February 1826 this division was designated by a diagonal line, drawn across the grasslands by government commissioners. To this division, the assembled Indian chiefs gave their assent and made their marks on the treaty paper at Prairie du Chien, Wisconsin Territory.

Article 1 of this treaty read, "There shall be a firm and perpetual peace between Sioux and Chippewas; between the Sioux and the confederated tribes of Sacs and Foxes; and between the Ioways and the Sioux." [3] This pronouncement was read to the assembled Indians with all the awful solemnity and finality of a Moses presenting the Commandments of God to the assembled Israelites. But the Indians knew that there was even less magic in the white man's paper than there was in the Indian's calumet. Shaky black marks painstakingly drawn on white parchment might seem powerful medicine to these commissioners, but they meant less to the Indian chiefs than the harsh reality of the white man's rifle. The treaty had said nothing about peace between the Indian and the white man. The latter would be ready, as he always had been, to bring on war in the name of peace.

Four years later, after many border skirmishes of the Sioux and their allies against the Sauk and the Fox, the commissioners again assembled the tribal leaders in Prairie du Chien. If a single invisible line across the grasslands, unmarked by a fence post or border stone and existing only on the white man's map,

---

3. George E. Fay, *Treaties and Land Cessions*, 25 vols. (Greeley: University of Northern Colorado Press, 1971), 24: 24.

would not be recognized by the Indians, then a wider mark on another map, cutting a swath twenty miles wide on each side of the old diagonal line would, perhaps, be more effective.

This treaty of 1830, on which the representatives of the Sioux, the Sauk, and the Fox made their marks with the goose quill, was part of the general Indian policy of that doughty old Indian fighter Andrew Jackson, who now sat enthroned in Washington as the Great White Father. Drive all the eastern Indians west, across the Mississippi into the grasslands and high plains, leaving the lakes, forests, and prairies of trans-Appalachia to the ever moving, restless farmer. Let the Mississippi be the perpetual boundary between two cultures that were irreconcilable. Surely there was enough land on either side of the river to satisfy both peoples.

Neither side was, in fact, to be satisfied for very long. Jackson's crystal ball of prognostication was as cloudy as Jefferson's had been in 1783 when he had hailed the Paris Peace Treaty, ceding to the United States all territory of the Old Northwest, as providing enough land for white Americans for a thousand generations. Jefferson's three millennia had been nearly consumed in forty years. Jackson's perpetual boundary was to last less than two.

It was the Indians who made the first move, as people in desperate straits are prone to do, no matter what the odds. The proud Sauk peoples of Illinois were not reconciled to giving up their lands and their great, hundred-lodge village of Saukenuk, the largest Indian village in the west, located at the juncture of the Rock River with the Mississippi, where the rivers teemed with fish and the flat lands grew good ears of corn and round, sweet melons. Saukenuk, the capital and pantheon of the Sauk nation, could not be given away by a simple mark on a piece of the white man's paper.

Those Sauks and their Fox allies who would not easily give up their homes and ancestral graves had an old leader to turn to in their moment of anger and despair. Chief Black Hawk, having fought in 1812 alongside the Shawnee Chief Tecumseh and the British at the battles of Frenchtown and Fort Meigs, had lived on through middle age waiting for the Great Spirit to send another leader with a prophet to drive back the white devils who kept coming across the mountains closer to his people's lands. Now in his sixty-fifth year, Black Hawk was still ready to fight rather than surrender his lands and capital to the white invaders. He was not impressed by all those pieces of paper that the white men held, going back in time to the Treaty of 1804, which the white men claimed gave them the right to take the lands of the Sauk and the Fox whenever they wished. Indian delegates, made drunk with white man's whiskey, could not, by a simple X mark, give up that which did not belong to them, but belonged to the Great Spirit who watched over them. Black Hawk, backed by his old companions who had fought with him as allies of the British nearly twenty years before, announced that in spite of the treaty of 1830, he and his people would return to Saukenuk in the early spring. The squaws would plant their fields, and the men would fish and hunt and tend the graves of their ancestors as they had done each spring since the Great Spirit had made them stewards of this land.

Black Hawk was old and still cherished the ancient hopes that had died with Tecumseh and his mystic brother the Prophet. The young men of his nation could see the present and the future as it was and would be, not as it should have been. They turned to a young leader, Keokuk, who counseled caution and collaboration with the white men across the river. After all, the land given them along the Iowa River was good land. The corn grew as well here as it did in the fields of Saukenuk. Only by accepting the inevitable could the Sauk and the Fox expect the white men to send soldiers to help them hold their present lands against the Sioux and the Chippewas.

So Black Hawk crossed the Mississippi in the spring of 1831 with but a part of his people—and those mainly women who wanted to return to their old lodges and till familiar soil again. They found the white settlers already moved in, and the army was there too, under the command of General Edmund P. Gaines. There were enough troops to drive Black Hawk and his band back across the Mississippi. Keokuk came over to Saukenuk to persuade Black Hawk's followers that resistance was useless. His conciliatory talk carried the day. The young chief persuaded Gaines to call one more meeting to reason with Black Hawk and his intransigent British Band, so-called because it

consisted largely of veterans, like Black Hawk, of the War of
1812. On 30 June 1831, Keokuk and Black Hawk, with their re-
spective followers, met with Gaines and his troops at the council house on Rock Island. Gaines again went over the old familiar ground, the treaties which had ceded all of Illinois to the
white men. Then Gaines's aide, Lieutenant George McCall,
read the prepared Articles of Agreement and Capitulation. By
the terms of this new treaty, Black Hawk and his supporters
were to recognize Keokuk's leadership of the Sauk nation, were
to move out of Illinois forever, and were to abandon any further
communication with the British in Canada. In return, the United
States would guarantee forever the Sauk and Fox lands west of
the Mississippi, and in addition, although not a formal part of
the treaty, Gaines would recognize the existence of the squaws'
cornfields already planted and would give to Black Hawk and
his women, corn from the army's stores equal to what the
squaws could have expected to reap had they stayed for the fall
harvest. Because of this codicil, given orally, the agreement of
1831 has been known in history as the Corn Treaty.

The reading being completed and the promise given, Gaines
began to call the names of the Indians present, for them to come
forward to make their mark. First came the name of Quash-
quame, Black Hawk's old ally and friend, then—the dramatic
moment—the name of Black Hawk himself. The old warrior
arose slowly, all the pain and humiliation of lost hopes written
in his face. He came forward to the table, grabbed the goose-
quill pen, and fiercely drew his X on the hated paper. "With a
force which rendered that pen forever unfit for further use . . .
I touched the goose-quill pen to this treaty, and was determined
to live in peace," Black Hawk would later write in his autobiography.[4]

The old chief returned to the new lands across the river, acknowledged the leadership of the young Chief Keokuk, and
looked forward only to a sad peace and an early death. But
dreams die hard, and old associates would not let him rest in

---

4. Quoted in William T. Hagan, *The Sac and Fox Indians,* (Norman: University of
Oklahoma Press, 1958), p. 133.

peace. One of the few young men who supported Black Hawk's old dream was a Sauk brave named Neapope. While Black Hawk was in Rock Island signing the Corn Treaty, Neapope was up in Canada talking with the British. He returned to say that the British would come down from Canada to help if Black Hawk would rally his people and take to the warpath again. More than that, Neapope brought the exciting news that to the Winnebagoes of the north the Great Spirit had given a new Prophet, a Prophet who looked to Black Hawk for leadership as the man of destiny. Neapope's siren call would have moved a far more stoical Ulysses than was Black Hawk to steer toward destruction. The old man aroused himself from the torpor of defeat and began to make new plans.

History has, at least, given a certain kind of dignity to the old warrior's last mad venture by calling it the Black Hawk War. It was not a war; it was a pathetic final act of defiance against reality. Nevertheless, it was to be of major consequence for all the Indians of the Middle West and for the grasslands that lay between the two great rivers.

Crossing the Mississippi a few miles below the old village of Saukenuk during the first week in April 1832, Black Hawk and his band headed north to follow the Rock River up to the Prophet's village in Illinois, where he expected to be joined by the Winnebagoes. From there, the plan was to follow the Rock River to its source in Wisconsin Territory, then to join forces with the British. There they would make their stand against the expected attack of the United States Army, drive it back, and reclaim all the lands of Illinois and Wisconsin for the triumphant Indians. General Henry Atkinson, commander of American troops in the western district, upon receiving word of Black Hawk's move into Illinois, at once called up the militia to pursue the old chief up the Rock River. It soon became clear that the British were not coming, indeed never had any intention of coming. Neapope had fantasized a wish into a promise. The Winnebagoes quickly retreated into a neutrality that would soon become open aid to the American army.

What followed was a long chase after Black Hawk through northern Illinois and southern Wisconsin Territory, during which neither the American militia nor the pursued Indians distinguished themselves with glory. Brief skirmishes, in which the militiamen were occasionally routed in panic, marked Black Hawk's slow movement north to a rendezvous with allies who never materialized. By the time Black Hawk's band reached Wisconsin, it was clear even to the old chief that the impossible dream was now finished. In a last desperate effort to escape the trap, Black Hawk swung his small, diminishing company westward, hoping to reach and cross the Mississippi, but at the mouth of the appropriately named Bad Axe River north of Prairie du Chien, the war came to its inevitable conclusion. The trap was closed. Black Hawk's hiding place was revealed by the faithless Winnebagoes, and he was sent in irons down the Mississippi to Jefferson Barracks in St. Louis, Missouri.

All the Indians of the region were to pay a price for Black Hawk's last venture. General Winfield Scott, representing the Great White Father, met with representatives of the Sauk and Fox at Fort Armstrong in Rock Island on 21 September 1832, and the terms were dictated. Keokuk was treated as summarily as if he had been the enemy rather than the great counselor of peace and conciliation. The Sauk and Fox were to give up their newly acquired lands along the Iowa and were to move farther west into the grasslands. In return for the eastern segment of the grasslands that only two years before had been given in perpetuity to the Indians, the American government would make thirty annual payments of $20,000 and assume existing Indian debts to the white traders of $40,000. The door had at last been opened. The camel had not only his nose but his front quarters inside the tent.

The equivocating Winnebagoes were not to fare any better. The white men now wanted their lands in Wisconsin Territory, and some Indian expert in Washington had the brilliant idea of moving the Winnebagoes out of the Wisconsin lands into the neutral zone in the grasslands, which divided the land of the Sioux from the now diminished lands of the Sauk and Fox to the south. Thus a new factor was introduced into the troubled area to make the once undisturbed and empty grasslands more populated and more bloody. Scorned by the Sauk, who blamed them

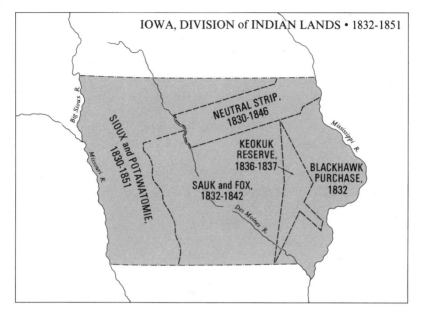

IOWA, DIVISION of INDIAN LANDS • 1832-1851

NEUTRAL STRIP, 1830-1846

KEOKUK RESERVE, 1836-1837

BLACKHAWK PURCHASE, 1832

SAUK and FOX, 1832-1842

SIOUX and POTAWATOMIE, 1830-1851

Big Sioux R.

Missouri R.

Mississippi R.

Des Moines R.

for encouraging and then betraying Black Hawk, and hated by the Sioux, who regarded them as yet another invader of the Sioux hunting grounds, the Winnebagoes were to be attacked from both sides. It was to protect these hapless middle men that the American government built Fort Atkinson for the protection of the Indian, on a high plateau overlooking the beautiful valley of the Turkey River.

No sooner had the terms of capitulation been announced than the familiar migration of the white farmers began again, and now, for the first time, they were to cross the upper Mississippi into the open grasslands that were called Scott's—or more popularly and ironically, Black Hawk's—Purchase. Three years later when a young army lieutenant, Albert M. Lea, led a small company of the First United States Dragoons into this newly acquired territory, he found over ten thousand white people already living there, a number which he generously inflated to "about sixteen thousand; . . . and there is every indication of a vast accession during the year 1836. Indeed large portions of the

States of Ohio, Indiana, Illinois, Kentucky, and Missouri seem
to be about to emigrate to this region.'' Lea was not surprised at
this rapid settlement, for he found the land to be ''one of great
beauty. It may be represented as one grand rolling prairie, along
one side of which flows the mightiest river in the world, and
through which numerous navigable streams pursue their devious
way towards the ocean. . . . Taking this District all in all, for
convenience of navigation, water, fuel, and timber; for richness
of soil; for beauty of appearance; and for pleasantness of climate, it surpasses any portion of the United States with which I
am acquainted.'' [5] Lea, upon returning East, wrote a little book
which he called *Notes on the Wisconsin Territory; Particularly
with Reference to the Iowa District.*

Lea had not only provided future immigrants with a useful
handbook of information, but he had given to the grasslands a
name—Iowa. Neither the Indians nor the later Iowa white
settlers could ever agree on the original meaning of the word;
some said it was a Sioux word meaning ''dusty face''; others
claimed it meant ''drowsy ones'' or ''he who paints pictures.''
But to the incoming white settlers, as well as to Lea, Iowa
meant ''here is the place'' or ''the beautiful land.'' Too beautiful certainly to allow the Indians to keep. Stories spread back
East of this new land called Iowa where the black soil went
down two feet, five feet—perhaps to the center of the earth.
Who could tell? The white men with their families poured into
Scott's Purchase and looked on to the West and wanted more.

No sooner had Fort Atkinson been built in the Neutral
Ground to protect the Winnebagoes from the Sauk and the
Sioux than the concerned Indian agent in the territory was writing to the commander of the troops at the fort to send troops immediately to drive out the whites who were invading the neutral
territory.[6] The white troops were as ineffectual as Black
Hawk in stopping the tide. Lea's prediction of growth within the
decade would prove to be too modest. New treaties, new forced

5. Albert M. Lea, *Notes on the Wisconsin Territory,* (Philadelphia: H. S. Tanner,
1836), pp. 14, 11–12.

6. Letter from D. Lowry, U. S. Indian Agent to Capt. E. V. Sumner, Fort Atkinson,
Iowa Territory, 22 July 1842, on display in the museum at Fort Atkinson, Iowa.

concessions in 1836, 1837, 1842, and 1846, and the last claims of the Sauk and the Fox to the land were purchased. By 1851 even the far northwest corner, still held by the Sioux, had to be abandoned. Less than twenty years after Black Hawk had set out on his last venture to drive the white devils out of Illinois and Wisconsin, the Indian story in Iowa was all but over. The Indians left behind only names on the land, of the chiefs Black Hawk and Keokuk, Decorah and Appanoose, and of the all but forgotten tribes—Winnebago, Pottawatomie, Sioux, Sauk, and, of course, the Ioways. Old names on the newly surveyed maps. That was all.

The land was now ours, but we were not yet the land's, "possessing what we were still unpossessed by." [7] That possession perhaps would come later, but in the meantime there were crops to plant, towns to plat, births, weddings and funerals to attend to. New graves to join those ancient mounds, shaped like the bear, the bird, and the lizard. The grasslands had become Iowa, the terra incognita had moved out of legend into the white man's geography and history books.

7. Frost, "The Gift Outright," p. 348.

2

We Occupy the Land
and Organize It

$\mathcal{D}$URING the one hundred and sixty years that elapsed between the day Jolliet and his black-robed companion followed the footprints along a riverbank to the camp of the Peorias and the sad moment when the young Keokuk had been forced by the folly of his elders and the land hunger of the white man to yield up the beautiful Iowa River valley, few whites had ventured into that broad expanse of grasslands between the two great rivers of the North American continent.

There was no flare of fireworks in these grasslands in 1776 to celebrate the Anglo-Americans' bold declaration of independence from their English monarch, nor was there any knowledge that the grasslands would soon have new and more covetous neighbors across the river. Philadelphia was still as remote as Paris or Madrid, and the prairie wilderness did not recognize any master except nature. The Indians may possibly have sold lead from their valuable mines on the high western bluffs of the great river to the white warriors, lead which may have found its way impartially into both the British redcoats and Continental blue coats. There may even be some basis of truth to the legend that a Frenchman, Jean Marie Cardinal, temporarily residing near the lead mines, tried to warn the Spanish in St. Louis that "the redcoats were coming" by paddling down the Mississippi in his canoe in the spring of 1780, but if so, existing documents do not support this attempt to give Iowa a place in the American Revolution. The inhabitants of the grasslands in 1776 could still afford to be indifferent to white men's distant quarrels.

In 1803 the long millennia of benign neglect for Iowa country were over. As soon as President Jefferson had overcome his constitutional scruples and had accepted the noble bargain for "the gift outright" that it was, he was eager to find out just what he had purchased. His personal secretary, Meriwether Lewis, and an army officer, William Clark, were commissioned to explore this vast territory. Lewis and Clark with twenty-three soldiers, three interpreters, and a slave, left St. Charles, Missouri, in the spring of 1804, heading up the Missouri River, noting, as they passed, the bluffs and the high prairie grass that lay beyond on their right as they pushed up the broad river to the north. On a promontory near the junction of the Missouri with a small river as yet without a name, they buried young Sergeant Charles Floyd, who had died of a ruptured appendix. This casualty, the only one suffered by the expedition in its 5,000-mile round trip, gave the area its first marked grave of a white man.

While Lewis and Clark were still pursuing the source of the meandering Missouri, Jefferson with the insatiable curiosity of the scientist mixed with the avidity of the newly titled landowner, arranged to have the upper Mississippi River explored to its source. General James Wilkinson, military governor of Louisiana, consequently commissioned Lieutenant Zebulon Pike to push up the great river to discover if its source lay within American territory. The Anglo-Americans were beginning to close in on both sides of the grasslands.

Pike, with a company of twenty men, laboriously poling and pulling his keelboat up the river, reached the mouth of the Des Moines River on 20 August 1805. From there on upstream, Pike found the land to be nearly as wild and devoid of human settlement as had Jolliet and Marquette 130 years earlier. Only on the river itself did Pike note the beginnings of a traffic that would bring an end to the isolation of the grasslands. He passed many pirogues of Indians, navigating with ease the tricky, shifting channel of the river. Some of the Indians attempted, in passing, to barter with the American soldiers, offering fish or venison for whiskey, but most kept their distance, and Pike noted with no little pleasure:

> It is surprizing what a dread the Indians, in this quarter, have of the Americans: I have often seen them go around islands, to avoid meeting my boat. It appears to me evident, that the traders have taken great pains, to impress upon the minds of the savages, the idea of our being a very vindictive, ferocious, and warlike people. This impression was perhaps made with no good intention; but . . . instead of operating in an injurious manner, it will have the effect to make them reverence at the same time they fear us." [1]

In the years that lay ahead the Indians might lose some of their reverence but none of their initial fear of these intruders from the east.

Pike also met a surprisingly large number of white traders, American and French, coming down the river to St. Louis. The river was becoming a major highway, but not until Pike reached Catfish Creek, some 398 miles north of St. Louis and over two hundred miles above the mouth of the Des Moines River, did he find the first and only white settlement on the west side of the Mississippi. This was the home of Julien Dubuque, the energetic and charming little French trapper who had come to this region from his native Quebec soon after the American Revolution to make his fortune.

Attracted to the lead mines which lay on both sides of the river, Dubuque, whom the Indians called Little Night, soon charmed his native hosts—by a happy combination of ingratiating pleasantries and simple tricks of legerdemain—into granting him the sole right to mine the area. In an agreement signed at Prairie du Chien on 22 September 1788, the Fox Indians accorded to Dubuque a permit "to work at the mine as long as he shall please, and . . . moreover, that they sell and abandon to him, all the coast and the contents of the mine discovered by the wife of Peosta (a Fox brave), so that no white man or Indian

1. Donald Jackson, ed., *The Journals of Zebulon Montgomery Pike*, 2 vols. (Norman: University of Oklahoma Press, 1966) 1:22.

shall make any pretensions to it without the consent of Sieur Julien Dubuque." [2]

It was an extraordinary concession on the part of the Indians, but Dubuque, knowing well the white man's disregard for Indian agreements, was not satisfied. He sought and finally obtained from the Spanish governor of Louisiana, Baron de Corondolet, legal possession of what Dubuque grandiloquently and with quite purposeful flattery named the "Mines of Spain." When all of Louisiana Territory passed to the Americans in 1803, Dubuque found it necessary to obtain still another grant from a new governing power. Entering into a partnership with the wealthiest and most powerful man in St. Louis, Auguste Chouteau, Dubuque was in the process of pressing his claims to the lead mines with the American government when Pike paid his visit to Dubuque on 1 September 1805. Although the little Frenchman warmly greeted the young American lieutenant with a field-gun salute, he was markedly reluctant to take Pike to see the mines, which, he said, were some six miles away, and unfortunately he had no horses available. Pike, who was under instructions to find out all he could about the operations and legal status of the famed mines, then posed several questions to Dubuque, who quite suddenly lost his usual volubility:

> What is the date of your grant of the mines from the savages?
> Answer: The copy of the grant is in Mr. Soulard's office in St. Louis.
> What is the date of the confirmation by the Spaniards?
> Answer: The same as to query first.
> What is the extent of the mines?
> Answer: Twenty-eight or twenty-seven leagues long, and from one to three broad. [3]

So it went. Pike left Dubuque's settlement at four o'clock in the afternoon, blessed with the miner's smiles and good wishes but not overburdened with any information about the mines.

2. Thomas Auge, "The Life and Times of Julien Dubuque," *Palimpsest* 57 (1976): 3.

3. Jackson, *The Journals of Pike,* 1: 19–20, 234.

For the next three years, Dubuque's mining camp remained the only white man's settlement in what is now Iowa. Dubuque continued to mine lead and ship it down the river to St. Louis, and largely through the efforts of his silent but powerful partner, Chouteau, his claims to the Mines of Spain were duly recognized in 1806 by the American Board of Commissioners meeting in St. Louis.

In 1808, the American army moved into Iowa country to build a fort to establish its control over the upper trans-Mississippi region. Dubuque at last had white neighbors west of the river, albeit some two hundred miles away. Leading an expedition of four keelboats laden with troops, First Lieutenant Alpha Kingsley was under instructions from the Secretary of War to build this first fort at the mouth of the Des Moines River, but Kingsley feared that the flat delta land would be flooded each spring. He pushed northward, past the Des Moines Rapids in the Mississippi until he came to a spot he liked. "The situation is high," he wrote to the Secretary of War in defense of his decision to violate instructions, "commands an extensive view of the river and adjacent country—also an excellent spring of water, and I believe there is no place on the river which will prove more healthy, and none more advantageous to the Indian trade." [4] The site may have appealed to Kingsley's esthetic and hygienic concerns, but any seasoned army officer could have told him that his choice was a poor one. Fort Madison, named for the newly elected President of the United States, provided an excellent view of the river, but unfortunately behind it lay a high ridge that held a commanding view of the fort. In case of a concerted attack, it could never be defended. Neither Kingsley nor his successor, Thomas Hamilton, could ever be sure when the Indians might move in force against it.

The full attack finally came in the summer of 1813, in the midst of Mr. Madison's ill-advised war to obtain Canada from the British. The attack came at the lowest moment for American fortunes in that war, with the western forts of Mackinac, Dear-

---

4. Quoted in Donald Jackson, "Old Fort Madison—1808–1813," *Palimpsest* 47 (1966): 13.

born, and Detroit already fallen to the British and their Indian allies. Far from gaining Canada, the United States was in danger of losing all of the Great Lakes and the upper Mississippi Valley region to the British. With the staggering loss of these key forts, no one in Madison's beleaguered government could give much thought to the plight of the insignificant little fort in the far-distant Iowa district. On 15 July 1813, the Indians attacked Fort Madison. Failing to take the fort by surprise, a party of Winnebagoes and Sauks lay siege. Commander Thomas Hamilton could now fully appreciate the folly of Kingsley's choice of a site. He wrote in despair to his commanding colonel at Fort Belle Fontaine near St. Louis that the besiegers encamped on the ridge behind the fort

. . . can actually . . . arrange for the execution of any plan they choose without being discovered. Of course they can come down upon us like a flash of lightening—to be ready to meet which, we are harnessed up day and night. . . . If I do not hear from you by the 20th of August and the Indians continue to harass me in the manner they appear determined to do, . . . I will take the responsibility on myself, that is if they will permit me to go away.[5]

The Indians continued to harass him, and no word came to the besieged Hamilton from his superiors in Missouri Territory. Sticking it out a few weeks beyond his proposed deadline, Hamilton finally took the responsibility on himself to abandon Fort Madison. Creeping out of the fort on hands and knees in the dead of night sometime in mid-September 1813—the exact date of evacuation is unknown—the garrison troops successfully reached the boats on the river. The last soldiers to leave the fort set fire to the buildings and stockade; then the boats moved quietly down the stream toward St. Louis and safety.

The grasslands returned briefly to their primeval isolation. They were once again free of white settlements, for Julien Dubuque had died three years prior to the abandonment of Fort Madison, and the Indians returned to work the mines that they had given up to him, and to send the crudely formed pigs of lead across the river to their tribesmen in Illinois. When the Ital-

5. Jackson, "Old Fort Madison," p. 60.

ian adventurer and first tourist to the region Giacomo Beltrami
visited in 1823, only the wooden mausoleum, which the Indians
had built to house the body of their beloved Little Night, gave
evidence that for twenty-five years a white man had lived in that
area and had mined its land. In 1832, at the time of the Black
Hawk Purchase, it is doubtful if fifty white people lived across
the Mississippi in the entire Iowa region, and most of those few
settlers who had dared to come lived in that area lying between
the Des Moines and Mississippi rivers, reserved for half-breeds
at the request of the Indians in 1824.

The Black Hawk Purchase took from the Sauk and Fox a
stretch of trans-Mississippi land fifty miles wide, extending
from the neutral zone line on the north to the Missouri boundary
on the south. News of this treaty quickly spread among the
farmers and adventurers of Illinois and the states to the east. It
was particularly noted that this Purchase included the mines of
Dubuque. Oklahoma has celebrated in its nickname the Sooners, those pioneers so eager for new lands that they beat the sig-
nal gun opening the land to white settlers. The Sooner phenomenon was not peculiar to Oklahoma. There were hundreds of
Iowa country Sooners who could not wait until 1 June 1833, the
date given to the Sauks and Foxes to remove themselves from
the lands ceded by the Purchase treaty.

Iowa country was now open for white man's business and
was rapidly being possessed by miners, farmers, shopkeepers,
craftsmen, and ferryboat men. But it as yet had no government.
This was dramatically demonstrated in the late spring of 1834
when an Irish immigrant miner named Patrick O'Connor without provocation shot and killed his cabin mate, George O'Keaf.
The enraged citizens of Dubuque hastily convened a court to try
O'Connor, who readily admitted the shooting, but rested his
defense on the simple statement, "Ye have no laws in this
country, and ye cannot try me." The jury decided otherwise
and, after a short deliberation, found him guilty and sentenced
him to death. The few friends that O'Connor had in the community, including a Catholic priest from Galena, Illinois, appealed
to the governor of Missouri and to President Andrew Jackson,
but both denied that they had any jurisdiction over the matter.
On 20 June 1834, the miserable O'Connor, who had had to

learn the hard way that on the American frontier justice could be a hastily improvised affair, was carted by wagon to a high mound in the mining camp and was hanged by the neck until dead.[6] Iowa country had had its first execution, and eight days later Congress, moving with remarkable speed, placed the area under the laws of the United States. The Iowa district was annexed to the Territory of Michigan and was divided into two counties, Du Buque and De Moines, courthouses were to be established in the towns of Dubuque and Burlington to register land claims, try civil and criminal cases, and to enforce the federal territorial laws of Michigan.

Iowa district at last had a government, but it was at best a tenuous and inchoate affair. The territorial capital was some six hundred miles away. It was as easy to communicate with the Capital in Washington as it was with the territorial governor in Detroit. Moreover, Michigan was at that moment attempting to set its boundaries and to prepare itself for statehood. Detroit had no time for, nor interest in, this remote Iowa district that had been so hastily and gratuitously given to it by Congress.

Two years later Congress created the Territory of Wisconsin, which was to include all of the Northwest Territory north of the state of Missouri and west of Lake Michigan to the juncture of the Missouri and White Earth rivers. Iowa district and Michigan parted company with mutual relief and no regrets; Michigan gained the statehood it sought, and Iowa found itself no longer on the remote fringes of territorial jurisdiction, but in the very center of the newly created Wisconsin Territory. Until a new capital for the territory could be built in Madison, the temporary capital of the territory was moved from Belmont, Wisconsin, to Burlington, Iowa, much to the anger and consternation of Dubuque, which, as the largest and richest town in the whole territory, regarded itself as the true center.

President Jackson appointed Henry Dodge of Mineral Point, Wisconsin, to be the governor of this new territory. It was an excellent choice, for Colonel Dodge was well known and respected throughout the region. He had played a conspicuous

---

6. Eliphalet Price, "The Trial and Execution of Patrick O'Conner," [sic], *Annals of Iowa,* 1st Series, 3 (1865): 569.

role in all of the military activities of the upper Mississippi Valley from the War of 1812 until the defeat of Black Hawk in 1832. In 1834 Jackson had selected him as colonel of the United States Dragoons, and Dodge had led his troops to the Red River Valley and the Rocky Mountains of Colorado. He quickly proved himself as able a civilian administrator as he had been a military commander.

Dodge, however, was not an Iowan, the name of the territory was Wisconsin not Iowa, and its capital would soon be relocated permanently east of the Mississippi at the City of the Four Lakes in the center of the Wisconsin district. Iowa and the entire trans-Mississippi area for which Iowa regarded itself the champion, would once again be on the periphery of government and power. It was time for Iowa district to push for its own territorial status. Henry Dodge had hardly settled himself in his temporary lodgings in a Burlington hotel when he was confronted with a convention of delegates from the newly created seven southern counties of Iowa district and the county of Du Buque, asking for territorial status. Resolutions to that effect were sent to the territorial legislature and to Congress.

Neither Dodge nor the territorial legislature opposed this secessionist move. Dodge wanted only to return to the beauty of his Wisconsin lakes and forests. "I have Had Office Enough to Satisfy one man," he wrote to George Wallace Jones, Wisconsin's territorial delegate to Congress, and he proposed that Jones be appointed governor of the new Territory of Iowa.[7]

Jones, who was in complete agreement with Dodge's suggestion, worked zealously for the Iowa Territorial bill in Congress. He pushed hard to get the bill reported out of committee in both houses, and he lobbied assiduously among his many friends in both chambers. Legend has it that it was he who sent a young woman, well known to many congressmen of that day for her beauty and charm, to the Senate antechamber on the day that the Senate began debate on the Iowa bill. She sent a note by a page to the Senate floor, requesting to speak to Senator John Cal-

7. Letter published in William J. Peterson, "Henry Dodge," *Palimpsest,* 19 (1938): 45–46.

houn, a known opponent of the bill. The gallant Carolinian responded to the call and thus being absent from the floor during the Senate's brief debate, was not able to raise his powerful voice in opposition to a bill creating out of the public domain still another free territory.

In the House, the Southern opposition to the creation of Iowa Territory was not so easily silenced. Representative Waddy Thompson from Calhoun's own state did not absent himself from the debate but vigorously led the forces against passage of the bill. He attempted to tie Iowa's territorial status with the annexation of Texas, which the Senate had blocked. No Texas, no Iowa, was his flat ultimatum. He was joined in his opposition by Representatives Samson Mason of Ohio and Charles Shepard of North Carolina, both objecting to the haste with which Congress was moving to disperse the population of the country to the far frontiers when people were badly needed in the East and South to develop industries and promote agriculture. Mason and Shepard were futilely bucking the irresistible tide of Manifest Destiny. The House, with only minor amendments, passed the Senate bill by a vote of 118 to 51. On 12 June 1838, President Van Buren signed the organic territorial act, creating the Territory of Iowa effective as of the Fourth of July, 1838.[8]

The news reached the people of Iowa on 30 June, just in time for the towns along the Mississippi River to celebrate a truly Glorious Fourth. In Dubuque, believing that their town would be the designated capital of the new territory and future state, the miners gathered to drink barrels of hard liquor, to cheer, and to give fair warning that this was to be a people's democracy. Chauncey Swan arose to propose a toast to "The Mercantile Aristocracy of DuBuque—May they never triumph over the Worker's Democracy of Miners." In far off Burlington, complacent in the knowledge that it was the capital, the more conservative farmers and townspeople gathered to toast themselves for their "industrious, enterprizing and patriotic natures" and to express the hope that they would be forever alert "to look out for

8. For a full account of the congressional debate over the Iowa Territorial Bill, see Kenneth Colton, "Iowa's Struggle for a Territorial Government," *Annals of Iowa*, 3rd Series, 21 (1937): 363–396.

snakes.'' And in the small community of Denmark, the center of transplanted New England Puritanism, the Reverend Asa Turner and his small band of devout Congregationalists, raised glasses of cold spring water, and then eighty-five of them signed the temperance pledge to "taste not, touch not, handle not, the accursed thing." [9] Iowa Territory, which five years before had not even had a name, was now on the map, a vast empire stretching from the Missouri border to Canada, from the Mississippi to the heartland of the Dakotahs. And in Iowa, the people in all of their wonderful diversity were beginning to congregate.

9. William J. Petersen, "The Birthday of the Territory," *Palimpsest* 19 (1938): 244–250.

3

We Proclaim the
Land a State

IT was generally assumed by George Wallace Jones and by his many friends in Iowa, who appreciated his tireless efforts on behalf of the Territorial bill, that he would be named the first governor of Iowa Territory. Unfortunately Jones, in the very midst of the debate over the Iowa Territorial bill, had participated as a second to Representative Jonathan Cilley of Maine in his ill-fated duel with Representative William J. Graves of Kentucky. On the third exchange of shots, Cilley had fallen mortally wounded, and the ensuing outcry from the public across the nation against "this barbaric custom" had forced Congress to appoint a special committee to investigate the duel and to make recommendations for action. The committee recommended that Graves be expelled from the House and that the two seconds, Henry Wise of Virginia and Jones be officially censured. After days of acrimonious debate, the House tabled the report without taking action.

President Van Buren was forced by public opinion, however, to turn a deaf ear to the petitions from Iowa for Jones's appointment, and instead, he first offered the nomination to Henry Atkinson, the military hero of the old Indian campaigns against the Sauk and Fox tribes. Atkinson, who had no interest in civil politics, promptly turned the offer down. Van Buren then of-

fered the governorship to Robert Lucas, twice governor of the
state of Ohio, who just as promptly accepted and was quickly
confirmed by the Senate.

The people of Iowa Territory knew nothing about the former
governor of Ohio other than his name and the fact that he was a
loyal Jacksonian Democrat. He had never visited the Upper
Mississippi Valley, had never fought in the old Indian wars of
that region, had taken no public stand on the territorial debates
of the past several years. The Iowans were naturally curious and
somewhat apprehensive over the man whom the fortunes of
Democratic politics had thrust upon them, and so a large crowd
turned out in Burlington to greet their new governor when he
walked down the gangplank from the steamer *Brazil* on the
morning of 15 August 1838. They saw a tall, gaunt man de-
scending briskly from the steamer. His iron-grey, thick hair
combed straight back from his high forehead, his cold blue
eyes, deepset under heavy eyebrows, his long, thin aquiline
nose, and strong, determined chin all gave him the appearance
of an Old Testament prophet incongruously placed in this rough
frontier settlement. There was no levity in the man, and no non-
sense either. He had arrived to take charge of the territory, and
Iowa had a governor it would not soon forget.

No one in that crowd awaited the governor's arrival with
greater interest than the territorial secretary, William Conway,
who had preceded the governor west by some three weeks. An
ardent Democratic newspaper editor from Pennsylvania whose
"rabidly violent and partisan" editorials on behalf of Jackson
and Van Buren had earned him the esteem of the White House
and the bitter enmity of the Whig opposition, Conway was a
man supremely confident of his own ability and aggressively
eager for the world in general and Iowa in particular to recognize it. Taking full advantage of that peculiar feature of congressional territorial legislation which made the secretary acting
governor in the absence of the governor from the territory,
Conway, in the three short weeks prior to the arrival of Governor Lucas, had established the judicial districts for the territory,
assigned the judges, and posted the dates when the courts would
convene. He had bought a home in Davenport, made friends

with the gargantuan Antoine Le Claire, who ruled the town of
Davenport like a feudal barony, and had let it be generally
known that if he had his way, Davenport would be the new capital of the territory. Conway had also just that morning finished
drawing up a state paper defining the legislative districts for the
territorial assembly and calling for a general election. It had
been a busy three weeks for the active acting governor, and he
was now prepared to present the governor with a *fait accompli*.
The territory had been organized legislatively and judicially.
Lucas could relax and let William do it.

Lucas recognized the challenge for what it was as soon as he
had stepped ashore. After a curt greeting to the assembled
throng, he asked Conway to see him alone in his hotel room.
An hour later, Conway was on board the same steamer, heading
north to his home in Davenport. Lucas could not undo the
judicial districting, but he did draw up his own list of legislative
districts, issued his own call for an election, and let it be known
that Conway had acted illegally during the previous three
weeks. There had been no vacancy in the governorship. It had
simply not as yet been filled. Now it most certainly was, and
Conway could tend to his own job of serving as secretary to the
legislative assembly when it met. Forcibly and quickly, Lucas
had met the first challenge to his authority. He knew he had not
heard the last of Mr. Conway, but he was also quite certain he
could handle him.

The next item on Governor Lucas's carefully prepared agenda
was a tour of the populated areas of the territory. Although the
citizens of Burlington had plans for a magnificent state dinner to
fête their governor, Lucas informed them that this would have
to wait. He was leaving immediately for Dubuque and on his return trip would stop at all the river towns between Dubuque and
Burlington in order to let the people see their governor and to
allow him to consider the possibilities for the location for the
territorial capital. It was a triumphal tour as each town displayed
its charms and advantages to win the nod of the governor. The
governor was clearly impressed with Dubuque, and it was
equally apparent that Davenport, the special preserve of Le-
Claire and Conway, would not win his approval. Ultimately

Lucas, in characteristic fashion, came to the conclusion that none of the existing towns would serve as the capital. None would be central to the future growth of the territory, and to pick one existing city would create lasting jealousies that could divide and embitter the entire territory. Instead, he would recommend to the territorial assembly that a commission be established to select a spot in the interior, preferably on the Iowa River near a good source of building stone for the creation of a new capital in the wilderness. The people of Iowa were quickly learning that they had an independent man as governor, one who was not susceptible to flattery and, although a Quaker, a man who showed no reluctance to fight and did not need a consensus of the meetinghouse to act.

Upon arriving in Iowa from Ohio, Lucas was immediately confronted with a border dispute with the state of Missouri. Missouri's northern boundary had originally been fixed by a line the surveyor John C. Sullivan had drawn in 1816 to mark the limits of the territory the Osage Indians had ceded to the United States. This line was to run due north one hundred miles from the juncture of the Kansas River with the Missouri, then due east to the Des Moines River and down that river to its juncture with the Mississippi. When Missouri applied for statehood in 1820, Congress had essentially accepted the Sullivan line as the northern boundary of the state, designating that this boundary should be the parallel of latitude which passed through the rapids of the river Des Moines, which was essentially the Sullivan line. The only difficulty was that the Sullivan line had not run parallel with the latitude line. Starting at the western point, Sullivan, by the time he had reached the Des Moines River, was two and a half degrees farther north. In 1837, at the time of the last Indian cession of land in northwest Missouri, the governor of Missouri appointed a surveyor, Joseph C. Brown, to draw a new line that would run parallel with the latitude line, beginning at the rapids in the Des Moines River. Brown found some rough water in the Des Moines River some sixty-three miles above the mouth, and deciding that this must be the rapids referred to, drew a neat parallel line west to the Missouri River from that point. This procedure produced a parallel line, to be sure, but a line considerably north of the old and long recognized Sullivan

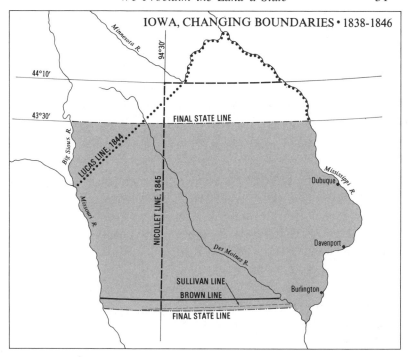

IOWA, CHANGING BOUNDARIES • 1838-1846

line. Missouri stood to gain some 2,616 square miles of territory from Iowa.

The discrepancy between the two lines lay in the interpretation of the phrase "the rapids of the river Des Moines." The difficulty with the interpretation Brown used, that the rapids referred to were in the Des Moines River, was the absence from the maps of the time of any notation of rapids in that river. Brown had had to search diligently along that river until he had found some rocky obstructions that could pass for rapids. At the time Sullivan had drawn his line, however, the phrase, "the rapids of the river Des Moines," had meant only one thing to any navigator in that region. It meant the Des Moines rapids that lay in the Mississippi River. It was an old phrase, first coined by the French as *les rapides de la riviere Des Moines,* referring to that fifteen-mile stretch of rough water known to every riverman as being the one major obstacle to Mississippi River travel between St. Louis and Prairie du Chien. It was to the head of those rapids that Sullivan had aimed, even if in so doing his line would be oblique instead of parallel.

With its new straight parallel line from the recently proclaimed Des Moines River rapids to the Missouri River, the state of Missouri would gain an additional fourteen-mile band of good farmland extending for 190 miles. It is not surprising that the Brown line found immediate acceptance in Missouri. The farmers living in the newly created County of Van Buren, however, considered themselves to be Iowans, and they had no desire to be annexed into Missouri. It was not just a question of regional chauvinism or the fact that they would now be subject to Missouri state taxes. An ethical problem of some importance was involved here. Missouri was a slave state, and many of the Van Buren farmers had deliberately settled north of the Missouri border in order to be citizens of a region that would be forever free of slaves. If this land were to become a part of Missouri, they would have to leave as a matter of conscience. Iowa's response to Missouri's new border line was to draw its own parallel line some fourteen miles south of the old Sullivan line and claim it as the true boundary between Missouri and Iowa. So matters stood when the organic act creating the Territory of Iowa was passed by Congress. Obviously some resolution had to be found. Congress, six days after the passage of the territorial bill, provided for a commission to determine the true southern boundary of the newly created Iowa Territory. President Van Buren selected Albert M. Lea, whose recently published little book was considered to be the definitive study of the Iowa district, to head the commission, and he asked Governor Lucas, who was still in Ohio, and Governor Lilburn Boggs of Missouri each to name a member of the commission. Lucas, as his first official act as governor, named Dr. James Davis of Burlington to serve, but Boggs, who felt the matter should have been settled by the Brown survey, refused to act.

After weeks of study, Lea, speaking for the truncated committee, reported that there were four possible boundary lines that could be considered by Congress: first, the old Sullivan line, long recognized as the boundary of Missouri; second, the newly drawn Brown line; third, the newly proposed Iowa line;

or fourth, a line as yet to be drawn which would correct the old Sullivan line so that it would be a true parallel and not an oblique line. Lea did state that at the time the Sullivan line was drawn, it seemed apparent that the rapids referred to were the Des Moines rapids that lay in the Mississippi, not some as yet undiscovered rapids in the Des Moines River, but beyond that, Lea refused to go. His conclusion was that Congress would have to determine which of the four lines would prevail.

Boggs, however, insisted that Congress had no authority over a sovereign state in determining its boundaries. If there was any question of validity, it was a matter for the courts, not the legislature, to determine. In the meantime, Missouri was prepared to assert its sovereign authority over its own territory. In August 1839, Sheriff Uriah Gregory of Clark County, Missouri, was sent into Van Buren County to collect taxes. The farmers refused to pay. Gregory returned in November with a sizable force, only to meet a larger force of enraged Iowa farmers, headed by Sheriff Henry Haffleman of Van Buren County, who promptly arrested Gregory for trespassing and took him off to Burlington for delivery to Governor Lucas.

Governor Boggs's response to Heffleman's action was to call up the militia. Some 2,000 Missourians responded to the call and prepared to move north into Van Buren County. A few impatient Missouri men, who could not wait for formal military action, entered the county and cut down three "bee trees," rich in honeycomb, which the local farmers treasured as a rare source of sugar. This precipitous action was to give to the whole imbroglio the mellifluous if inappropriate name in history of the Honey War. There was, alas, more vinegar than honey in this civil conflict.

Governor Lucas, who regarded Boggs's call for the militia as an act of war not against the Territory of Iowa but against the people of the United States, promptly called up three divisions of Iowa militia to support the United States marshal in his efforts to protect the rights of the citizens in that area. Writing to Van Buren's Secretary of State John Forsyth on 13 December 1839, Lucas stated his position succinctly, "We are still acting on the defensive and will continue to do so," but he added with pointed emphasis that Missouri's show of force "cannot intimidate us, or drive us from a faithful discharge of our duty to the United States." [1] It was a motley crew of Iowans, hastily assembled from Burlington, Davenport, and even as far away as Dubuque, who, armed with ancient blunderbusses and ceremonial swords, marched south in December to join the embattled farmers of Van Buren County. The stage was set for a civil war in microcosm.

The Iowans found no Missouri militia north of the old Sullivan line, however, and fortunately, if there was little sweetness in this Honey War, there was some light among the moderates on both sides of the border. The Clark County court, acting quite independently of Governor Boggs, issued an order to disband the Missouri militia. The Iowa assembly, meeting in the Old Zion church in Burlington, was in an equally conciliatory mood, and passed a resolution asking that both Governors Boggs and Lucas suspend military action until the issue could be settled by a competent tribunal. Although Lucas promptly vetoed the resolution on the grounds that it had referred to difficulties existing between the State of Missouri and the Territory of Iowa when in reality it was a dispute between the State of Missouri and the people of the United States, nevertheless, the bellicose passions of the moment had been broken. Sheriff Gregory, released from protective custody was sent home, and there were no further attempts to collect Missouri taxes in Van Buren County. In spite of the continuing intransigence of the two governors, the border became relatively quiet.

The issue was referred to Congress over the Missouri governor's protests, and there it languished for six years. It was still unresolved when Iowa became a state in 1846. With Iowa's statehood, the boundary question could properly be considered a dispute between two sovereign states, for which the Constitution provided that the Supreme Court should have original jurisdiction. Congress on 4 August 1846, even before Iowa was officially admitted into the Union, eagerly and happily referred the

1. Letter published in Carroll J. Kraus, "A Study in Border Confrontation: The Iowa-Missouri Boundary Dispute," *Annals of Iowa,* 3rd Series, 40 (1969): 98.

question to the Supreme Court, and Missouri formally brought suit against Iowa for all land up to the Brown line.

In February 1849, Associate Justice John Catron, speaking for a unanimous Court, essentially found for Iowa by accepting the Sullivan line, which for many years had been recognized as the northern boundary of Missouri. Governor Lucas, by then in retirement in his home at Plum Grove, could once again take satisfaction in his firmly held belief that a show of might could bring about the right.

Compared to the threatened war with Missouri, the other problems that arose during Governor Lucas's three-year term seemed minor. Secretary Conway continued to be a source of trouble and vexation to the proud, intractable governor. He refused to approve the voucher providing for the purchase of furniture for the governor's office, claiming that the expenditure was not authorized by the territorial statutes. More alarming to Lucas were Conway's efforts to unite those disgruntled legislators who resented Lucas's vetoes into a cohesive political coalition to pressure the national administration into removing the governor from office. Lucas retaliated by seizing the Great Seal of the Territory of Iowa from Conway's office and refusing to approve of any legislative acts until the assembly showed some disposition to work with its chief executive. In November 1839, the Conway-Lucas quarrel was abruptly and completely resolved in the governor's favor by the sudden death of the secretary, stricken with "bilious fever," which no doubt was complicated by apoplectic rage. For Lucas, Conway's unexpected death was a relief, certainly, but it was almost too easy a solution. Lucas would have preferred forcing the resignation of Conway, and seeing him retire into ignominious defeat. But with Conway out of the picture, Lucas had little more difficulty with the territorial assembly.

The other major concerns of Governor Lucas were to push ahead with the building of the new capital in Iowa City, to extend county government to the ever expanding Iowa frontier line, and to enter into negotiating with the Sauk and Fox for the ceding of their remaining land in Iowa to expand these frontiers even further.

Under the able direction of the acting commissioner from Dubuque, Chauncey Swan, who not only adapted and revised the original architectural plans of John F. Rague, but also almost single-handedly pushed and bullied the suppliers, contractors, masons, and carpenters into action, the new stone capitol was far enough along in construction for Governor Lucas to attend the laying of the cornerstone on 4 July 1840. It was not until 1842, however, after Lucas was out of office, that the building was sufficiently enclosed for the territorial legislature to assemble there. Finally, in 1851, the cupola and the central spiral staircase were completed, and the contract was closed. This magnificently conceived and beautifully proportioned building was to serve the territory and the state of Iowa for only fifteen years as capitol before the state government was moved to Des Moines. The building has continued to serve the University of Iowa and the people of Iowa as the most esthetically pleasing example of architecture in the state. For this structure alone, Robert Lucas's governorship should be appreciatively remembered.

When Lucas became governor in 1838, there were twenty-one designated counties in Iowa Territory, which the Wisconsin territorial legislature had created following the cessions of land in 1836 and 1837. Many of these counties, however, existed in name only. They had no government, and their boundaries were only vaguely delineated. Four were of gigantic size, taking in lands of the Sauk, Fox, Sioux, and Chippewa Indians, which had not as yet been ceded to the United States. Buchanan, Benton, and Keokuk counties extended from their eastern boundaries across the entire Iowa district to the Missouri River, and Fayette County extended north and west to take in the upper quarter of Iowa, nearly all of Minnesota, and two-thirds of the Dakotas. The 140,000 square miles within its borders gave Fayette the distinction of being the largest single county ever created in the United States. Under the prodding of Lucas, the territorial legislature organized those interior counties that had a population large enough to justify county governments. County seats were built, county officials were elected, and courts were convened.

Lucas also entered into negotiations with the Sauk and Fox to persuade them to give up their remaining lands in central and southern Iowa and to depart from the territory forever. Before he could accomplish this, however, there was a change in the national administration: Van Buren, blamed for the depression of 1837, failed in his bid for re-election. The Whig party elected its first president, William Henry Harrison, who, upon taking office, adopted with alacrity the very Jacksonian spoils system that he and his party had vigorously attacked for the past eight years. Lucas went out of office along with Van Buren and was succeeded by John Chambers, a Henry Clay Whig from Kentucky. Lucas retired to his farm at Plum Grove, near Iowa City, where from his front yard he could keep an eye on the continuing construction of the capitol he had begun. Although he nurtured some small hopes that, with the return of the Democrats to power, he might again be appointed territorial governor and have the honor of bringing the Territory of Iowa into the Union as a state, it was not to be. When the Democrats did regain control of the Presidency in 1845, Lucas was considered too old for the position. President Polk appointed James Clarke, Henry Dodge's son-in-law, as Iowa's last territorial governor. Clarke had succeeded Conway as Lucas's secretary in 1839, and had he still been around, Conway would surely have found wry humor in the fact that it was a territorial secretary after all who had won out over Lucas for the governorship.

Van Buren had done well by Iowa in selecting Lucas as the first territorial governor. His three appointments to the territorial supreme court were equally felicitous. Joseph Williams of Muscatine, Thomas Wilson of Dubuque, and Charles Mason of Burlington as chief justice, were three of the ablest jurists in Iowa's history. Mason in particular, not only in his rulings from the bench, but also in his codification of the territorial laws, done at the request of Governor Lucas, gave a distinction to the judiciary branch of this frontier region that was not surpassed by any other territorial or state court in the land. Lucas's report on the capitol to the territorial legislature in 1840 upon his return from laying the cornerstone might well serve as a appraisal for Iowa's first government under his and Mason's administrations:

"I must say that, so far as the work has progressed, it [has been] done in the most substantial and workmanlike manner." [2]

From the moment the Territory of Iowa was created, it seemed apparent that Iowa's territorial status would be of brief duration. So rapid was the influx of settlers into this rich land, even before it could be surveyed and land sales offices established, that the territory's population was doubling every two years. As early as 1839, Lucas urged the second meeting of the territorial assembly to begin preparations for statehood. He even provided the assembly with a map showing the boundaries he proposed for the state, making it a curious trapezoidal sovereignty, bounded on the northeast and the east by the Mississippi River, on the south by the still disputed boundary with the state of Missouri, on the west by the Missouri River, and having for its northern boundary a domed peak that would be created by drawing a line from the juncture of the Missouri with the Big Sioux River diagonally northeast to St. Peters [Minnesota] River and then northeast down that river to its juncture with the Mississippi at the point where the city of St. Paul is now located. This proposal, Lucas insisted, would provide the state with its true natural boundaries, the Mississippi, the Des Moines, the Missouri, and the St. Peters rivers.

Lucas, as usual, was a commander far in advance of his troops. The legislative assembly in 1839 was still trying to organize a territory. It was not ready to think about statehood. Again in 1840, when the recently completed census showed Iowa to have a population of 43,000, exclusive of Indians, Lucas reiterated his position, and this time the assembly did agree to put before the people the question of calling for a convention to write a state constitution by including this question on the ballot of the August election. The people decisively and emphatically rejected the idea of statehood by voting 2,907 to 937 against calling a convention.

The major argument against statehood at this early date was a financial one. John Brown, a farmer in Indiana who was con-

2. "Unpublished Message by Governor Lucas, July 14, 1840," *Annals of Iowa,* 3rd Series, 3 (1897): 210.

sidering moving to Iowa Territory, spoke for the large majority of Iowans when he wrote to a friend who had already moved to Iowa that he regretted reading in the paper Governor Lucas's advocacy of statehood.

> While Iowa remains a Territory, the Genl. Government pays all the Territorial expenses, which I consider a matter of much importance to the people at present, as they have no land taxable yet nor will have soon . . . consequently, you will have nothing but personal property to tax. . . . And furthermore, while it remains a Territory, Congress will make appropriations for improvement of the roads and rivers. I hope therefore that, Gov. Lucas's recommendation will not be complied with. . . ." [3]

It wasn't, but still the idea would not die. The official position of the Whigs in Iowa, once their party had captured the Presidency in 1841, was to oppose statehood, knowing full well that the Democrats were in the majority in the state. With a Whig President, their party would have the territorial governorship and all of the appointive offices, but with statehood, the Democrats of Iowa could elect all of the state offices no matter who might control the federal government. It was therefore with consternation that the Iowa Whigs read the first message of their Whig-appointed territorial governor, John Chambers, to the territorial assembly in 1841, urging consideration of a state constitutional convention, couched in the same exhortatory language as that of Governor Lucas. But once again, the people of Iowa in the election of 1842 overwhelmingly defeated the governor's proposal to call a constitutional convention.

By 1844, however, the population of the territory was approaching 80,000. It was apparent to all that statehood could not be much longer delayed. The financial argument against statehood, moreover, had been largely vitiated by the Distribution Act of 1841, by which Congress provided for a distribution of federal funds received from the sale of public lands to the several states in the Union. None of this largesse went to the territories, and the proponents of statehood argued cogently that the

3. "Letter of John Brown to Gideon S. Bailey, 1 December 1839," published in *Annals of Iowa*, 3rd Series, 8 (1907): 147.

distribution funds Iowa would receive as a state would more than offset the expenses of a state government for the immediate future. With this tempting carrot dangling before their eyes, the territorial assemblymen voted to bring the issue once again to the people, and the people, voting in township elections in April 1844, by a substantial margin reached out for the same carrot and approved the calling of a constitutional convention.

The worst fears of the Whigs were realized in the subsequent election held to select delegates to the constitutional convention. Of the seventy-two delegates chosen, fifty-one were Democrats and only twenty-one, Whigs. The convention, meeting in the capitol in Iowa City in October 1844, within a month wrote a constitution that reflected the Jacksonian spirit of the majority. There was a provision guaranteeing religious freedom for all, even for atheists who wanted freedom from all religion. District judges were to be popularly elected, and state supreme court judges were to be elected by the General Assembly for a specified term—no life-tenured judges by executive appointment for democratic Iowa. Banks, to most of these hard-money Jacksonian delegates, were highly suspect institutions, which locked their doors and pulled down their shades in the middle of the afternoon to carry out their nefarious practices in secrecy. Consequently, there were to be no banks or any other corporations chartered in the state of Iowa except by a specific act of the General Assembly, and even then, each individual charter would have to be approved by the voters of the state. The convention cheered when Delegate Jonathan Hall moralized that "a Bank of earth is the best Bank, and the best share is a Plow share." [4] This was frontier democracy in its most unabashedly naked form.

The boundaries for the proposed state caused the least amount of discussion at the convention, for almost all of the delegates accepted without question the "natural" boundaries of Iowa as proposed by Governor Lucas five years before. The convention, generally proud of its handiwork, adjourned on 1 November,

4. Quoted in Benjamin F. Shambaugh, "The Convention of 1844," *Palimpsest* 15 (1930): 112.

and the constitution along with a formal request for statehood was sent to the territorial delegate in Congress Augustus Dodge for congressional action. The convention had provided that Congress should first approve of the constitution and then it would be submitted to the people of Iowa in April 1845 for final approval.

Congress was eager to act upon a petition from Iowa for statehood. This time there would not be the Southern opposition that there had been when Iowa applied for territorial status, for standing in the wings was the Southern slave territory Florida. Florida had been waiting since 1838 to become a state, but it had become an unwritten law in Congress that no territory could join in the grand state waltz of the Union unless it first found a partner of the opposite section to accompany it in the dance. In 1800, prior to the time that sectionalism had become an issue in national politics, there had been sixteen states in the Union, and quite by chance, eight were Northern, eight Southern. Ohio had gained admittance in 1803, followed in 1812 by Louisiana, the first state to be created out of Mr. Jefferson's noble bargain. By then people were beginning to count very carefully the couples on the floor. Indiana and Mississippi were paired in 1816–1817, followed by Alabama and Illinois in 1818–1819. When Missouri applied as a slave state in 1820, it looked as if the dance might end up in a brawl until Massachusetts consented to relinquish its Down East district of Maine to provide a partner for the Show Me state. Michigan had been hurried into statehood so that it could be embraced by Arkansas. As Florida had grown more than weary of its wallflower status, Iowa's bid was eagerly accepted. It seemed highly appropriate that the last slave state east of the Mississippi should be accompanied into the Union by the first free state west of the Mississippi. Both Congress and President Tyler promised quick action. A bill granting statehood to both Florida and Iowa was quickly reported out of committee and came to the floor of the House for what would appear to be a perfunctory debate. By joining Florida and Iowa together in a single bill, the unwritten law of sectional equality was to become a written condition.

The giant shadow of Texas cast a gloom over this convivial

gathering. Texas had been waiting to be annexed as a state since it had achieved its independence from Mexico nine years before. Its previous bids had been rejected in the Senate, where a treaty of annexation required a two-thirds majority vote. Now, however, wily President Tyler had devised a new method to admit Texas into the Union, not by treaty, but by a joint resolution of Congress, which required only a simple majority in both houses. The resolution to admit Texas provided that at any time Texas so desired, she could divide herself into five separate states without any further generative action from Congress. If the North were to find partners for all of these potential little new Texases, then it behooved Northern congressmen to divide into as many states as possible all of the Louisiana territory that lay north of the 36° 30′ parallel, which according to the Missouri Compromise should be forever free of slavery. It was hoped that at least five states could be created out of the Wisconsin-Iowa territories. That could not be done if the House were to accept the proposed Lucas boundaries for the State of Iowa. Consequently, Representative Alexander Duncan of Ohio arose to offer an amendment to the bill altering the boundaries of Iowa to what he called even more natural boundaries. He had a map that was part of a hitherto neglected report which a French cartographer Joseph Nicollet had made for the United States Geological Survey in 1841. Nicollet had not only drawn the topography of the region, but he had quite gratuitously sketched in boundaries for five possible states in the upper Mississippi Valley. Iowa was to be bounded on the west not by the Missouri River, but by a straight line drawn from the Missouri border north along the longitude 94° 30′, to the juncture of the St. Peters and Blue Earth rivers and then straight east on the 45th parallel to the Mississippi. These boundaries would create a neat rectangle of a state where, according to Nicollet, "the uniform direction of the waters, together with the similarity of climate, soil, resources, and avenues to market, are well calculated to give to the inhabitants of this State a homogeneity of character and interest highly conducive to their well-being." [5]

5. Quoted in Ruth Gallaher, "J. N. Nicollet, Map Maker," *Palimpsest* 26 (1945): 298.

Duncan's amendment found immediate support among his northern colleagues. Some Southerners saw through the ploy and threatened to have Florida divided into Panhandle and Peninsula. In the interest of getting the bill through Congress that session, however, both the House and the Senate accepted the bill as amended by Duncan, and President Tyler signed the bill on 3 March 1845, just one day before his term expired. On his last day in office, Tyler also signed the joint resolution of Congress annexing Texas into the Union. In spite of a diminished Iowa, to which they objected, the Southern congressmen could feel satisfied that they had carried the day.

If Congress was satisfied, Iowa was not. Although technically it might be argued that Iowa had been admitted as a state as of 3 March 1845, the people of Iowa still had to give their approval to the constitution that Congress had so quickly amended and then approved, and the people of Iowa did not like the way their new state had been changed. Although Delegate Augustus Caesar Dodge, belying his imperial name, was ready to accept defeat and urged the people to ratify the constitution because he was convinced that Congress would not, under any circumstances, consider a larger area for the state, the people thought otherwise. In spite of Dodge's pleading, backed up by the leaders of the Democratic party and by John Chambers, the maverick Whig governor, the people rejected the constitution and statehood by a narrow margin in the April election. The arguments of the Whigs, led most effectively by their party leader, William Penn Clarke, against some of the provisions in the constitution respecting the chartering of banks and the popular election of judges undoubtedly had some impact upon the electorate, but the main reason for rejecting the constitution was the Duncan amendment, reducing the size of the state to a little over half of that which Lucas had originally proposed. Most Iowans were sympathetic to the Northern position in Congress in wanting more free states than slave states. But like the nation itself, Iowa was torn between sectional interests, which tended to restrict and confine, and Manifest Destiny, which sought expansion and natural boundaries, and this was the year of Manifest Destiny.

The 1844 constitution having been rejected, Iowa was in the

curious position of being in the Union as far as Congress was concerned, but out of the Union by the action of its own people. There was nothing else to do but to call another constitutional convention. The second convention, like the first, was dominated by the Democrats by a two-to-one margin, a clear indication that what had defeated the ratification was not Whig arguments on banking and judges so much as the Big Iowa arguments of three young Democrats, Theodore Parvin, Enoch Eastman, and Frederick Mills, who had deserted their party leadership to lead the campaign against the amended constitution.

Meeting in Iowa City in May 1846, the delegates to the constitutional convention were aware of the fact that that great compromiser in the House, the Little Giant from Illinois, Stephen A. Douglas, had already come up with a compromise solution to the boundary question. He proposed that Iowa be bordered on the west by the Missouri and Big Sioux rivers and on the north by the 43° 30′ parallel. Iowa would lose the Minnesota River valley with its pointed cupola, but it would regain the Missouri River. Although Congress had yet to act on Douglas's proposal, the Iowa convention quickly adopted it as its own, restated all of the earlier controversial provisions on banking and elective judges, and then provided that this time the people would vote on the constitution *before* submitting it to Congress.

Congress by this time was weary of the whole Iowa question. Douglas's suggestion appeared reasonable to most Northerners, who were eager to get one more free state in the Union as quickly as possible to offset both Florida and Texas. Duncan, to be sure, still protested. If Iowa couldn't be separated from the Missouri River, then let it be cut in two horizontally along the 42° parallel. He claimed, surprisingly enough, that he had a petition from the citizens of Dubuque urging this as a settlement. This proposal would have placed Dubuque outside the state of Iowa, but evidently there were still some diehards in that town who continued to dream of Dubuque's being a state capital, if not of Iowa, then of a new, smaller state to the north. Duncan's suggestion was quickly dismissed, however, and an act establishing the boundaries as proposed by Douglas and the Iowa constitutional convention passed both houses of Congress and was signed by President Polk on 4 August 1846, just one day after the people of Iowa, by the narrowest of margins, had ratified the 1846 constitution in their general election.

Iowa at last had its natural boundaries, not as grandiose as Lucas had envisioned, but a state properly rectangular, and above all, Mesopotamia was still intact. It looked good on the maps. Indeed, of all the states, Iowa most closely resembles the familiar form of the contiguous territory of the United States. Drawn to a scale of 1 to 10, Iowa, like the United States is three units east-west, to two units north-south, and is bordered on both the east and west by water. In Lee County, projecting below Missouri, Iowa even has its own shorter and more pointed Floridian peninsula.

Upon receiving news of the approval of the constitution by the Iowa general election, Governor Clarke immediately called for an election of state officials to be held in October. The Democratic and Whig parties meeting in state conventions on two successive days in September both selected dark-horse candidates for the governorship. The Whigs chose Thomas Mc-Knight, receiver of the United States land office in Dubuque, a Democrat until 1842, when he changed his party affiliation to hold on to his job. He was not one of the leaders of the Whig party, but he had the distinct advantage of being from Dubuque, where his party badly needed votes. The Democratic choice was an even greater surprise: Ansel Briggs, a former Whig, who had been a stagecoach driver from Jackson County. He had held several county offices, and in 1842 had served one term in the Fifth Territorial Assembly. He was, however, little known to the general public, a point the Whigs emphasized by circulating the story that he had been chosen because on the day the Democrats convened, a new steamboat, *The Governor Briggs,* named for the governor of Massachusetts, arrived in Iowa City, and a majority of the delegates had considered this an auspicious sign from heaven. So it proved to be, for Briggs, in a close election, won over his Whig opponent and carried with him the entire Democratic ticket.

Throughout the two-year struggle for Iowa's statehood there

had been a failure of synchronization between Congress and the people of Iowa. In 1845, Congress had admitted Iowa into the Union, but Iowa had continued to regard itself as a territory. Now in 1846, following the approval of the constitution by the general election, Iowa, regarding itself as a state, disbanded its territorial offices and inaugurated Briggs as governor. But Congress still had to approve the constitution and formally to admit Iowa into the Union. This enabling bill finally passed the House early in December and the Senate on Christmas eve. President Polk signed it on 28 December 1846. The birth pains had been protracted, but Iowa was at last the twenty-ninth state of the Union.

Four years later, Iowa along with the other states in the Union was requested to furnish a block of marble, inscribed with a message of its own choosing, for the towering obelisk that was being erected as a monument to George Washington. A proper slab of marble was found in the stone quarry of Moses Root near Keosauqua, and a joint committee of the two houses of the Iowa legislature invited suggestions from several prominent persons in the state as to an appropriate inscription to be carved on the stone. The suggestion accepted by the committee came from Enoch Eastman, the Young Turk of the Democratic party who had led the fight against the ratification of the 1844 constitution. His winning entry read:

> Iowa.
> Her affections, like the rivers of her borders,
> flow to an inseparable Union.[6]

Eastman's reference to "the rivers of her borders" was no idle poetic metaphor. Everyone knew how hard he had fought and the political ostracism he had faced in his own party to secure those river borders. Now in that tense year of 1850 when sectionalism threatened the dissolution of the Union, Eastman's pretty sentiment of tying the rivers to an inseparable Union was far more defiant than it was sentimental. It struck a responsive chord in the state, for Iowa was determined that the rivers on

6. "The Origin of a Famous Inscription," *Annals of Iowa,* 3rd Series, 1 (1895): 661–663.

her borders should not be cut by any hostile, alien boundary. Iowa's affection for the Union was as physical as it was metaphysical. That affection would soon be tested in physical combat.

4

We Come to the Land
to Possess It

*T*HE land was now ours—its boundaries set. Another star in the ever more crowded blue field, a marble stone in the Washington monument, a name on the map. Now the people must come to till the fields, to dam the streams, and build their towns, to be possessed by the land they now possessed. And come they did in an increasing flow. John B. Newhall, a Burlington merchant and self-appointed publicity agent for the entire state, in writing his book, *A Glimpse of Iowa in 1846,* sought to encourage immigration into Iowa by the time-honored salesman's pitch of urging the reader to run not walk to his nearest riverboat or covered wagon and head west to Iowa before all the best land was gone:

> The writer of these papers, frequently having occasion to traverse the great thoroughfares of Illinois and Indiana, in the years of 1836–8, the roads would be literally lined with long blue wagons of the emigrant slowly wending their way over the broad prairies . . . —often ten, twenty, and thirty wagons in company. Ask them, when and where you would, their destination was the "Black Hawk Purchase." [1]

1. J. S. Newhall, *A Glimpse of Iowa in 1846* (reprinted Iowa City: State Historical Society, 1957), pp. 12–13.

Even if one dismisses these early accounts of migration into Iowa as examples of the promoter's predilection for Münchhausen exaggeration, one cannot be unimpressed by the cold statistics of Iowa's population growth during the seventeen years from 1833, when the land was first opened to settlement, until the first federal census taken after Iowa became a state. With at most only fifty illegal squatters in its territory at the time of the Black Hawk Purchase, Iowa by 1850 could boast of nearly two hundred thousand inhabitants. By the time of the next decennial census, the population of Iowa had again more than trebled. The amateur demographers and prophets of Iowa confidently predicted that within the next hundred years the population would exceed five million. Only then, in 1960, would Iowa be ready to cry "enough" and to consider the necessity for zero population growth.

In the meantime, the more the merrier. The gates were not only open wide, but the press, state officials, and private individuals were prepared to promote actively the state's enticing charms in order to keep the people coming. The various westward passages became common knowledge. If the immigrant and his family were in a hurry to reach the promised land and if they had the necessary capital and an easy access to the great waterways leading into the interior of the country, they could come by boat. If from New England or New York, they could come by way of the Erie Canal to Buffalo, then across Lake Erie to Cleveland and down the Ohio Canal to Portsmouth on the Ohio River. There they could join those who had already boarded the steamers in Pittsburgh and together steam down the Ohio to Cairo and up the Mississippi past St. Louis to Burlington, Davenport, or Dubuque. The entire water trip might take a month, but this was lightning-quick compared to the wagon and cart journey from interior Pennsylvania or Ohio or even farther east across a third of the continent from the Great Smokies of Carolina or the Blue Ridge mountains of Virginia.

Where did they come from, this seemingly unending parade of people that marched into Iowa during the quarter century prior to the Civil War? And why did they come, leaving behind farms and families and friends in the settled East? The first question is easier than the second for the historian to answer, for in the federal censuses beginning in 1850, the birthplaces of the inhabitants of the state are duly noted.

Because of Iowa's later unswerving adherence to the Republican party, because of the strength of the abolitionist movement in Iowa just prior to the Civil War, because of the many little Iowa towns with their large, white frame houses, crowned with Salem widow's walks and shaded by elm trees, and because of the Congregationalists, who were far more conspicuous than their actual numbers would suggest, the belief was prevalent in the late nineteenth century that Iowa's first settlers and its early territorial and state leaders came mainly from New England. It was a historical myth that the social and political leaders of the 1880s and 1890s, seeking cultural respectability, were not reluctant to preserve and propagate.

The data available to us, however, do not substantiate the claim that Iowa was a newer New England, a more fertile "Massachusetts on the Mississippi." There were, to be sure, a few small communities, such as Denmark and Grinnell, which were indeed transplanted New England villages, but even there, these Congregational pioneers found much prejudice against "the Yankee foreigner" among their rural neighbors. Reuben Gaylord, a young minister from Connecticut who established the second Congregational church in Iowa at Danville, reported back to the Home Missionary Society in 1839:

> Being a stranger, it was necessary to move cautiously at first. . . .
> Moreover, prejudices are easily excited, and hard to be allayed. I
> am called an "educated man" and a "Presbyterian." Then the term
> "Yankee" is sometimes as repulsive to a Western man as like poles
> of a magnet.[2]

The census data show clearly that Gaylord and his Yankee brethren were indeed a minority in Iowa at least by 1850. Of the 192,000 persons living in Iowa as recorded by the federal census of that year, only 5,500 or 2.87 percent had been born in one of the six New England states and could properly be called

2. Quoted in Truman O. Douglass, *The Pilgrims of Iowa* (Boston: The Pilgrim Press, 1911), p. 36.

Yankees. Surprisingly enough, Vermont, which had the second-smallest population of the New England states, had contributed the largest number of its natives to Iowa's population. The four Middle Atlantic states of New York, Pennsylvania, New Jersey, and Delaware provided nearly five times as many native-born citizens to Iowa as had New England: 24,516 persons or 12.75 percent of the population. From the border slave states of Virginia, Maryland, Kentucky, Tennessee, and Missouri had come an even larger number of natives to Iowa: 26,824 persons or 14 percent of the state's total population. Virginia and Kentucky had each contributed far more persons to Iowa's population than all of the six New England states combined. The Southern states of North and South Carolina, Georgia, Florida, Alabama, Mississippi, Louisiana, and Texas had collectively sent almost as many of their native population to Iowa as had New England: 4,059 persons or 2.11 percent of the total. The great bulk of Iowa's immigrant population, however, had been born in the five states of the old Northwest Territory—Michigan, Ohio, Indiana, Illinois, and Wisconsin: 59,098 or 30.74 percent of the total population. Of these states, Ohio had contributed the largest number, 30,713 persons, with 19,925 Hoosiers giving Indiana second place as a source of Iowa's immigrant population. The flat Midwest accent and the Southern drawl, which were to give Iowa its speech patterns, stood in no danger of being drowned out by the nasal twang of the New England Yankee.

One of the first social historians to dispute the belief that New Englanders had dominated the first settlements in Iowa was Professor Frank I. Herriott of Drake University, who, in a series of articles appearing in the *Annals of Iowa* in 1906, attempted to lay to rest once and for all the myth of Iowa's being a western colony of the states lying east and north of the Hudson. Herriott offered as concrete evidence the fact that most of the early territorial officials, army commanders, and other citizens notable enough to have had their birthplaces a matter of historical record had been born or had grown up in such states as Virginia, Kentucky, Pennsylvania, or Tennessee. By searching army records and membership lists of territorial assemblies and constitutional conventions, he could find few First Families of Iowa who had their origins in Massachusetts, Connecticut, or Rhode Island. But Herriott was lacking in complete data. Much of his argument that Iowa's demographic roots lay south of Long Island Sound was based upon subjective reasoning and Herriott's own deep-seated prejudices. Being as dedicated a New Anglophile as the very myth-mongers he was attempting to refute, Herriott denied Iowa's New England heritage largely on the grounds that its early political institutions and culture were not sufficiently democratic or libertarian to be of Yankee origin. Local government found its basic unit not in the democratic and honest township government of New England but in the autocratic and corrupt county rule of the South. Iowa, in his opinion, was essentially anti-intellectual; it starved its school system, derided "book larnin'," and rewarded mediocrity. Herriott wrote:

> If one thing more than another characterizes the New Englander, it is respect for law and his resort to the processes of the law for the suppression of disorder and violence. Coupled with, if not underlying this marked trait, are his sobriety, his love of peaceful pleasures and his reserve in social life. In the early history of Iowa we find much of the boisterous carousal in country and town . . . gross disregard of law and order, frequent in election contests, flagrant corruption and considerable practice in Judge Lynch's court. . . . There is in the Iowan's character and in his life a noticeable trait that we may designate Languor, a certain inclination to take things easy, not to worry or fuss even if things do not satisfy. . . . This is clearly not a characteristic of the New Englander.[3]

And clearly Professor Herriott was a regretful myth slayer. He would have greatly preferred a different Iowa from that which he felt the first settlers had given him and in which he and his Yankee brethren must forever be aliens in their own land.

Later more scientific and less passionate demographic studies of the origins of Iowa's pioneer population have essentially substantiated Herriott's highly subjective findings. Using the census data available to them, John Louis, Frank Garver, Allan Bogue,

---

3. Frank I. Herriott, "Whence Came the Pioneers of Iowa," *Annals of Iowa*, 3rd Series, 7 (1906): 373–376.

and Mildred Throne, in their detailed studies of individual counties and townships, have shown that the sources for Iowa's
American-born stock remained remarkably constant over a
thirty-year period and throughout the state, from the southeast-
ern counties of Washington and Wapello to the western counties
of Shelby and Woodbury. Although the federal census data do
not provide information on previous places of residence other
than place of birth, Throne and the others have shown that by
noting places of birth of the immigrants' children, which the
manuscript census records do show, the diligent researcher can
trace many settlers living in Iowa in 1850 back to their first
entry into the region during territorial days. By using the same
data, one can also frequently chart the moves of the immigrant
across the country, before the census taker finally caught up
with him in Iowa, by noting where each of his several children
was born. Indeed, it could be argued that for many of these
early immigrants into Iowa, their place of birth was not very
meaningful, for they had often lived during childhood and early
adulthood in several states before reaching Iowa. Mildred
Throne has found in her study of the population of Wapello
County in 1850, only twenty-two percent had moved directly
from their native state to Iowa; sixty-six percent had moved
once to another state before coming to Iowa; eleven percent had
lived in two states other than their native state before entering
Iowa; and one percent had moved three or more times. Analysis
of the data in the other counties and townships studied show
much the same pattern of movement.[4] A familiar pattern for the
Iowa immigrant was to have been born in Virginia, Kentucky,
or Ohio, to be married in his native state, then to move to Ohio
or Indiana, where the first child would be born, then on to Iowa,
where the birth of an additional child or children would be duly
recorded by the census taker.

4. Mildred Throne, "A Population Study in an Iowa County in 1850," *Iowa Journal of History,* (hereafter referred to as *IJH*), 57 (1959): 305–330. See also John J. Louis, "Shelby County: A Sociological Study," *IJH* 2 (1904): 83–101; Frank H. Garner, "The Settlement of Woodbury County," *IJH* 9 (1911): 359–384; Allan Bogue, "Pioneer Farmers and Innovation," *IJH* 56 (1958): 1–36; and William L. Bowers, "Crawford Township (Washington County) 1850–1970," *IJH* 58 (1960): 1–30.

From the data found in manuscript census records, church membership lists, election returns, and newspapers, what kind of composite picture can be drawn of the typical immigrant coming into Iowa in the years between 1838 and 1850? There is a slight probability in favor of the person being male. (Of more than 190,000 persons in Iowa in 1850, 100,000 were males, 90,000 females; but certainly there was not the preponderant male population considered typical of a frontier area). The immigrant would undoubtedly be white, and would most typically be between the ages of twenty-eight and thirty-five. (Again, the frontier population of Iowa is surprising in that it was not as youthful as generally believed). He would probably have been born in the United States, for there was only one chance out of ten that he would have emigrated from a foreign country. If foreign-born, he would more likely have come from one of the west German states than from any other part of Europe, with Ireland and England the second- and third-best possibilities. There was a better chance in 1850 of the foreign-born immigrant's being Dutch than Scandinavian, for several hundred Netherlanders had followed Dominie Henry Scholte to central Iowa, when that dedicated Calvinist divine founded his community in Pella in 1847 for reformers of the Reformed Church. The great Scandinavian migrations from Norway and Sweden to Iowa would not begin until the 1860s and 1870s. There would be little likelihood that the foreign-born immigrant would have come to Iowa from any of the southern or eastern countries of Europe. In all of Iowa in 1850, there were fewer than five hundred of the Mediterranean and Slavic peoples.

The typical immigrant to Iowa, whether American or foreign-born, would probably be married, would have two to three children, and would have been and in Iowa would continue to be a farmer. He would operate a farm of 160 acres and would have, by 1850, a third to a half of it under cultivation. He would most likely be a Protestant by religion and quite probably a Democrat in politics. His major concerns would be the weather, his legal claim to the land he was already cultivating, adequate transportation to get his surplus farm produce to a market, the ready availability of credit but at the same time the maintenance of a sound currency. He would be highly suspicious of bankers, lawyers, and most politicians. The only professional man for whom he would have much respect would be his own local minister. He would be wary of the reforming ideologue and fanatic, but generally tolerant of the eccentric as long as the latter's idiosyncratic behavior did not impose itself upon him. He was quite satisfied with his majority status, but did not object to religious, political, or ethnic minorities as long as they were content to remain minorities and keep their distance. Racial minorities, however, were quite another matter. The Indian had to be driven out and the black man should not be allowed in. The typical Iowan had no love for slavery or for the slave. This was white man's country by conquest and occupation, and he intended to keep it that way.

As to the more difficult question of why the immigrant had come to Iowa, there is no easy answer. For the foreign-born immigrant, the reasons could in many instances be rather precisely stated: famine in Ireland, religious disaffection in Sweden or Holland, military conscription or political persecution in Germany, technological or agricultural displacement in Scotland, England, and Wales. These were the major factors that had pushed the emigrant out. He was pulled to Iowa by letters from relatives and friends who had preceded him, by translated newspaper stories and emigrant guidebooks, which had told of the richness of the easily obtained land, and of the political and religious freedom that prevailed.

For the much larger number of native-born Americans who left established homes in Virginia, Pennsylvania, Ohio, and Indiana the reasons for change were not so simple or so easily understood, even by the immigrants themselves. It was not often hunger or the need to escape political or religious persecution that drove them from their original homes, but the many accounts of Iowa's rich land undoubtedly influenced them. Some had gone heavily into debt in their former places of residence and they had found it simpler to declare bankruptcy with their feet rather than by legal action in the courts. Some Southerners, in moving, were registering an individual protest against their region's "peculiar institution," which they found as abhorrent as the European emigrant had found monarchy, military conscription, or an established state church. But for most native-born Americans, it was not a case of their being pushed by their environment into moving; instead, they were pulled by vague, only partially understood psychological urges into making the trek westward; curiosity, adventure, ambition, dissatisfaction, claustrophobia, restlessness. These were nomads and the children of nomads, for whom getting there—anywhere or nowhere—would always be more than half the fun. They would settle a state and then they or their children would move on to a new wilderness, and still the land continued to stretch on west before them for another fifty years. When finally the open land did give out, their descendants would buy motor homes and move not in a linear track but in a circular pattern across the whole continent, still searching for that which they could not name and did not even care to find.

Iowa was quickly settled by these restless, searching European and American immigrants coming from the East. As historian Mildred Throne has said,

> The frontier period was compressed within a very few years.
> . . . The frontier procession, as described by [Frederick Jackson] Turner, marched single file: "the buffalo following the trail to the salt springs, the Indian, the fur-trader and hunter, the cattle-raiser, the pioneer farmer—and the frontier has passed by." In Iowa, this procession was hardly single file—the movers trod on each other's heels, or walked side by side.[5]

Iowa, in achieving its settlement, had benefited greatly from the migratory impulses of the residents of the eastern states. The state was opened, organized, and settled in less than one generation by immigrants from the eastern and southern states. But Iowa was also to be afflicted by the same high attrition rate that prevailed in Ohio and Indiana. Of the 829 farmers living in Wapello County in 1850, according to Throne's findings, only 377 or forty-five percent were still there ten years later. The others had moved on to newly opened lands in the western part of the state or had crossed the Missouri into the frontier of the Great Plains and the Rocky Mountains.

5. Throne, "A Population Study," p. 330.

Iowa had hardly become a state when the whole nation was seized with gold fever in 1849, and Iowans, like Americans everywhere, rushed west to realize the golden promises of California. Even that champion booster of Iowa's charms, J. B. Newhall, was to pack his horsehair trunk and start the long trip westward toward the gold fields on the American River. His was a short trip, however, for he died miserably of cholera in a hotel room in Independence, Missouri. Too few Iowans heeded the moral of his unhappy story, and each successive discovery of gold in the next twenty-five years—Colorado in 1850, Nevada in 1860, Idaho and Montana in 1863, the Black Hills of South Dakota in 1874—drained away some of Iowa's population. Nor was all that glittered in the prospective emigrant's eye gold. There were the wheatlands of Kansas, the grazing lands of Nebraska and Dakota, and the long trail winding into the wonderful Willamette Valley of Oregon. Nomads might be invited into Iowa, but they could not be held there.

For many newcomers into the state, Iowa was never considered as a home but merely as a thoroughfare, a wide valley that had to be traversed in order to reach a Zion that did not lie in this Mesopotamia. In the very year that Iowa became a state, its land was to be crossed by hundreds of covered wagons, the advance guard of the twenty thousand Latter-day Saints living in Nauvoo, Illinois. After the murder of their prophet, Joseph Smith, the Mormons, weary of combatting the hostility of their gentile neighbors, first in New York, then in Ohio, Missouri, and now Illinois, were ready to heed the command of their new Moses, Brigham Young, and follow him westward beyond the pale of civilized bigotry to establish the State of Deseret in the Great American Desert. These first Mormon trailblazers crossed southern Iowa in the late winter, spring, and summer of 1846, using roads for the first hundred miles, and then making their own trail west to the high bluffs of the Missouri, following the ridges and high ground as much as possible, building camps at Richardson's Point, Centerville, Garden Grove, and Mount Pisgah, digging wells and planting gardens for the thousands who would come after them.

This was one group of immigrants to the state who were neither welcomed nor encouraged to stay. The remarkable Mormon exodus across Iowa was to continue for the next fourteen years; first, all of the Saints of Nauvoo in heavy, lumbering wagons, following the trail of their leaders, and later the new converts from the Eastern seaboard and from England and Scandinavia, who came by rail to the end of the road in Iowa City. Here they took a more northerly route than their predecessors across Iowa to Council Bluffs, walking and pushing handcarts, which contained all their worldly goods, progressing along the thousand-mile trail that led to Zion and glory.[6]

Year after year they kept coming. As late as 1857, Edward L. Peckham, a botanist on a sight-seeing trip west from Brown University in Providence, Rhode Island, passed several groups of Mormons while he was crossing Iowa.

> There were many young girls, wearing large straw bonnets. . . . They were making nosegays as they went along. Some were quite pretty, and evinced some modesty, but the older women exhibited great indignation at being chided for their belief in polygamy. . . . Of the men, some were indifferent, some smiled and some laughed, but no one said a word. [As the stagecoach passed] . . . the immigrants struck up one of their sacred hymns, their voices being wafted over the plains with a strange and thrilling power." [7]

So they passed across Iowa, singing their hymns and digging ever deeper ruts into the already blazed trail. Some of the Mormons, to be sure, never left the state. There were many hundreds who found graves in the open grasslands; a few grew weary and, knowing they could not continue across the interminable plains to Zion, exchanged their faith for Iowa farmlands; and a sizable number refused to accept the leadership of President Young and particularly his advocacy of plural marriages. These Mormons, calling themselves the Reorganized Latter-day Saints, established their own community at Lamoni on the Missouri border, where they founded a college they named Graceland. There their descendants have remained, holding fast to

6. I am indebted to Porter French of Grinnell, Iowa, who has explored and found traces of the Mormon trails across Iowa.

7. Diary of E. L. Peckham, excerpts printed in *Palimpsest* 6 (1925): 238–239. The diary was originally published in its entirety by the National Historical Society in *The Journal of American History* 17 (1923): 225–235; 341–353; 18 (1924): 39–50.

what they claim is the true faith of their prophet Joseph Smith—
Iowa Mormons, at peace with their gentile neighbors but forever
alienated from the Utah Saints. Most of the thirty thousand
Mormons who crossed Iowa in the decade and a half prior to the
Civil War, however, hurried through as fast as the oxen or their
own legs would carry them, leaving behind a trail still discern-
ible on the Iowa landscape and a legend of one of the most extraordinary planned marches in all human history.

During these same years of the Mormon crossings, Iowa was
to receive still another band of immigrants whom it had not invited with newspaper propaganda and emigrant handbooks. This
group needed no guidebooks. It knew the land well and unlike
most Mormons, these people were coming into Iowa to stay.
When Governor Chambers signed a treaty with the Sauk and
Fox Indians in 1842, which stipulated that all members of those
two tribes were to leave Iowa by May 1845, most white settlers
breathed a sigh of relief and said "Good riddance." They hoped
never to see a red man in that part of Iowa again. But the Sauk
and Fox felt a quite different emotion. They sorrowed over the
beautiful lands that they had possessed such a short time. A few
refused to leave, hiding out in the unsettled lands along the
Iowa and Des Moines rivers. For the great majority who went
across the Missouri into the dry plains of Kansas, however, life
was intolerable. There were no streams to fish, and game was
small and scarce. Proud hunters of elk and deer, trappers of
beaver and otter, they were now miserable snarers of prairie
dogs and grubbers after field mice and beetles. It occurred to
some of the leaders of the Fox (Mesquakie) tribe that having
failed utterly in trying to arrest the advance of the white man
with peace pipes, parleys, or tomahawks, perhaps the only way
left was to play the white man's own game. Why not use their
annuity money and buy Iowa land just as if they were white immigrants from Holland or Ohio? So in 1856, Chiefs Ma mi nwa
ni ka and Ha pa ya sha raised $735 and came into Iowa as
buyers of land. They found in Tama County three brothers,
Philip, David, and Isaac Butler who were willing to sell them
80 acres for that amount, thus realizing a rather handsome profit
on $1.25-an-acre land. But as the Indians might have expected,

there was, as always, a catch in the white man's laws when applied to Indians. Indians were not legally persons. They could not own land any more than black slaves could. Surprisingly enough, however, the Indians had some friends among the white men who were willing to send petitions and lobby the state legislature for a law which would permit the Indians to become residents of Tama County and to obtain land, providing the governor would purchase the land in their name and that he and all succeeding governors of the state would serve as trustees for the Indians. Even more surprisingly, the legislature in special session in the fall of 1856 passed this bill, and Governor James Grimes, who was a sympathetic friend, quickly signed the bill and assumed trusteeship for the Indians. The Mesquakies were now legal persons, placed in the same category as children and idiots who needed guardians, but recognized as the legal owners of land in the white man's capitalistic society. The glad word went out to Kansas, "Bring your annuity money and come back to Iowa. We can buy more land and hunt and fish in the Iowa Valley again." But still the white man had his tricks to play. The Great White Father in Washington was not so sympathetic as the Little White Father in Iowa City. The Mesquakie chiefs had come up with a dangerous idea that could play havoc with the nation's Indian policy. Abruptly, all annuity payments were canceled for any Indian living outside of his designated reservation in Kansas. For the next ten years the Mesquakies, crowded into their eighty acres that could not be taken away from them, but with no money to buy more, lived a miserable existence. Always on the brink of starvation, for the small amount of land they held could not feed all of them, they peddled their beadwork in the small towns of the county and surreptitiously fished and hunted on lands they did not own. Mostly they had to beg from their increasingly hostile white neighbors in order to stay alive, but they would not give up. Finally in 1866, Secretary of the Interior James Harlan, an Iowan himself, rescinded the administrative order and agreed to the payment of annuities to the Mesquakies living in Iowa. After that, their lot improved somewhat. More land was purchased, until eventually the Mesquakies owned three thousand acres, for which they paid, on an average $30 an acre, about twice as much as their white neighbors were paying for their land. The Mesquakie Tama Indians no longer faced starvation, but they continued to live in poverty. The old way of life, of winters spent in trapping and hunting was forever gone. But at least a piece of the land was once again theirs. They could look at the river and the wooded hills beyond and that was good. Even better, at their annual powwows held each August they could tell their visiting relatives from Kansas and Oklahoma how for at least once in history the Indian had played at the white man's own gaming tables and had won.

The Mesquakie Indians had been fortunate that the bill enabling them to establish residency and purchase land had come to the Iowa legislature in the fall of 1856. Had it been delayed six months, the results could well have been different, for in the spring of 1857, most Iowans were not feeling very kindly toward any Indian. On 8 March in the far northwest corner of the state on the outer fringe of the frontier, along the shores of the beautiful "Great Lakes" of Iowa occurred the Spirit Lake massacre. Before the day was over, thirty-four settlers, living in isolated cabins on the shores of Okoboji and Spirit lakes, lay dead. When their bodies were discovered the following day by one of the settlers returning from a trip for supplies, the story was quickly spread to Fort Dodge and points south, and a thrill of horror ran through the state.

Part of the horror of the event lay in the fact that the massacre was so totally unexpected. Iowa's Indian problem was considered to have been finally and completely settled when in 1851 the Sioux had ceded their last remaining claims to Iowa land and had supposedly withdrawn from the state across the Big Sioux River into the Dakotas. Not all of the Sioux had left in that year, but those who remained had confined their hunting and trapping activities to the borders of the state, a safe distance from all but the most advanced and daring of the white settlers. Indeed, all of Iowa had seemed to be so secure from any possible Indian uprising that the army had abandoned Fort Dodge, the most northern military outpost in the state in March 1853, sending the troops farther north to Fort Ridgely in Minnesota

Territory. Those few foolhardy whites who in the mid-fifties had pushed north and west of the frontier line of settlement, however, should have had sufficient warning that there might be trouble. Isolated bands of Sioux were not uncommon throughout the area, warriors and hunters who gave no indication that they had ever heard of the treaties of Mendota and Traverse des Sioux, which had ceded their land to the white man in 1851.

In January 1854, there had occurred the tragic and brutal murder of the Sioux Chief Sintomniduta, along with his wife, mother, and children, by the disreputable whiskey seller and horse thief, Henry Lott, on the appropriately named Bloody Run in Humboldt County some twenty-five miles north of the abandoned military post at Fort Dodge. Historians have argued ever since as to whether or not Sintomniduta (or Sidominadota, as the name is sometimes spelled) was the blood brother of Inkpaduta, the Wahpekute Sioux who was to lead the Spirit Lake attack. But this is a white man's argument that to an Indian would be quite irrelevant to the case. Both men were leaders within the Sioux nation, and an attack upon one Dakotah chief was an attack on his entire people. The story of Lott's brutal attack at Bloody Run had been widely circulated among all of the subgroups of the Sioux region.

The winter of 1856–1857 was one of the worst in Iowa's history. From early December on, the snow had lain deep across the prairie. The frequent blizzards and bitter cold had isolated most Iowa communities, and food had to be carefully rationed, particularly among lonely settlers living on the fringes of the frontier. The winter had been equally difficult for the Indians, trying to hunt and trap in the same region. Game was scarce, and travel was often impossible. In late February, however, the weather moderated somewhat. Inkpaduta and his small band of fourteen hunters, who had spent the winter near the Big Sioux, decided to head inland to the northwest, searching for game and any other provisions they might obtain from the white settlers.

Inkpaduta, like his father before him, was something of a renegade among his own people. Noted for his bravery and skill in battle, he had never been willing to accept tribal discipline in times of peace or acknowledge the authority of the council or a superior chief. Except during a great intertribal war, he preferred to live apart from his Wahpekute brothers, surrounded by a few young men who would acknowledge his supreme authority. He had had frequent contact with whites in the area, and had even formed a close friendship with one of the first settlers in Woodbury County, Curtis Lamb, whom he taught to speak his Siouian dialect. There was nothing in his earlier history that would have singled him out among many other leaders of small bands of Sioux for the role he was to play in history.

On 13 February 1857, Inkpaduta and his men arrived in Clay County some fifty miles to the south of Lake Okoboji. Here, near the future town of Peterson, a few white settlers had staked out claims. A young girl, Jane Bicknell, recorded in her diary the panic she felt when the Indians suddenly appeared at her parent's farm demanding food. The Indians took all the flour and cornmeal they could find and then, before departing, in a sudden frenzy slit open the comforters and pillows on the beds and scattered the feathers over the ground.[8]

As the Indians headed north, the frenzy within them grew. They were particularly outraged to find evidence of white settlers on the shores of the three lakes which they and their people had always held in reverential awe. The largest of these lakes was called Minne-Waukon, Spirit Waters, a lake so sacred that no Indian would ever fish or put a canoe in its waters. Now on their shores were several log cabins of white settlers, with the fenced-in appearance of permanent occupancy. So, no matter whether it was Sintomniduta's murder by Lott, or the plump goose-feather pillows of the Bicknells, or the sight of rails fencing in the shores of Okoboji and Minne-Waukon, the breaking point had been reached. The Indians went from one cabin to another, killing men, women, and children indiscriminately. It was the sudden madness of murder that had no immediate cause of provocation from the victims, but it was also the cold sanity of murder prompted by the perpetrators' long premeditation over many causes. The last, bad chapter of white-Indian relations in Iowa had been written with blood on the snow.

Taking three married women and a young single woman,

---

8. Excerpts of Jane Bicknell's diary quoted in Curtis Harnack, "Prelude to Massacre," *The Iowan* 4 (Feb.-March 1956): 36–39.

Abbie Gardner, as captives, Inkpaduta and his band headed north into Minnesota Territory. When the word of the massacre reached Fort Dodge, a hastily assembled company of militia set out to rescue the captives and avenge the slaughter. But Inkpaduta was never apprehended, and the expedition, first trapped by swollen spring streams and later caught by sudden subzero weather, ended in disaster. Most of the men were thankful to have escaped from this futile chase with their lives. Two of the women taken by Inkpaduta were later killed by their captors, but Margaret Marble and young Abbie Gardner were eventually ransomed, the only survivors of the Indian attack.

In the long history of interracial conflict on this continent the Spirit Lake massacre is not a very significant one. Many more unprotected whites were to be massacred a few years later in southern Minnesota and a great many more Indians were to be brutally slain at Wounded Knee and Sandy Creek before the long conflict was over. But in the history of Iowa, Spirit Lake looms very large. Kept alive by the graphic reminiscences of Abbie Gardner, by scholarly articles, by poems and novels, the legend has persisted within the folklore of the people. The whites had moved in, so the Indians were forced to move out, and Spirit Lake was the final bitter farewell of the Indians to the land they had named Iowa—"Here is the place"—but not their place after all.

5

We Bring Our Ideals
to the Land

QUITE by chance, the State of Iowa came into being precisely at a time when the nation politically, socially, and intellectually was in ferment. No period in American history has been more caught up with the excitement of change and reform than were the fourth and fifth decades of the nineteenth century. It was a time when millennial hope outran temporal reality, and the spiritual frontiers of regeneration were advancing at an even faster pace than were the physical frontiers of human settlement. The old cakes of custom, carefully baked according to the tested recipes of Calvin, Locke, and Newton, had grown hard and stale. Now a new, yeasty mix was being stirred up and kneaded by many hands. The batter sent up many gaseous bubbles that could only burst and dissipate, but nevertheless the dough continued to rise, and eventually all America would serve as its oven.

Only a minority of Americans actively participated in this wildly eclectic reform movement, but no one, no matter how isolated, could ultimately escape its influence or ignore its demands. Most of the immigrants into Iowa had not come to create a new Zion or to set the prairies on fire with radical reform. The typical pioneer could have stated his hopes and ideals rather simply: to get land, to better his own and his children's condition, and to be left alone in the process. He was ready to fight to keep what he had or to get what he wanted but not for any abstract concept that had no immediate bearing upon his life. He demonstrated his patriotism on the Fourth of July, his politics on election day, and perhaps his religious beliefs on Sunday. For the rest of the year he was quite content to live and let live and leave well enough alone. But the crusading age in which he lived would not let him off so easily as that. Preachers and politicians, temperance lecturers and abolitionists, eccentric purveyors of panaceas and idealistic communalists all conspired to disrupt his life and to drag him, willy-nilly, into the whirlpool of ideological dispute.

First came the preachers, in the very vanguard of the procession into the state. The Catholics could lay first claim to Iowa by right of historical precedent, for Father Marquette had undoubtedly observed the first Christian rites on Iowa soil in 1673. But the Catholics during the next one hundred and thirty years of occupancy had done little to exploit their initial advantage. No Catholic missions had been established in Iowa, no attempts made to convert the sparse Indian population. It was not until the land was opened to white settlement and the eager miners, including many Irish Catholics, had rushed into Dubuque mines that the Roman Catholic church made definite plans to establish a church in Iowa. Father Pierre Jean DeSmet, who was later to achieve fame as a Catholic missionary on the Great Plains, arrived in Dubuque in July 1833 and formed a committee of laymen to collect money for the building of a church. As DeSmet was eager to move westward, it was left to the gifted and urbane Father Samuel Mazzuchelli, son of a wealthy Milanese family, to come down from his mission in Wisconsin in 1835 to supervise the building of St. Raphael's in Dubuque, the first Catholic church in Iowa. The indefatigable Mazzuchelli, an amateur architect as well as a skilled politician and zealous missionary for the Catholic faith, was successful during his eight years of residency in Iowa in designing, building, and, most important, filling seven churches before returning to his native Italy in 1843. The Third Provincial Council of Roman Catholic bishops, meeting in Baltimore in 1837, recognized the growing strength of Catholicism in Iowa by creating the diocese of Dubuque, and in 1839 the French aristocrat Mathias Loras arrived in Dubuque from Mobile, Alabama, to become Iowa's first Catholic bishop.

The Methodists quickly emerged as the major champions for Protestantism in contending with the Catholics for religious power in Iowa. Peter Cartwright, the venerable spokesman for Methodism in the Midwest, visited Iowa in 1834 and immediately saw the potential that existed there for saving souls for John Wesley's church. Three months later he sent a young circuit rider, Barton Randle, into Dubuque to confront the Catholics head on in their own stronghold. Not concerned with the niceties of architectural drawings and the need for an expensive stone structure as was Mazzuchelli, Randle solicited funds wherever he could find someone who might give a quarter or half-dollar to the cause. In a short time he had raised $244 from the people of Dubuque, including contributions from three black slaves who each gave twenty-five cents, to build a log-cabin church. Within eight weeks the structure was completed. On 25 July 1834, the first church in Iowa was open for religious service. "We raised the meeting house with a few hands and without spirits of any kind," one of the church members proudly noted in his diary.[1] Three years later a much more elaborate brick church was built in Burlington and soon became affectionately known throughout the territory as Old Zion. This church was not only the center for Methodism in southeast Iowa but it also served as the temporary capitol for the Wisconsin and later Iowa territorial legislatures until a new capitol could be constructed in Iowa City.

Church buildings were not essential to the cause, however, for Methodism was, of all major Protestant denominations, the best suited in its organization and by practical experience for proselytizing on the frontier. It was prepared to deliver its message wherever the people could be found—in individual homes, grocery stores, taverns, street corners, or in the open fields. Barton Randle preached his first sermon in Peru, a little village

1. Quoted in Ruth A. Gallaher, "The First Church in Iowa," *Palimpsest* 7 (1926): 7.

just north of Dubuque, in a pool hall, which, for small Midwestern towns was often the only den of iniquity of which they could boast. The owner, out of respect for the good reverend's sensitivity, had discreetly covered the billiard table with a white sheet. Inspired by the draped table's resemblance to a coffin, Randle preached an impassioned sermon on the death of sin in Peru. The owner was so shaken by the minister's eloquence that he promptly sold the hall with all of its nefarious equipment and donated the proceeds to further the cause of Methodism.

Not every sermon had as immediate and positive an effect as this, but the rapid progress that the Methodists made in these early frontier days in winning converts to their religion was impressive. Unlike most other major denominations, Methodism was not dependent upon trained theologians to conduct its religious services. It was quite prepared to use lay exhorters as well as young ministers to spread the word of its gospel by riding circuit to round up the wandering sheep. From the first days of settlement, the Methodist church became the largest single religious denomination in Iowa, a pre-eminence which it was never to lose.

Prior to Iowa's achieving statehood in 1846, most of the major religious organizations in America had sent ministers into the territory and had established churches. The Baptists built their first church at Long Creek, near Burlington, in 1834, and the Presbyterians at Sugar Creek in Lee County two years later. The Congregationalists claim the honor of being one step ahead of both the Catholics and the Methodists in conducting the first religious service in Dubuque in the summer of 1833, but this apparently was a one-day wonder. It was not until Asa Turner came to Denmark in 1838 that the first permanent Congregational church was established in Iowa.

The story of transplanting Congregationalism from its secure base of power in New England to the rough, no-holds-barred, spiritual free-for-all on the Iowa frontier dramatically reveals the problems that some of the long-established denominations had in adapting to a totally different environment. Refusing to use untrained laymen to ride circuit and to perform ministerial functions as did the Methodists, and lacking the clerical resources of

Roman Catholicism to draw upon, the Congregationalists, Episcopalians, and Presbyterians were unable at first to compete very effectively with either of the two major denominations on the frontier. Lonely, isolated ministers like Asa Turner in Denmark and the Presbyterian missionary Launcelot Bell in Burlington pleaded desperately with the American Home Missionary Society, which the two denominations shared, to send them ministerial help to establish new churches. But the frontier was wide, and the society could not find enough theological students willing to leave the security of the East for the uncertain hazards of the far west to satisfy the demand.

One can then well imagine Turner's surprise and skepticism when, in the spring of 1843, he received a letter from twelve young students at Andover Theological Seminary informing him that they were considering the possibility of forming themselves into an Iowa Band and coming to the Iowa frontier, each to establish a church and together, they hoped, eventually to found a college. They asked in their letter some very practical questions: What is the weather like? What kind of clothes should we bring? Is it safe to bring wives with us to the frontier? Turner's response was prompt:

> I am happy to hear that a reinforcement from Andover is talked
> of. I hope it will not end in talk, but I fear. . . . Don't come here
> expecting a paradise. Our climate will permit men to live long
> enough, if they do their duty. If they do not, no matter how soon
> they die. . . . Come prepared to expect small things, rough things.
> Lay aside all your dandy whims boys learn in college, and take a
> few lessons of your grandmothers before you come. Get clothes
> firm, durable, something that will go through the hazel brush
> without tearing. . . . Get wives of the old Puritan stamp . . .
> those who can pail a cow and churn the butter, and be proud of a
> jean dress or a checked apron.

And then he added in a despairing postscript, "But it's no use to answer any more questions, for I never expect to see one of you west of the Mississippi river as long as I live." [2]

The challenge had been thrown at them, and the Iowa Band

2. Quoted in Douglass, *The Pilgrims,* pp. 54–56.

immediately laid plans to meet in Albany, New York, on 4 October. Eleven of the twelve kept their rendezvous, and three weeks later they arrived in Iowa ready to build their churches and to bring New England culture to the wilderness. In the true Congregational spirit, Turner refused to assign them to posts but insisted that each young minister choose his own location in which to labor as a latter-day Pilgrim. So the eleven scattered over the whole wide territory that had been opened up to settlement—from Garnavillo in the north to Farmington, close to the Missouri border, from Muscatine on the Mississippi to Ottumwa on the very fringes of the western settlement. All but one survived the first five years of frontier existence, and within that time each had not only established his own church, but the ten together, along with Turner, had founded Iowa College in Davenport, modeled on a modest scale after their own beloved undergraduate colleges of Amherst, Bowdoin, Union, and Yale. It would appear that they had successfully fulfilled the promise they had made to each other in the library at Andover in the spring of 1843. The letters that one of the band, William Salter, faithfully wrote during these years to his fiancee back in New England and the journal entries he recorded reveal how difficult it had all been and how uncertain these young men felt about their success in bringing spiritual and cultural enlightenment to the frontier. They had the will certainly. Salter wrote Mary Ann Mackintire:

> I shall aim to show that the West will be just what others make it, and that they which will work the hardest and do the most for it shall have it. Prayer and pain will save the West and the Country is worth it. . . .

There were prayers and pain a plenty, but sometimes Salter wondered if the West really wanted to be saved after all.

> In so new a country where so many other interests absorb the minds of men, the objects in which we are engaged are very much slighted. . . . Whole communities [are] filled up with families who are Universalists or ignorant persons [and] who had never been brought up to respect the Sabbath or attend public worship.

Back in New England, these self-confident young men may have smiled indulgently at Turner's patronizing counsel to put aside the "dandy whims boys learn in college," but they were now discovering that it was not easy to cast aside two centuries of culture in order to meet the west on its own terms. They may have expected their chosen communities to welcome them with open arms as the bringers of light and salvation, but in despair, Salter wrote:

> Bellevue is one of the most abandoned places I was ever in—a most dreadful population. The only evidence I have that I have preached the truth among them is that they hate me. I can assure you that it is very trying to know how to get along with the wicked men here. . . . Oh, if we had such settlers as New England first had, we might hope that this wilderness would bud and blossom. But alas, the wicked and the worldly and the backsliders are the main settlers of this country. . . . I preached a Thanksgiving sermon this week to a very small congregation. Most of the people were in the fields husking corn.

Always there were the Methodists and Papists crowding in ahead of him and winning converts. "The Methodist Circuit Preacher was here at 6 p.m.," Salter noted, "and organized a class of ten members. They are too disposed to be sectarian and push a little with their horns." [3] The Methodist exhorters might be scorned for their deplorable manners, but the Congregationalists and Episcopalians were ill prepared to compete with them. Although Turner repeatedly warned Salter, Erastus Ripley, and others that their sermons were too scholarly, too filled with classical allusions, they found it difficult to change. Most of the band were to stay the rest of their lives in Iowa, Salter himself setting a ministerial record for Iowa that still stands by serving his congregation in Burlington as pastor for sixty years, but they remained always transplanted Yankees, who spoke of Massachusetts and New York as home. To the end of his life Salter insisted that people in Iowa could not even say the name

3. Salter's letters to Mary Ann Mackintire and Salter's Journal 1843–1846, edited by Philip D. Jordan, were published in their entirety in *Annals of Iowa*, 3rd Series, 24, Part 2 (1943): 105–185.

of their own state correctly. It should be pronounced I-O'-WA, with the accent on the second syllable, as every cultured New Yorker knew.

The Presbyterians and Baptists soon proved to be far more adaptive to the frontier than the Congregationalists, Episcopalians, or Unitarians would ever be, but no other Protestant sect could overcome the initial advantage and strength of the Methodists. On the eve of the Civil War the 1860 federal census showed the following religious box score for Iowa: the Methodists in a comfortable first place, with 90,000 members and 35 percent of the total church membership for the state; the Presbyterians in second place with 43,000 members and 17 percent of the total church membership; the Catholics third with 31,000 members, 12 percent of the total membership; the Baptists a close fourth with 28,000 members, 10 percent of the total; and the Congregationalists a poor fifth, with 19,000 members, which was less than 6 percent of the state's total church membership. Exceeding by far the total number of members of all the religious denominations combined, however, were the 418,000 residents who belonged to no religious organization whatsoever. Nearly two out of every three Iowans remained unmoved by Methodist exhortations, Congregational culture, or Catholic ritual. They continued to be "absorbed in so many other interests . . . in their fields husking corn" on Thanksgiving or on the Sabbath day. To Salter they were "wicked, worldly, and backsliding," but the pioneer farmer, had he had the advantage of Salter's education, might well have flung back at the Andover seminarian a quotation from his own beloved classics, *"Laborare est orare."*

Many of the minor religious sects in Iowa did not depend upon circuit riding and mass conversions to impose their ideals upon the land. These communicants came in groups to buy land and establish their own ready-made congregations; the Dutch Reformers under the leadership of Dominie Scholte in 1847; the Quakers, who came into east central Iowa in the early 1850s; the Mennonites, entering Johnson and Washington counties in the 1860s and 1870s; and the River Brethren who came from Pennsylvania in 1877 to scattered parts of Iowa. Of all the immigrants who came into Iowa bringing with them intense religious ideals, these small pietistic sects were undoubtedly the most content with their situation. Their religion was so deeply engrained within them as to be inseparable from all of the daily tasks of living. They welcomed into the fold anyone who might seek them out, but because they were not interested in proselytizing, they never experienced the frustrations of the Catholic or Protestant missionaries, whose exhortations so frequently fell on deaf ears. On the other hand, because they already had found a faith that could not be moved, they were not troubled, as were their unregenerate neighbors, by those who would seek to convert them. They were left alone and were quite at peace in their isolation.

Finally, there came to Iowa those small groups of Utopian Communitarians for whom the ideal they had grasped was so totally absorbing that everything else must be subordinate to it. These were the genuine radicals in the true meaning of that word, for they sought to strike at the very roots of existing social institutions. They regarded all of the major religions as being nothing but organized hypocrisy. Of what use was all of this talk of conversion and regeneration of the individual through prayer, baptism, and ritual when the very people calling themselves saved served as money-changers in capitalistic temples, chaplains and soldiers in murdering national armies, and solons in corrupt legislatures. The individual could be saved only if society was saved, and these ideologues would regenerate society by providing it with models of totally different institutional structures, which it could emulate.

Some of these radical communities that bubbled up out of the leavened mass of nineteenth-century reform dismissed all formal religion as being irrelevant to the question of social salvation. These were the socialist groups who in those pre-Marxian days manifested their Utopian ideals in many forms: Fourier Phalanxes, Owen co-operatives, and Transcendental work farms. The most notable of these experiments in Iowa was that of the Icarian colony in Adams County, near the present town of Corning. Here the last remnants of those who had pursued the dreams of the French Utopian socialist Etienne Cabet from

France to Texas to Nauvoo, Illinois, gathered in 1860 in the hope that at last the long *Voyage en Icarie* could terminate in a safe harbor in the unlikely empty grasslands of western Iowa. Here they were determined to make a reality of the 1789 French rallying call to revolution, but there were always, among the Icarians, more liberty and equality than there was fraternity. Torn apart by internal dissension over such questions as the right of the individual colonists to own their own private fruit and vegetable gardens, the right of women to vote in their assembly meetings, and the wisdom of admitting new converts into the society, the colony kept splintering away into dissident factions. When William Alfred Hinds, a student of American Utopian socialism and himself a former member of the Oneida colony in New York, visited Icaria in 1876, he found only eighty-three persons left, out of an original five hundred members, and he knew he was looking upon a dying experiment. Two years later an Iowa court revoked the original charter for the colony, and two separate Icarias then emerged, each with its own charter and settlement. The more radical group lasted only a few years more before its members drifted off to California, still pursuing their evanescent dreams. The more conservative, pro-private-garden faction continued to exist as "La Nouvelle Communauté Icarienne" until February 1895 when the last few aging communists voted reluctantly but unanimously to dissolve the society and divide their assets. The voyage was at last over, but the memories of radicalism lingered on in the Corning area long after the last *Cabétiste* was laid in his grave.

A Fourier Phalanx from Watertown, New York, was also established in Iowa, some nine miles south of Oskaloosa in 1843, but it lasted less than two years and was totally forgotten by history until 1930, when a diligent researcher in early land claims came upon a claim entered in the Mahaska County abstract book by the Fourier Association of Iowa for several sections of land in Scott township. A more successful and longer lasting secular communal society was established at about the same time in Clayton County in northeast Iowa by eight Germans and one Frenchman from St. Louis. Purchasing 1,400 acres of land in the beautiful valley lying between the Volga and Turkey rivers, they named their settlement Communia, a socialist community for farmers, artisans, and manual laborers. It soon attracted the attention of a German refugee, Wilhelm Weitling, a former follower of Cabet who, after organizing thirteen communistic societies in Switzerland and being imprisoned for his efforts, had fled to New York, where he established the Workers' League of America. Promising the leaders of Communia that he would provide new skilled recruits and much needed cash if the Workers' League were given a share of the property, Weitling managed to get himself elected president of the community and to transfer the entire assets of the colony to his labor organization. Funds and recruits from New York, Philadelphia, and Baltimore did come to Communia and for a few brief years in the early 1850s, the settlement prospered. Ambitious plans were made for the building of factories, gristmills, and additional towns, but as so often happened, factional disputes disrupted the community. Weitling himself left in disgust, and urged his Workers' League to send no more colonists or funds to Communia. After nine years of existence, the society was divided among those who still remained in the area. Another novel experiment in communal living had ended in failure.

Most of these early Utopian experiments in socialism had been indifferent but not openly hostile to organized religion. When William Hinds, in visiting Icaria, asked if the community had not exalted communism into a religion, President Sauva replied, "You are perfectly right in supposing that we elevate the principle of Communism . . . into the place of religion; but Christianity in its primitive purity is held with us in great esteem; and of personal opinion in matters of religion there is in Icaria the greatest tolerance, provided its expression does not result in trouble and disorder to the Community." [4]

At least one colony established in Iowa during this period, however, did not share Sauva's tolerance toward individual Christian beliefs. This was Abner Kneeland's notorious settlement of Salubria, which was established in Van Buren County

---

4. Interview quoted in William Alfred Hinds, *American Communities*, (Oneida, N.Y.: Office of the American Socialist, 1878), p. 74.

near Farmington in 1839. Kneeland, born in Gardner, Massachusetts, in 1774, had traveled a very long road of Protestant belief from Scottish Presbyterianism to a born-again Baptist conversion, to Congregationalism, and finally to Universalism. He served with considerable distinction as a Universalist minister in Boston for many years. Eventually, however, he was to find even the mild, liberal tenets of the Universalist church too restrictive, and he abandoned his Boston pastorate in 1829 for what he called a rational free enquiry after truth. He became editor of a weekly paper, *The Investigator,* and devoted the columns of this journal to the advancement of many causes: the cooperative movement, the abolition of slavery, and above all else, attacking organized religion. An editorial of his written in December 1833 finally brought him to the attention of the authorities. He stated as his credo:

> Universalists believe in a God, which I do not; but believe their God with all his moral attributes (aside from nature itself) is nothing more than a chimera of their own imagination. . . . . Universalists believe in the resurrection of the dead, in immortality and eternal life, which I do not; but believe that all life is mortal, . . . and that no individual life is, ever was, or ever will be eternal.[5]

Under an ancient and nearly forgotten statute, Kneeland was tried and convicted of blasphemy. After a long court fight and several re-trials, and in spite of the support given him by Emerson, William Ellery Channing, Theodore Parker, William Lloyd Garrison, Bronson Alcott, and other Massachusetts luminaries, Kneeland was finally sent to jail for sixty days, the last person ever to be imprisoned in Boston for blasphemous writings.

His incarceration convinced Kneeland that liberty was dead in Massachusetts and that he must pursue his free enquiry in a totally new environment. In the spring of 1839, at the age of 65, he came to Iowa to found his colony. Although a close associate of both Robert Dale Owen and Frances Wright, Kneeland did not intend to build a socialistic co-operative commonwealth, but rather an association of free people who, living outside the

5. *The Investigator,* 20 December 1833, quoted in Mary R. Whitcomb, "Abner Kneeland: His Relations to Early Iowa History," *Annals of Iowa* 6 (1904): 346.

confines and threats of organized religion, could pursue truth as they wished. Kneeland wrote enthusiastic letters back to his friends in the East urging them to join him:

> Even aside from the persecution I have endured in my native state, I know of no place in Boston that could afford me half the pleasure, as to the beauty and grandeur of the scenery, as it does to sit in my front door here and look across the Des Moines River; to see the large branching trees on the nearest bank and the beautiful green forest on the opposite side—this wonderful country which is destined to outvie everything which can be even imagined in the East.[6]

A few like-minded seekers joined him in Salubria within the next three years, and Kneeland, intoxicated by his initial success at colonization, decided to enter Iowa politics and run for a seat in the upper house of the territorial assembly. He quickly discovered that Massachusetts had no monopoly on religious bigotry. In a rare display of unity, Whigs and Democrats, Methodists, Congregationalists, Presbyterians, and Catholics, all combined their forces to defeat him. The ardent young ministers of the Iowa Band, in particular, saw in Kneeland the very embodiment of that spirit of wicked, atheistic worldliness against which they had dedicated their lives. It was almost as if God had provided them with a Lucifer in corporeal form to inspire them to greater efforts in their missionary work. Ephraim Adams at Mount Pleasant, Daniel Lane in Keosauqua, and Harvey Adams at nearby Farmington all preached impassioned sermons against this infidel who would "substitute Paine's *Age of Reason* for the family Bible, dance for the prayer meeting, and the holiday for the Sabbath." [7] It was the old drama of the Puritan attack on Thomas Morton's Merrymount re-enacted in a new setting. Once again the maypole, joyfully raised to celebrate freedom from dogma, was hacked down. With the death of Kneeland in August 1844, there was no health left in Salubria, and the colony quickly disappeared.

Most of the radical religious experiments in communal living

6. Whitcomb, "Abner Kneeland," p. 353.
7. Ephraim Adams, quoted in Whitcomb, "Abner Kneeland," p. 357.

were as short-lived in Iowa as were the secular Utopian communities. A small band of German Swedenborgians, led by a German shoemaker, Hermann Diekhover, came into Iowa County from St. Louis in 1851 to establish a communistic society that would live according to the philosophic precepts of their great Swedish mentor. They called their colony Jasper, taking the name from Revelation 21:19,

> And the foundations of the walls and of the city were adorned with all manner of precious stones. The first foundation was jasper.

The name proved to be a prophetic inspiration, for within two years the material substance of their prosperity became more precious to them than their social beliefs. The colony in 1853 voted overwhelmingly to abandon communism for the hard, gemlike tangibility of private land ownership; and Diekhover, who had argued in vain against this decision, returned heartbroken to his cobbler's bench in St. Louis.

The one exception to the general pattern of failure among these Utopian communal societies was that of the Community of True Inspiration, which came, over a ten-year period from 1855 to 1865, from Ebenezer, New York, and settled in Iowa County not far from the defunct Swedenborgian colony of Jasper. These were German Pietists who had broken away from the Lutheran church in the early 18th century and had for the next one hundred years endured religious persecution and legal prosecution from their state and neighbors. In the nineteenth century they had found a new source of inspiration and a leader in the person of a young carpenter of Ronneburg, Christian Metz. It was Metz who convinced the members that they could find peace only in the New World. In 1843 they began to come in small groups to western New York and southern Canada to live in a communal society, but the land they had purchased lay too close to the rapidly growing city of Buffalo, so once again the inspired Metz took his people westward, this time to the empty lands of Iowa. Here they built their seven villages of Amana, tilled their 26,000 acres of rich farmland, and re-established their communal society, which was to last for another eighty years, longer than any other communistic group in America except the Shakers.

IOWA

A photographer's essay by Joe Munroe

Photographs in Sequence

Many factors contributed to the success of Amana. The True Inspirationists were able to reconcile the kind of individual pietism of the Quakers with a discipline of leadership comparable to that of the Mormons. The Amana Society was not fragmented by atomistic individualism nor oppressed to the point of revolt by the authoritarian rule of its elders. It also achieved a happy balance between the demands of communal living and the individual's desire for personal possessions. All lands, mills, factories, tools, and livestock were held in common. Tasks were assigned to each adult within the community, and the people worked in their common fields, prayed in their community churches, and ate in their common dining rooms as a collective society. The old socialist dream "from each according to his ability, to each according to his need" was a living reality in Amana. But after each day of communal living, upon finishing the evening meal, each family went to its individual home, where every man, woman, and child had his or her own room that could be furnished with one's own personal possessions. Here was a sanctuary within the communal hive that allowed for individual privacy and family cohesion.

Although living in communities apart from the rest of society, the people of Amana never insisted, as did the Amish, upon emphasizing their separate distinction to the point of an eccentricity, which would alienate them from their neighbors. There were no rigid taboos in diet, dress, or education. The society was quite receptive to technological changes and improved methods in agriculture and industry. The railroad was not only accepted, it was actively sought by the elders of the society. One reason for the society's purchasing the small nearby village of Homestead, which was already in existence at the time of the Inspirationists' arrival, was that it was to be a station on the trans-state Mississippi and Missouri Railway line.

The size of the society was also a contributory factor to its success. Beginning with 800 people in 1845, the colony grew to a maximum population of 1,800 by the turn of the century. Unlike so many smaller communal groups, which were not large enough to sustain the venture, Amana had a diversity of skills and interests great enough to sustain a viable economy. Nor did it insist upon maintaining its exclusiveness to the point that it would not admit outsiders as hired hands when there was a shortage of labor or of special skills. As early as 1855, additional labor had been brought in to help build Amana, and these "outsiders" not only stayed, but their numbers increased. Many of Metz's letters indicate that he was unhappy with this dependence upon hired hands, but it is significant to note that the society was flexible enough to accommodate itself to the necessities of a practical labor situation without losing its sense of community identification and its reason for existence.[8]

For nearly a century, Amana thrived and held fast to the communistic ideals of Metz and Barbara Heinemann, the society's two "Instruments of Inspiration." When the distinguished American economist Richard T. Ely visited Amana in 1902, he wrote enthusiastically on the success of its communal economy. "Amana comprises more than half the communists of the United States and in studying Amana, we are examining the largest and strongest communistic settlement in the entire world," he could with accuracy report in that pre-Leninist age. Already Ely could sense, however, that the outside world was having its distracting influence upon the colony, particularly among the young people. "The seclusion of Amana is necessarily yielding to the influence of the American environment. . . . Will the solvent of American life destroy this prosperous community?" He thought that it inevitably would. "It has lasted sixty years. It may last sixty years longer, . . ." but Ely was doubtful.[9]

Ely's doubts about the continuing existence of this communal society were well justified, for even before World War I, there were signs of trouble in this rural paradise. Although there is evidence in the records to indicate that the society had always had to deal with the few who sought to shirk their assigned tasks, the number of drones within the communal hive increased in the first decades of the twentieth century. Many families after 1900, moreover, while still availing themselves of the products of the communal kitchens, were abandoning the communal din-

8. I am greatly indebted to Jonathan Andelson, Assistant Professor of Anthropology, Grinnell College, for his help to me in writing this account of the Amana Society.

9. Richard T. Ely, "Amana: a Study of Religious Communism," *Harper's Monthly Magazine* 105 (1902): 659–668.

ing rooms in favor of eating in their individual homes. Above all, it was the automobile which was to change the Amana lifestyle. It not only brought the outside world into Amana, it also lured the society's young people out. They left the community to take jobs in Cedar Rapids, Iowa City, and more distant places, returning only for short visits in order to show off their new cars and to invite their friends to come away with them.

The Supreme Court of Iowa, in the first decade of the twentieth century, upheld the right of the Amana Society to be communistic in its organization as being a proper exercise of religious freedom and the right to voluntary association. This decision, written by Chief Justice Scott M. Ladd, was especially notable in that Ladd was himself a distinguished scholar in property law and a staunch defender of private property rights. Judge Ladd's court was, unfortunately, far in advance of the general public in its defense of civil liberties. For there was a growing resentment from outside neighbors, particularly in nearby Marengo, toward this Germanic communistic colony, a hostility that reached its peak of xenophobic hysteria during and immediately after World War I, when anyone using the German language was suspected of being a spy and any communal sharing was not only regarded as being un-American but as being probably inspired by Red Bolsheviks.

Pressed by an increasingly hostile outside world and pulled by its own young people, the society could only forestall, not avert, the inevitable conclusion. It was far too late, even if they had wished to do so, for the Amana elders now to attempt to seal off their community from the corrupting influence of the outside world as had the Old Amish in Kalona and Hazelton. The Amana Society suffered as severe an economic crisis in the agricultural depression of the 1920s as did its capitalistic neighbors, with the collapse of the midwestern wool market and the decline in grain prices. As the depression deepened in 1931, the elders with characteristic resolve decided to take drastic action. A committee was established to study and make recommendations for a change in the communal structure. Insisting that Metz and Heinemann had never considered communism as an end in itself, but only one means of working and living within the faith, the committee recommended that the communal society be turned into a capitalistic corporation with each member of the society a stockholder. The farmlands and factories would become the property of the corporation and wages would be paid to all those employed by the society. Individual families would be encouraged and assisted in buying their present homes or building new ones. The communal kitchens would be closed. Amana, in short, would become a co-operative company town in which the workers and their families would be the owners of the corporation. The elders and the entire society voted unanimously to adopt the report, and so in June 1932, ironically in the very year that many Americans were seriously considering the possibility of moving in the opposite direction, Amana abandoned communism and adopted a capitalistic structure. Under capitalism, the seven villages of Amana have continued to thrive. Tourists by the thousands come each year to dine in the colony's restaurants and to purchase the fine furniture and woolen goods of its factories. The word "Amana" is probably best known today throughout the United States, not for its past history, but as a trade name for refrigerators, air-conditioners, and micro-wave ovens, an industry which the society established in 1937 but later sold for several million dollars to an outside corporation. Amana has prospered under capitalism, the faith has been kept, but the old way of life has been lost forever. This loss surely is a source of regret to some, but no one would desire to return to the communal past. Of the many experiments in communal living begun in the nineteenth century, Amana remains as the one outstanding example of success both in sustaining a communistic society for ninety years and then in adapting itself to a changing world. Its star shines all the brighter in the history of Utopian societies because of the contrast it presents to all the hundreds of little candles that were lighted by both religious and secular communal reformers only to flicker and go out. The average life span for all of these communities was probably no longer than three years. Most have been lost to history, their names "written in water" or at best as a single entry in a county abstract book.

But what of the more notable experiments such as Brook Farm, New Harmony, Zoar, and, in Iowa, Icaria, Salubria, and Communia? Have social historians paid unwarranted attention to these noble failures? Most of these historically renowned communities were equally short-lived and all of them, as Ralph Albertson points out in his study, were economic failures. They had inadequate capital and they frequently overextended themselves, buying more land than they needed or could take care of, building mills and factories without having an adequate labor force or proper managerial skills.

It could also be argued that they failed in their primary purpose of reforming society by setting a radical example of change. When Mary Whitcomb in 1903 went to Farmington to do research on the history of Salubria, she found that the Farmington Congregational Church had been built upon land given by the Kneeland family, and Abner Kneeland's own granddaughter was teaching Sunday School in that church! For an old man who had preached that there was no immortality for anyone, this was perhaps an appropriately wry conclusion to his story. And in Clayton County the descendants of Communia are now conservative and highly successful farmers, dedicated to the principles of free enterprise and usually voting a straight Republican ticket. Are we then in our frequent retelling of the histories of these radical communities simply celebrating meaningless failures and pointing up the absurdity of man's millennial hopes and dreams? Albertson would argue otherwise. He suggests in the conclusion to his study that we need instead to re-examine our meanings for the words "success" and "failure." "That culturally and educationally they were worth all that was invested in them is the opinion of many of the ex-participants. That they sent out their people into the common life of the country to be good citizens no one will question." [10]

One can carry Albertson's reasoning even further and argue that these societies not only benefited those who participated in them but that they also had an impact upon society in general that cannot be evaluated simply by counting the number of converts they won, in measuring the length of time they survived, or in relating what has happened to their descendants. The influence of these Utopian dreamers was far more subtly pervasive

10. Ralph Albertson, "A Survey of Mutualistic Communities in America," *IJH* 34 (1936): 438.

than their opponents realized. In a negative way they promoted
the cause of reform in America by the very radicalness of the
positions they took. In contrast to their extreme and widely
diverse attitudes toward marriage, sex, dietary and sumptuary
laws, and the private ownership of property, the advocates of
temperance, pacificism, penal reform, woman's rights, and even
the abolition of slavery seemed moderate and reasonable. More
positively it can be argued that these radicals were the yeast
needed to raise the consciousness of America for needed social
reforms. They co-operated with the more orthodox religious ide-
alists, the Congregationalists and Quakers, in circumventing the
Fugitive Slave Law and in promoting the abolitionist cause.
Some of these groups by example added strength to the Methodist and Baptist forces fighting for temperance, and within their
own societies, they frequently established models of sexual
equality which provided evidence in support of the conten-
tions of Lucretia Mott, Amelia Bloomer, and Elizabeth Cady
Stanton. By daring to protest with direct action the conventional
wisdom of their society, they helped to prepare the land for the
more successful reform movements that would follow after the
Civil War: radical reconstruction, the Social Gospel, populism,
and progressivism. If they had done nothing else, these communal societies deserve credit for giving to Iowa a much needed
ideological diversity, which might in part compensate for its
lack of racial and ethnic diversity.

Benjamin Spaulding, the Iowa Band's representative in Ottumwa, celebrated the news that the Fourier Phalanx in nearby
Mahaska County had failed by writing in his journal, "It is truly
a matter of gratitude to God that so many mistaken schemes are
falling to the ground." [11] But God's ways can be inscrutable,
even to those who believe themselves to be his special emissaries. Posterity might express its gratitude in quite a different
manner—not that "so many mistaken schemes" had failed but
rather in thankfulness that they had ever existed. Certainly
Iowa's history has been the richer for having had them.

11. Quoted in Philip D. Jordan, "The Iowa Pioneer Phalanx," *Palimpsest* 16 (1935):
225.

6

We Fight for the Land

O N May 1850, Augustus Caesar Dodge, the senior senator from Iowa, arose in the United States Senate chamber to express his strong support for the series of bills that Henry Clay had introduced in an effort to allay the sectional tensions arising over the question of slavery. It was with no little interest that his colleagues, the galleries, and the press listened to the senator from Iowa, for he represented the only state west of the Mississippi in which slavery was prohibited, "the one free child of the Louisiana Purchase" as the more poetically inclined journalists had dubbed Iowa. Dodge did not equivocate. In denouncing Representative David Wilmot's attempt to prohibit slavery in the territory recently acquired from Mexico, Dodge placed the entire blame for the controversy arising out of "Wilmotism" upon what he called "the fell spirit of abolitionism . . . As for this compromise, I will vote for it because I wish to get the subject from before us. I am sick, sore, and tired of it." [1]

A few days later, he was joined by his colleague from Iowa, Senator George W. Jones, in enthusiastic support of the compromise measures. Henry Clay's five bills sought to satisfy both North and South by: first, admitting California as a free state; second, allowing the New Mexico and Utah territories to deter-

1. *Congressional Globe,* Part I, 31st Cong., 1st Sess. (May 28, 1850): 1085.

mine for themselves the question of slavery within their borders; third, settling the boundary dispute between New Mexico and Texas in New Mexico's favor, but in compensation, authorizing the federal government to assume Texas's external debt; fourth, abolishing the slave trade in the District of Columbia; and fifth, passing a new and much more stringent fugitive slave law. It all balanced beautifully on paper: two and a half points for the North; two and a half points for the South, and peace for the entire nation. The difficulty lay in the fact that neither the North nor the South felt that the five points were of equal importance. The South regarded it a poor bargain to give up any hopes of establishing slavery in California for the remote possibility that New Mexico and Utah might opt for slavery. Northern liberals and radical abolitionists were outraged by an equation that gave the same weight to abolishing the auction block (but not slavery) in the nation's Capital with a Draconian law that would open up every Northern state to search and seizure by Southern slave hunters, backed by the strong arm of federal marshals.

Iowa's two senators, however, were obviously as pleased with what proved to be Clay's last balancing act as was that old master juggler himself. Four years later, Dodge would boast on the Senate floor that "Iowa is the only free state which never for a moment gave way to the 'Wilmot Proviso.' My colleague [George Jones], who never dodges a responsibility or fails to perform a duty, voted for every one of the compromise measures . . . including the fugitive slave law—the late Senator Sturgeon, of Pennsylvania, and ourselves, being the only three senators from the non-slaveholding section of this Union who voted for it. Since then, my colleague has been returned to this body without any objections, so far as I have heard, from either Democrat or Whig, on account of his votes to which I have referred." [2]

Dodge and Jones basked in what they regarded as the warm security of a safely Democratic state. Iowans did not like slavery, and neither did their two senators, but on the other hand,

2. *Congressional Globe*, Appendix, 33rd Cong., 1st Sess. (Feb. 25, 1854): 382.

Iowans were not abolitionists. They were not crusaders. Let the South keep its slaves south of the Mason-Dixon Line, the Ohio River, and the Iowa border, and all would be well. Let the Whig party be torn apart by Cotton Whigs and Conscience Whigs; the party of Jefferson, Jackson, Cass, and Douglas would endure, and a Democratic state legislature in Iowa would continue to return its obligingly reasonable and compromising senators to Washington, two voices of sanity in an increasingly fanatical city. Dodge and Jones would continue to work for railroads for Iowa, for low tariffs, sound money, and against powerful banking interests. This is what Iowa wanted, at least so Dodge and Jones reasoned in 1850, and they were probably right.

But had the two senators been more careful students of Iowa election returns, they might not have sounded quite so complacent in their Senate speeches nor have cast their votes with so positive an assurance that their voice was indeed the voice of all the people and hence the voice of God. It was quite true that since achieving statehood, Iowa had consistently elected only Democrats to Congress and to the governorship and other state offices. But to count only final victories without measuring the strength of the opposition can be misleading and dangerous. Iowa was Democratic, but not safely so. The Democrats tended to ignore the fact that for four of the eight years of its territorial government, Iowa's appointed governor had been a Whig. Through the power of patronage and influence in Washington, the Whig governor had been able to build a solid party, ably assisted by many of the territory's leading newspaper editors and businessmen. The result was that the first legislative assembly of the state elected in the fall of 1846, was so closely divided between the Whigs and Democrats that for over two years, it was impossible for the legislature to elect a United States senator. It had not been until December 1848 that Dodge and Jones had finally secured their election and could take their seats in Washington. In the presidential election of 1848, the first to occur after Iowa had become a state, the Democratic electors obtained a plurality but not a majority of the popular vote. The Democratic candidate, Lewis Cass, received 49.7 percent of the

Iowa vote; and the Whig candidate, Zachary Taylor, 45.6 percent. It was the abolitionist-tinged Free Soil party that held a potential balance of power with 4.6 percent of the popular vote. Should the Whigs of Iowa try to lure the Free Soilers with a more vigorously stated opposition to slavery, the Democrats could be in serious trouble.

As it turned out, however, this election proved to be the last presidential victory for the short-lived Whigs. Divided over the question of slavery, the party would soon disintegrate and out of its ruins would grow a new and vigorous sectional party. The Democrats were not able to take much consolation from the disarray of their Whig opponents, for they, too, at both the state and national level had to confront the same divisive forces. In the gubernatorial election of 1850, at the very time that Dodge in Washington was speaking glibly of the happy Democratic consensus which existed in his state, back home the Democratic candidate, Stephen Hempstead, was defeating his Whig opponent by only two thousand votes out of a total of twenty-five thousand votes cast. Iowa, prior to the Civil War, was definitely a two-party state. Quite obviously any major political crisis—national or local—could easily upset this rather delicate balance. Small wonder that Iowa's Democratic senators had rallied to the support of their Whig colleague's compromise bills.

With the passage of Clay's compromise in the summer of 1850, the great crisis over "Wilmotism" seemed to have passed. Congress in the name of popular sovereignty had willingly delegated its long-accepted power to determine the question of slavery in the national territories to the residents of the territories obtained from Mexico. Still the issue of slavery would not go away. Neither the abolitionists nor the slaves themselves would let it. Dodge might have thought that with the passage of the compromise bills, he had "got the subject from before us," but in Iowa the abolitionists were becoming bolder, speaking out in the pulpit and in the press and increasingly obtaining the attention if not the sympathy of both Whigs and Democrats. In 1852, for the first time, a Whig was elected to Congress from Iowa. John Cook had won in the normally heavily Democratic Dubuque district by attracting a large part of the

German vote with his outspoken support for free land for free men.

The runaway slave from Missouri and points south also brought the issue of slavery in its most personal form directly to Iowa. Much has been written about the development of the undergound railroad in Iowa in terms so extravagant as to convey the impression that this covert operation of transporting fugitive slaves across Iowa moved with the dispatch, efficiency, and regularity of timetable that would have been the envy of the Rock Island or Burlington railroad lines. Many families living in southern and central Iowa would, at a much later date, boast of the hundreds of slaves they had helped on the way to freedom. These memories are romantic exaggerations. There are, of course, no statistics on the number of fugitive slaves who entered Iowa during the two decades prior to the Civil War, but it is safe to assume that legend has multiplied their numbers many times over. The risks were too great to attract many passengers to this northbound subterranean line. Over a period of time, a rather loosely organized line of movement was developed across Iowa, from the little Congregational village of Tabor in the southwest corner of the state, to the Quaker settlement at Earlham, and then on east through Des Moines, Lynnville, Grinnell, Iowa City, and Springdale to Clinton or Muscatine on the Mississippi River. But of necessity there had to be many spur lines, much more make-shift than the established main route, to meet the demands of a spontaneous traffic that could not be organized. It was the solitary slave, never having heard of the "Tabor Line," but suddenly deciding on his own to make a bolt for freedom, whom an Iowa farmer would find cowering in his barn. Looking into that frightened black face, the farmer would see the true countenance of slavery and would then have to come to grips personally with the moral issue that slavery presented. Should he obey his nation's laws and turn the poor wretch over to the authorities or should he listen to the mute appeal for humanity and help the slave to escape his bondage? The poison of the South's "peculiar institution" was spreading; it could not be contained in one section, and there was no antidote in congressional compromises.

James Connor in his essay, "The Anti-Slavery Movement in Iowa," correctly emphasizes the fact that Iowa was never pro-slavery, as so many earlier historians had claimed, basing their judgment on the large number of Southern immigrants into Iowa in 1830s and 1840s. What is not noted by these historians is that many of these Southern immigrants had come from the mountain areas of Virginia, Kentucky, and Tennessee, where the hostility to slavery was strong. They had left the South to escape slavery, not to serve as its advance agents in the Midwest.[3] They carried with them a prejudice against blacks, but this was a prejudice that was in no way confined to the slaveholding states of the South. It is a great mistake to confuse racial prejudice with proslavery sentiment, as so many post-Civil War Northern historians have done. Had these two attitudes indeed been synonymous, then the Southern slaveholders' ascendancy would have been complete and the entire nation would have been proslavery, for both sections overwhelmingly held in common a belief in white racial supremacy. It was the manner in which the two sections, by historic circumstance, expressed their prejudice that created the sectional difference; the South would maintain white supremacy by keeping the blacks in slavery; the North would maintain the same prejudice by keeping the blacks out of their lands.

In the first year of its territorial existence, the government of Iowa, both in its legislative and in its judicial branches, had issued two official and seemingly contradictory statements in respect to the black man in Iowa. In January 1839 the territorial legislature passed "An Act to Regulate Blacks and Mulattoes." This bill provided that no black or mulatto person could take up residence in the territory without first obtaining a court document certifying that he was a free person and then posting a five-hundred-dollar bond to assure the community that he would not become a criminal or a county charge. This repressive Black Code has been a major piece of evidence for those historians who have insisted that Iowa initially was pro-slavery in sentiment.

3. James Connor, "The Anti-Slavery Movement in Iowa," *Annals of Iowa,* 3rd Series, 40 (1969) 343–376; 450–479.

Six months later, however, the Iowa supreme court in the very first case to come before that body for adjudication rendered an opinion that would seem to reflect a quite different attitude toward blacks. This was in response to a suit for a writ of habeas corpus that has become known in history as "The Case of Ralph, a person of color." Ralph, who had been a slave in Missouri, had persuaded his owner, a man named Montgomery, to allow him to go to the lead mines of Dubuque to work for wages in order to purchase his freedom. By the terms of this agreement, Ralph was to pay Montgomery over a two-year period the sum of $480, his purchase price, for freedom. Ralph quickly discovered, however, that the lot of the wage laborer, particularly if he was black, was not as fortunate as he had anticipated. It took all of his meager earnings simply to provide for the basic necessities of life, and he was unable to send any money back to Montgomery in Missouri. After waiting for more than two years without receiving any payment, Montgomery decided that Ralph had no intention of paying, and sent two slave-catchers to Dubuque to bring Ralph back into slavery. As soon as Ralph was arrested, an antislavery Irishman, Alexander Butterworth, interested himself in the case. On behalf of Ralph, he applied to the district court for a writ of habeas corpus. The judge of the district court, Thomas Wilson, who was also an associate justice of the territorial supreme court, at once perceived the importance of this case and had it transferred to the higher court for a full hearing. David Rorer, one of the most able lawyers in the territory, and himself a former slave owner from Arkansas who had become an outspoken critic of slavery, offered his services free of charge to Ralph. Quoting from both Blackstone and the Bible, Rorer denounced slavery as being an unnatural state repugnant both to the laws of nature and to the laws of God. Rorer found a sympathetic audience in the three territorial justices. Speaking for a unanimous court, Chief Justice Mason ruled that inasmuch as Ralph had been given permission by his master to come to Iowa, he could not be regarded as a fugitive slave. And since he was not a fugitive, the law provided no recourse for his former master to reclaim him. The Territory of Iowa, by congressional action of 1820, did not per-

mit slavery; consequently, Ralph, as a resident of Iowa, could
not possibly be a slave. Montgomery might have a legal claim
to the $480 due him, but he could not enforce that claim by
reducing Ralph to the status of a slave. Anticipating by nearly
twenty years the infamous Dred Scott decision, the three territorial justices of Iowa came to a diametrically opposite conclusion. None of the Iowa justices questioned the right of a black
to have standing in court, and all three were in agreement that
Congress had the constitutional power to prohibit slavery in any
territory, and that established residence in a free territory was of
itself an act of manumission. Theirs was a remarkable judgment, and had Chief Justice Taney and a majority of his
brethren on the United States Supreme Court chosen to use the
Case of Ralph as a precedent for determining the Case of Dred
Scott in 1857, American history could have been given quite a
different turn.

Although it might be argued that the territorial legislature and
the judiciary in 1839 reflected opposite points of view, neither
the repressive racial bigotry of the legislative enactment nor the
surprising liberality of the judicial opinion was inconsistent with
the views held by most Iowans at that time. Blacks were not
welcome in the territory, but if they were able to establish
residency there, it must be as free men not as slaves. These two
official pronouncements of Iowa's territorial government offer
striking evidence of the compatibility of antislavery and anti-
black sentiments.

It is safe to say that most Iowans would have been content to
put the entire question of slavery into a deep freeze and to have
the nation abide by the great compromises of 1820 and 1850.
But a moral issue as volatile as slavery could not be stabilized
and fixed for all time. Not only would the fugitive slave and the
abolitionist Congregational minister keep the issue alive, but the
Iowa farmer himself, in seeking further territorial expansion and
a transcontinental railroad, would serve as an agent of agitation
for a continuing controversy over slavery. Like an evil incubus,
slavery lay on top of and penetrated every issue of national importance from the time of our war with Mexico in 1846 until the
Southern guns finally opened fire on Fort Sumter in 1861. Any

proposal to dredge the Mississippi River channel, to build a railroad across the Great Plains, to open the trans-Missouri lands to white settlers, or even to offer the nation's thanks to its victorious general who had stormed the heights of Chapultepec must be confronted with the leering, obscene visage of slavery. Escapism was an impossibility, but Iowa continued to cling to its illusion of isolation until the last possible moment.

That moment finally arrived in 1854, and ironically it was Iowa's own Senator Dodge who, by introducing a bill to organize the Territory of Nebraska, was to destroy the last hope that the issue of slavery could be isolated and ignored. As introduced by Dodge in December 1853, the bill would have created one vast territory lying between the 37° and 43° parallels west of the Missouri River to the 104° longitudinal line. No mention was made in Dodge's bill on the question of slavery in the territory, but as all of this territory lay north of the 36° 30' line established in the Compromise Act of 1820, the assumption was that this would be free territory, just as Iowa and Minnesota had been.

The Southern congressional leaders, however, had no intention of allowing yet another vast territory to be created out of the Louisiana Purchase that prohibited slavery. And Dodge's close friend and colleague, Senator Stephen A. Douglas of Illinois, had no intention of allowing the Nebraska bill to be defeated by a controversy over any moral issue so abstract and academic as the possible existence of slavery in the Great Plains area. Douglas and Dodge wanted a railroad from Chicago to Council Bluffs, Iowa, that would serve as the necessary connecting link with a transcontinental railroad that would be built across Nebraska and on through Utah to the Pacific Coast. This could be done only if Nebraska were organized as quickly as possible to offset the New Orleans–Texas claims for a southern transcontinental route. The Missouri Compromise of 1820, Douglas reasoned, was a small price to pay for Illinois's and Iowa's imperial railroad dreams. So Douglas rushed in with an amendment to Senator Dodge's bill: a proposal to divide the territory into two parts—Kansas and Nebraska, to repeal the Missouri Compromise, and to allow the settlers in both new territories to determine for themselves the question of slavery. The necessary Southern notes were obtained, and the Kansas-Nebraska bill became law in May 1854.

Neither Douglas nor Dodge could have anticipated the political storm that their bill would arouse within their own states. Both must have felt that their constituents would be as willing as they were to buy an immediate economic gain for their states with a promissory note of popular sovereignty. They both were quickly to discover how out of touch they were with thousands of their constituents. Douglas would later ruefully comment that soon after the passage of the Kansas-Nebraska Act it would have been possible for him to travel from Chicago to Springfield in the dead of night, his way lighted by his own effigies being burned by an enraged citizenry. Douglas was powerful enough to survive the storm of abuse in Illinois and to win re-election to the Senate in 1858, but Dodge was not so fortunate in withstanding the anger of his constituents. The Kansas-Nebraska Act ended his successful political career in Iowa. He even had to endure the open opposition of his father, Henry Dodge, the senior senator from Wisconsin, who spoke and voted against his son on the Kansas-Nebraska bill.

In Iowa, the news of the repeal of the Missouri Compromise, to which the state owed its initial free status, shook the entire political structure with a seismographic reading of force 8. Old party alignments toppled, and the delicately balanced political scale, which had been slightly weighted in favor of the Democrats, now swung to the side of the Whigs. But it was not the old Harrison-Clay type of Whigs who added weight to that side of the scale. It was a new brand of Whigs, who openly courted the Free Soilers and abolitionists. Many were novices on the political scene, Congregational and Methodist ministers, newspaper editors, and even women such as Amelia Bloomer, Delia Webster, and Annie Savery, "strong-minded women" who correctly identified sexual discrimination with racial oppression. Some, like William Penn Clarke, had long been active in politics, but always on the fringes of power because of their extreme antislavery positions. Now all of these diverse groups could be brought together into one coalition, united in a single cause, which, if properly publicized and exploited, could have wide political appeal.

Much has been written on the divisive effect that slavery had on American politics in the decade prior to the Civil War, and certainly it was over the question of the extension of slavery that both of the two great national parties were to divide and collapse. Not enough attention, however, has been given to the opposite effect slavery had on the American political scene. Paradoxically, the issue of slavery was both a centrifugal and a centripetal force. As it shattered old alignments, it also served as a coagulant to bring together many different and heretofore hostile elements. In Iowa, recent German immigrants and xenophobic nativists, Irish saloon keepers and cold-water temperance reformers, Methodist circuit-riders and Congregational scholar preachers, West-Point-trained army reservists and Quaker pacifists—all now found themselves bound together in their common opposition to the extension of slavery. Never has the old cliché "politics makes strange bedfellows" had greater validity than in the years immediately after 1854. But a new bed was needed if former Democrats, Whigs, Know-Nothings, and Free Soilers were all going to climb in and lie comfortably together. In Illinois, Michigan, Indiana, Wisconsin, and Iowa, spontaneously formed protest meetings were being held in the early spring of 1854 that, taken collectively, would provide a new party in which all of these diverse elements could bed down.

As the anger mounted in Iowa over the proposed repeal of the Missouri Compromise, the hapless Democratic party felt honor-bound to support Senators Dodge and Douglas, and their doctrine of popular sovereignty. The Whigs, on the other hand, had a great opportunity to capitalize upon the growing opposition in the state to the possible extension of slavery, providing they pushed aside the old compromising leadership that had long dominated their party. Loudly insisting that a new issue of transcendent importance called for new leadership, the antislavery faction of the Whig party at the state convention held in Iowa City on 22 February 1854 was powerful enough to force through the nomination of James W. Grimes for governor. Then very cleverly, in what was an open bid for co-operation if not fusion with the recently organized Free Democracy party, they nominated that party's candidate for superintendent of public instruction, George Shedd, for the same office on their ticket. The triumph of the antislavery Conscience Whigs was now complete.

The Whigs had chosen wisely in selecting James Grimes as their candidate for governor. A prominent Burlington lawyer and railroad promoter, Grimes had been active in Whig politics since his arrival in Iowa in 1836. As a friend of William Salter and a member of his church, Grimes had long had close ties with the Congregational hierarchy in Iowa and was entirely sympathetic to its antislavery position. Although repeatedly denying the charge that he was an abolitionist, Grimes was definitely allied to the extreme antislavery forces in the state. Now his time had come. Realizing that if he were to defeat the Democrats he must have the united support of all the antislavery people in the state, Grimes went as a humble petitioner to Denmark to ask the ruling clique of the Free Soil—Free Democracy party, Asa Turner, George and Curtis Shedd, and George F. Magoun, the future president of Iowa College (now known as Grinnell College), to drop their candidate, Simeon Waters, and to endorse Grimes. He was given a warm reception by these stalwart abolitionists, and with Waters's willingness to be sacrificed, the merger was quickly accomplished.

Grimes, in return for the endorsement, issued a formal position paper upon which he would base his campaign. In blunt language, he brought the issue of Kansas-Nebraska directly home to the people of Iowa:

> If there is one State in the Union more interested in the maintenance of the Missouri Compromise, it is the State of Iowa. . . . With a slave State on our western border, I see nothing but trouble and darkness in the future. . . . I do not attempt or desire to interfere with slavery in the slave-holding States . . . but, with the blessing of God, I will war and war continually against the abandonment to slavery of a single foot of soil now consecrated to freedom.[4]

The great number of Iowans who had long sought to keep slavery isolated and remote but who were now troubled and out-

4. Quoted in Connor, "The Anti-Slavery Movement," pp. 373–374.

raged by the prospect of being slowly encircled by the "peculiar institution" had found a powerful spokesman in the lawyer from Burlington.

Even so, Grimes did not win the election by a landslide. He needed all of the Free Soil votes he got to defeat his Democratic opponent Curtis Bates by a little over 2,000 votes out of a total of 44,527 votes cast. Of equal importance to the Whig party, which was now rapidly revamping itself into the Republican party, was the fact that it won enough seats in the Iowa General Assembly to oust Senator Dodge and to elect James Harlan of Mount Pleasant to the United States Senate.

In the months that followed his election to the governorship, the trouble and darkness that Grimes had predicted would result from the Kansas-Nebraska act was indeed visited upon his unhappy state. Iowa and Missouri became the two great staging areas for hundreds of Free Soilers and proslavery men, hell-bent for Kansas where they could participate in Douglas's popular sovereignty contest with their ballots and their bullets. John Brown, peripatetic tanner from Connecticut, Pennsylvania, and Ohio, who quickly emerged as a fanatical leader of the antislavery forces, has had his name historically linked with the states of Kansas and Virginia, but he is also an integral part of the history of Iowa in these troubled years. It was in Iowa that this stern disciple of Old Testament morality was to find his one sanctuary, a secure base to which he could retreat to rest, recruit new followers, and make plans for future operations.

Between the time when he first went to Kansas in August 1855 to join his five sons who had preceded him, and February 1859 when he headed east for his ill-fated appointment with history at Harpers Ferry, Brown visited Iowa at least four times, staying with abolitionist friends at Tabor, Des Moines, Grinnell, and Springdale. Here in this last named small Quaker village in Cedar County, which he first visited in the fall of 1856, coming directly from the bloody fighting at Ossawatomie, Brown was to establish his Iowa headquarters for the next two years. The attraction that the militant Brown and the gentle pacifistic Quakers of eastern Iowa had for each other was so curiously unnatural as to defy rational explanation. Bound together only by their common aversion to slavery, the Quaker farmers living peaceably

along the Pedee Creek west of the Cedar River and Bloody Old
Brown, the Scourge of God, found in each other that which they
needed for these tumultuous times. For the Pedee Quakers,
Brown was apparently a surrogate instrument of destruction,
destroying with violence that which they themselves hated but
were forbidden by their religion to attack. For Brown, the few
months he spent living quietly at various farmhouses near
Springdale and West Branch were moments of sanity to remind
him of the pastoral peace he had once known before madness
had gripped him and his nation.

It was to Springdale that he returned in November 1857 to
make plans for the final assault upon slavery that he had been
slowly formulating in his mind. He brought with him a band of
ten men including his own son Owen and a fugitive slave, Richard Richardson. A well-to-do farmer, William Maxson, welcomed Brown and his men into his home, and the group spent
the next five months there, engaged in military drill and study
during the day and conducting a mock legislative assembly for
the ''State of Springdale'' in the evenings. Here in a district
school building, legislative committees were formed and bills
repealing the Fugitive Slave Law and granting the franchise to
women were introduced and solemnly voted on. It was, in all, a
surrealistic dress rehearsal of John Brown's planned drama for
the future.

Quite naturally, such activities attracted wide attention and
comment in this peaceful Cedar River valley. Young boys
watched excitedly the sharp drill maneuvers in the green pastures of Maxson's farm, and their elders observed with quiet
satisfaction the legislative enactments of the Springdale school-
house assembly. Two young Quaker brothers, Edwin and
Barclay Coppoc, were especially infatuated by these activities,
and were soon admitted into the secret councils of the visiting
band.

Brown returned to Springdale for the last time in February
1859, bringing with him eleven fugitive slaves whom he was
personally conducting to Canada. Here the final plans were dis-
cussed for the attack on Harpers Ferry. The Coppoc brothers
were told to be ready to join him at a moment's notice. They

obediently sold their livestock in order to have funds in hand for the expected trip east. The word from Brown reached them in mid-July, and, according to Springdale legend keepers, Barclay announced to his mother, "We are going to start to Ohio today."

"Ohio!" she exclaimed. "I believe you are going with old Brown. When you get the halters around your necks, will you think of me?"

"We cannot die in a better cause," was Barclay's simple answer.[5]

When Brown finally collected his band of twenty-two men in Maryland during the last week in July 1859, it included, in addition to Edwin and Barclay Coppoc, four other Iowans, the largest contingent from any one state. Iowa had sent its first men off to civil war.

While Brown was training his small band in Springdale for action on the battlefield, Governor Grimes was organizing forces for a full assault on the Democrats on the political front. Almost imperceptibly and without fanfare, the old Whig party of Iowa had merged into the new Republican party, and in 1856 its triumph was complete. It carried both houses of the Iowa legislature by over two-to-one margins; it elected its two candidates to Congress; and it gave its four electoral votes to the dashingly romantic Republican candidate for President, John C. Frémont.

Grimes and his fellow Republicans were prepared to take full advantage of their victory, for their political program included more than the single issue of continuing opposition to the extension of slavery. High on their priority list was a proposal to write a new constitution for the state. These antislavery Republicans, who were also ambitious capitalists, were determined to eliminate the hated constitutional restriction on banks and other corporations in the state. They were also eager to write into constitutional law a provision that would move the capital from Iowa City to Des Moines in the center of the state. This move would not only provide an additional incentive for further

5. Quoted in Pauline Grahame, "Springdale Recruits," *Palimpsest* 41 (1960): 30.

railroad construction but it would help secure the political support of the rapidly growing population in the western part of the state. Consequently, Grimes pushed the proposal to call a constitutional convention as soon as he took office, and in the general election of August 1856 the voters gave their approval to a convention by a vote of 32,790 for and only 14,612 against.

The thirty-six duly elected delegates, twenty-one Republicans and fifteen Democrats, met in Iowa City on 19 January 1857 to begin their deliberations for a new constitution. The convention completed its work within six weeks and produced a constitution that, with less than forty amendments, has endured to the present time. The constitution that this convention wrote was essentially a compromise doctrine. First, it balanced the demands of the new aggressive capitalists against the old radical populists' fears of monopolistic capital. The constitution authorized the general assembly to create "corporations or associations with banking powers," and a "State Bank with branches," but no such law "shall take effect . . . until the same shall have been submitted, separately to the people, . . . and shall have been approved by a majority of all the electors voting for and against it at such election." [6] The people could still block the establishment of any banking corporation, and as a further check upon expansive capitalistic ventures, particularly in the area of railroad promotion, the constitution set a limit on the bonded indebtedness of cities and counties, a debt which could not exceed five percent of the value of taxable property. Second, the convention balanced the demands of the central and western parts of the state for the constitutional determination of the location of the state capital in Des Moines with a provision that there should be one state university and that it must be permanently located in Iowa City. Bowing to the Jacksonian democratic spirit, which was still strong in the state, the convention shortened the term of the governor and all other elective executive officers to two years, and it provided for the popular election of all judges, including supreme court justices.

6. Text of the Constitution of the State of Iowa (1857) reprinted in Benjamin Shambaugh, *The Constitutions of Iowa*, (Iowa City: State Historical Society of Iowa, 1934), p. 329.

On the vexing question of racial equality the convention wrestled with its deeply ingrained prejudices, and unhappily the prejudices largely won out. The black citizens of Iowa did get constitutional recognition that the "due process" clause applied to them. For the first time, their testimony was now to be acceptable in all state courts, and they had a right to trial by jury even though they themselves could not sit on a jury. Nor could any black hold state office or serve in the state militia. Over the protests of the few genuinely egalitarian abolitionists in the convention, the new constitution still restricted the vote to white male citizens, twenty-one years of age or older. The most that Rufus Clarke and John Parvin could obtain in the way of a compromise was that an amendment to the constitution striking the word "white" from the suffrage clause would be offered to the people at the same time the constitution itself was presented for ratification. This amendment was subsequently defeated by an overwhelming vote of 49,387 to 8,489. The convention neatly dodged the question of public education for blacks and Indians by voting down a proposal to establish "separate but distinct" schools for the races, and simply provided "for the education of all the youth of the state through a system of common schools," thus leaving to each school district the freedom to handle the integration of the races in its own way. As Iowa's historian Leland Sage has observed in his evaluation of the convention's work in respect to racial equality, "To put it bluntly, the 'first free state in the Louisiana Purchase' was not very free; the Negro was 'north of slavery,' just that and little more, with perhaps a small degree of advancement over the views expressed in 1844 and 1846." [7]

The convention completed its task on 5 March 1857, and the result of its labors went to the people for approval. By a scant 1,630 votes out of some 79,000 votes cast, the people of Iowa ratified their new constitution. The large negative vote was not too surprising. What the delegates gave with one hand they seemed to take away with the other. Elitism had been carefully

7. Leland Sage, *A History of Iowa* (Ames: Iowa State University Press, 1974), p. 136.

balanced with populism. No one, regardless of status, could be totally satisfied with the result; no one had been totally rejected.

This constitution was very nearly rejected by the voters because it failed to satisfy anyone fully, but it has endured for one hundred and twenty years precisely because it was a compromise document. It has permitted growth and change because it is vague and often contradictory. Unlike many other Midwestern states, Iowa did not find it necessary in the 1870s to rewrite its constitution in order to place a more effective popular control over railroads and other monopolistic corporations. That power had already been given to the general assembly and the people. The constitution's racially and sexually discriminatory features could and would be rectified by an amendment process that required only a simple majority vote in the general assembly and among the voters of the state, a much simpler and more democratic process than is the amending of the United States Constitution. The quite undistinguished delegation that met in Iowa City in the winter of 1857 had built a far better edifice than anyone, themselves included, had reason to believe at the time.

Having successfully accomplished his major goals of building the Republican party into a successful statewide organization and of getting approved a constitution that he and his party could live with, Governor Grimes was ready to move on to a higher office. After only one term as governor, he retired in 1858, and was succeeded by the quite colorless and unenergetic Ralph P. Lowe of Keokuk. Grimes immediately turned his attention to getting his party's backing for the United States Senate seat still held by George W. Jones.

By 1858, the day of reckoning for Jones had at last come. The senior senator from Iowa, who had once so proudly boasted of his votes for the Compromise of 1850 and the Kansas-Nebraska Act, had been in no way affected by the rapid course of events that had changed his state from being Democratic to becoming Republican. Remaining stubbornly loyal to the disastrous Kansas policies of President Buchanan, Jones could no longer command support even within his own party. The Democrats unceremoniously dumped him and chose Benjamin Samuels as their candidate for the United States Senate. But with a solid Republican majority in both houses of the Iowa General Assembly, the result was a foregone conclusion. Grimes easily won the Senate seat over Samuels by a vote of 64 to 41. Iowa, which only four years before had been represented in the Senate by two of the most conciliatory Southern appeasers from any of the Northern states, was now to be represented by two of the most outspoken antislavery men in the United States Senate. Although Harlan and Grimes were never to be very close personally, to the nation they presented a single united front in opposition to the Buchanan administration and the Taney Court. Iowa had moved rapidly from isolation to the very vanguard of sectional partisanship.

As the nation continued to lurch from one sectional crisis to another, moving inexorably toward disaster, the Republican party in Iowa skillfully exploited each outrage, the Dred Scott decision, the proslavery Lecompton constitution in Kansas, even the mad raid of John Brown on Harpers Ferry, to consolidate and enlarge its political power. For the state general election to be held in October 1859, the Republicans eliminated the ineffective Governor Lowe as a candidate for re-election by nominating him as a justice for the Iowa Supreme Court, an office that by temperament and training he was much better suited to fill. To replace Lowe as governor, the party made the rather surprising choice of Samuel Kirkwood, a state senator from Iowa City, a former Democrat and miller from the state of Ohio. Lacking new leadership for their beleaguered party, the Democrats turned once again to Augustus Caesar Dodge, hoping that his four years of exile as minister to Spain would have erased the memory of his unhappy association with the Kansas-Nebraska act. The Republicans would not let the voters forget, however, and although Dodge conducted a vigorous campaign, the hitherto unknown Kirkwood won fifty-eight of the ninety-two organized counties and carried with him to victory all of the Republican candidates for state office, including the three supreme court justices. The Republicans now controlled all three branches of the state government and had elected all four representatives to the two houses of Congress.

It would be difficult to imagine a greater contrast in personality than that between the outgoing and incoming Republican governors. The quiet, scholarly, and cautiously apolitical Lowe had been replaced by an untutored, bluntly outspoken man of the people. Often crude and ungrammatical, Kirkwood's state papers and formal speeches remain as refreshing a delight for readers today as they were for the audiences to whom they were addressed. Kirkwood never equivocated, never dodged an issue to play a political game with the voters, and to the surprise of all, his manner of operating proved to be amazingly good politics. Kirkwood was a worthy successor to Governors Lucas and Grimes, and Iowa was fortunate to have him in the chief executive office during the tragic years that lay ahead.

Almost immediately upon assuming office in January 1860, Kirkwood was confronted with a sectional issue that would test his skill and courage and attract the attention of the entire nation. John Brown's body, one month after its burial, had not yet begun "a-mouldering in its grave," but his spirit was certainly on the march across the land. Young Edwin Coppoc of Springdale had died on the gallows along with his quixotic hero, but his brother Barclay had not been in the roundhouse at Harpers Ferry on that fateful morning when Colonel Robert E. Lee's troops battered down the doors. Escaping from the Maryland farmhouse that he had been left to guard, the younger Coppoc, along with Owen Brown and three other companions, had managed to get north into Pennsylvania. Then after weeks of hiding during the day, traveling at night, and eating raw corn stolen from fields along the way, Coppoc managed to make his way back to Iowa where, emaciated and near the point of exhaustion, he appeared in Springdale to be welcomed as a hero. Governor John Letcher of Virginia, learning of Coppoc's arrival home, sent his agent Charles Camp to Des Moines on 23 January 1860 to deliver formal extradition papers to Governor Kirkwood, requesting the return of Coppoc to Virginia for trial. To the surprise and consternation of Camp, Kirkwood refused to honor the papers, finding them "fatally defective" in not specifically charging Coppoc with the crime of treason and in not offering any evidence that Coppoc was in the state of Virginia on the morning of the raid. An enraged Governor Letcher had to draw up new extradition papers to meet Kirkwood's objections, but by the time these papers were received and honored on 10 February 1860, Coppoc, with Kirkwood's apparent connivance, had escaped to Ohio, where he remained in hiding until the outbreak of the war and the secession of Virginia enabled him to return in safety to Iowa. Kirkwood emerged from the affair as a hero to the people of his own state and to abolitionists everywhere. Young Barclay, however, was not to escape martyrdom. While crossing the Platte River near St. Joseph, Missouri, in August 1861, the troop train on which he was riding plummeted off the bridge, which had been sabotaged by Rebel guerilla forces. Barclay Coppoc became one of Iowa's first casualties in a war that the young Quaker considered holy.

After his successful encounter with the governor of Virginia, Kirkwood could do nothing wrong in his home state. He and his party looked forward eagerly to the approaching presidential election which they felt confident could be won by any candidate whom the party might nominate. To the second national convention of the Republican party, which was to convene in Chicago in May 1860, the Republicans of Iowa sent thirty-two delegates, each with one-quarter of a vote. It was a marvelously eclectic group of Iowans that set off for the Wigwam in Chicago in early May: old antislavery Whig politicians like William Penn Clarke, who in heading the delegation found to his own amazement that recent events had propelled him from the periphery to the center of the political scene; the aristocratic Dominie Henry Scholte of Pella and John Brown's good friend Josiah B. Grinnell; young men like William B. Allison, James F. Wilson, and William P. Hepburn, whose successful political careers lay in the future; and one or two wonderful eccentrics like the Baptist clergyman John Johns dressed in blue denim and a white tasseled stocking cap, who, lacking any money for his transportation, had walked the three hundred miles from Skillet Creek in Webster County to Chicago. Governor Kirkwood was there, not as a delegate, but as an assiduous convention worker for his good friend Abraham Lincoln. John Kasson, the able state chairman of the Republican party in Iowa, served the convention with such distinction in drafting a platform that he was to win the high praise of Horace Greeley's *New York Tribune.*

Iowa's votes for a presidential candidate were as widely disparate as were its delegates. As the delegation was never polled, the anonymity of the votes would later permit nearly every delegate from Iowa to remember fondly that he had had the good sense to cast his vote for Lincoln, but the official tally of the first ballot shows that no other state scattered its votes in so many directions as did Iowa: Lincoln 2 (which meant 8 delegates did vote for him), Seward 2, Cameron 1, McLean 1, and Chase 1. On the second ballot, Lincoln jumped to 5 votes among the Iowa delegation, thanks to Kirkwood's efforts, Seward held steady at 2, with Chase and McLean still hanging on with ½ vote each. On the third and final ballot, Iowa was still divided with the Seward men still casting 2 votes and Lincoln picking up only McLean's ½ vote. Only when Lincoln's nomination was assured, did Iowa's thirty-two delegates finally achieve unanimity for their neighbor Illinoisian.

In the campaign that followed, one could find little evidence in Iowa that the nation was engaged in the most fateful presidential election in its history. Borrowing all of the log-cabin, hard-cider razzle-dazzle that the Whigs had used with great effect to elect the vacuous Harrison in 1840, the Republican Wide Awake clubs held torchlight parades, barbecue picnics, and rail-splitting contests for Honest Abe. They played up the planks in the Republican platform for free homesteads and federal aid to railroads, and for the first time they attempted to mute somewhat the dangerous issue of slavery, insisting that Lincoln was not a fanatical abolitionist. The Democrats tried to tar the Republicans with prohibition and Know-Nothing nativism, issues with which they had considerable success among the Germans and Irish in the Dubuque area. Above all, the supporters of Douglas presented their candidate as the one truly national figure, the only one of the four presidential aspirants whose election would not mean the disruption of the Union. But the contest was never much in doubt. Lincoln received 70,118 votes and carried 60 counties, Douglas got 55,639 votes and 25 counties, and the other two candidates, Breckenridge and Bell each received only a handful of votes. Iowa's four electoral votes were added to Lincoln's impressive total. A Northern sectional candidate had been elected, and seven Southern states promptly seceded before he could be inaugurated President.

Iowa's senators and representatives in Congress took no part in the last-ditch effort to find one more compromise which might save the Union and prevent war. Henry Clay was dead, Jones and Dodge were discredited in their own state, and the hour for compromise had passed. The two congressional delegations from the states of Iowa and Maine had the distinction of being the only ones that voted unanimously against every proposal offered to avert the crisis. When the war came in April 1861, it brought almost a sense of relief to the people of Iowa that at last the long years of tension were over, and a clean, swift, final resolution could be effected upon the battlefield. Democrats and Republicans alike joined in a spontaneous outburst of enthusiasm to "Rally Round the Flag, Boys." In Lincoln's first call for 75,000 troops, Iowa's assigned quota was only one regiment, consisting of ten companies, or approximately 800 men. It was very quickly oversubscribed, as young men left the farms and towns to sign up for duty. Rallies were held on the steps of the Old Stone Capitol in Iowa City to recruit university students, and at Iowa College, which only two years before had moved from Davenport to the abolitionist town of Grinnell, nearly the entire male student body marched off to war.

No other period in Iowa's history has been so thoroughly researched and analyzed as the four years from 1861 to 1865, and quite properly so, for no other event, not even the Great Depression of the 1930s, was to have so profound an impact upon the state as the Civil War. It was the great determinant of our political structure and in many important ways of our social attitudes for the next one hundred years. In these respects, the Civil War was as important to Iowa as it was to Alabama or Mississippi. It created a one-party state with all the implications that that historical fact has politically, socially, and economically. It was the great temporal landmark by which thousands of Iowans would fix their family calendars, and our museums and courthouse squares are filled with the artifacts and memorials of that conflict.

Iowa during the four years of civil war was to furnish to the Union cause 70,000 soldiers, Nearly half of all men of military age in Iowa were in the service at some time during the war. Of the soldiers and sailors sent to war, few states paid a higher cost in lives lost than did Iowa: 3,540 were killed or mortally wounded in battle; 8,498 died of disease; 515 died in prison camps of disease or starvation; 8,500 were seriously wounded. In a recent study of Iowa's casualties in the Civil War, Robert Dykstra found that more Iowa troops died from disease than were killed on the battlefield because Iowans were mainly employed in the lower Mississippi Valley and in Georgia, where disease was the great killer, and were not utilized to any great extent in Virginia, Maryland, and Pennsylvania, where the worst carnage occurred on the battlefield.[8]

During the four years of war, Iowans fought at Wilson's Creek and Pea Ridge to keep Missouri in the Union. They were with Grant at Fort Donelson and went on south with him to Shiloh, Iuka, and Corinth. With Grant they encircled, laid siege to, and conquered Vicksburg, opening the Mississippi to the sea. Iowa regiments marched with Sherman to the sea and then north to Columbia, South Carolina. Few had entered the war with any thought of freeing the slave. Most of them had enlisted because of peer pressure and a craving for excitement. S. H. M. Byers, a young private from Oskaloosa, with honest candor wrote: "I had gone into the army for adventure as well as patriotism, and I was forever trying to get into the lines where the real adventures were going on. I foolishly wanted to see men killed in battle, and to take a real chance of being killed myself."[9] Byers could describe adventure precisely enough, but patriotism is a more difficult concept. It meant the flag and the Union; it meant keeping Iowa's great border rivers in their en-

8. Robert R. Dykstra, "Iowa: 'Bright Radical Star,' " in James C. Mohr, ed. *Radical Republicans in the North* (Baltimore: Johns Hopkins University Press, 1976), p. 171.

9. S. H. M. Byers, "How Men Feel in Battle," *Annals of Iowa*, 3rd Series, 2 (1896): 440.

tirety within one country; it meant not having an alien nation on your southern and western flanks; it meant one hundred years of past history as a nation.

But patriotism also meant cold and hunger, disease and death. Fear and numbed exhaustion soon replaced the pounding heady excitement these young men had felt at the recruiting rallies and as they boarded trains in Iowa City or Keokuk to take them south to Jefferson Barracks in St. Louis. They were marching to war across their own land, across states whose names and physical features they had memorized in fourth-grade geography classes, but war can turn any land into an unknown terrain, and the old familiar names of Missouri, Tennessee, Mississippi and Georgia became as hostilely alien and exotic as Manila, Chateau-Thierry, Iwo Jima, and the Mekong delta would be to their descendants. These teen-age youths, quickly aged into campaign veterans, expressed these emotions well in their songs, "Just Before the Battle, Mother," and "Tenting Tonight on the Old Camp Ground," and in their diaries and letters home. These are the documents people save, and the archives of Iowa, public and private, are filled with these graphic historical records, which spell out the meaning of civil war. Some of these journals of personal experience transcend their authors' amateur limitations of style and grammar and the unbelievably difficult environment in which they were written and become pieces of enduring literature. Stephen Crane was never more eloquent in describing a young man's experience of going into battle than was a young Mormon recruit from Mills County, William Kelley, in recording in his journal what it meant to be in the advance guard of Union troops scouting out the enemy around Decatur, Tennessee:

> It was still dark when the call came to "rise and shine." The word was passed around that there was a river a few rods ahead of us. There would be no stopping at the river because we would be quite exposed and an easy target for the guerillas who were thought to be near. We were told that we would have to undress at our camp before we started if we wanted to keep our clothes dry. What a choice. It was cold, the ground and trees covered with frost and the ground was frozen hard. But wet clothes, soaked through to the

skin, stay cold and offer no comfort to the wearer. . . . It was
generally decided that the lesser of two evils was to strip and carry
our belongings on our heads and shoulders. . . . The frozen ground
cut into our feet but luckily the cold numbed our feet which helped
to dull the pain from the tough walking. . . . My feet were hurting
me more and more and I was getting chilled through so that my
teeth began to chatter.

The men ahead resembled a war party of pale, ghostly Indians on
the warpath. . . . Lynch who was just ahead of me . . . started
down a short incline when suddenly his feet flew out from under
him and he landed hard on his backsides with a loud splat. . . . I
hurried as best I could to aid him and get him on his feet while he
got his wind back. . . . Some of the fellows who were behind us
caught up with us. Suddenly, they broke out in great convulsive
laughter. One of the boys pointed to Lynch's backsides and roared,
"Where did you get the decoration, Lynch? Are you wearing it to
keep yourself warm?" There, hanging to his rear was a giant
sycamore leaf, looking like it had been carefully placed there to
cover him up. . . . I thought I would add a bit more to the fun and
I would christen him. I edged close to him from the rear so he
couldn't see me, held my hand over his head and pronounced in a
very serious, ministerial tone, "I christen thee 'Adam Hindside.' "
"Where do you get this Adam stuff?" he growled. I replied, "Easy
enough. You are wearing Adam's apparel a 'fig leaf' but you aren't
wearing it in front. You have it on your hindsides." All this
raucous talk and laughter would have alerted any Reb within a mile
of our whereabouts but there evidently were none nearby for we
made it to the river finally without any action from the enemy. The
river proved to be over half a mile from our camp . . . so we were
cold, footsore and mad as hornets when we finally got there. . . .
As we waded in to our armpits . . . it was so cold one could not
tell it from a searing blast from a fiery furnace. . . . We struggled
up the bank on the far side, dried ourselves off as best we could
with our hands and tried to get into our clothes. Everyone was
shaking so from the cold we could hardly pull on our clothes and
our teeth were chattering so that no one could be understood when
we tried to talk. . . . We surely must have presented a most
militarylike appearance this morning straggling along that road
through the woods, naked, half-frozen and dispirited. Some army.
. . . After we crossed the river rations were issued to us. . . .
Then we marched about 4 miles west of town where we camped for

the night. I was exhausted. The ague still was clinging to me. . . .
I was sick with a fever all night.[10]

This little journal, hurriedly scrawled by campfire light,
presents the true indictment of war in all of its cruel absurdity,
the comradeship and humor of boys at play combined with the
pain and suffering of men on the long hunt to kill their brothers.
Small wonder that as the war dragged on year after year, the
song most often sung by the soldiers in the field was no longer
the rousing "Rally Round the Flag, Boys," but the plaintive
refrain, "We are tired of war on the old Camp ground, Many
are dead and gone."

Those who had remained at home were also to be permanently scarred by this, our first total war. Superficially, a great
many Iowans appeared to be fully engaged in their old peace-
time pursuits, undisturbed by distant battles at Champion's Hill,
Chickamauga, and Gettysburg. Population continued to expand
(Iowa was allotted four additional congressional seats in 1862),
roads were built, new fields tilled, and Senator Harlan worked
as assiduously in Congress for railroad promotion as he did for
Radical Republican war measures. Many Iowans in the
northwestern part of the state were far more concerned with the
Sioux uprisings in southern Minnesota in 1862 than they were
with Rebel victories at Manassas and Fredericksburg. They demanded and got a deployment of Iowa troops from the Southern
battlefront to Sioux City to protect them against an enemy that
was far more real to them than Stonewall Jackson.

There was also an attempt to continue politics as usual, with
the Democrats bravely contesting every election only to suffer
humiliating defeat in each encounter. For rebellion and war had
made ordinary political opposition very nearly impossible. The
only safe Democrat was the drum-beating War Democrat, and
the only good Democrat in many Iowans' view was the Democrat who had converted to Republicanism. The so-called Peace
Democrats held to their views only at their own peril. One of

10. *Civil War Experiences: The Journal of William H. Kelley 1864–1865*, privately
printed. I am indebted to Edmund G. Kelley, William's grandson, for making this valuable journal available to me for quotation.

Iowa's most colorful prewar Democrats, and unquestionably the greatest orator in the state, Henry Clay Dean, was very nearly lynched by a mob in Keokuk for his opposition to the war, and Iowa's former senator, George Jones spent several months in prison for having "treasonably" continued a correspondence with his old friend Jefferson Davis. Spurred on by the rabble-rousing proclamations of United States Marshal Hubert Hoxie who would gladly have instituted a reign of terror, complete with guillotine, against any dissidents, many an Iowa community eagerly searched its woodpiles and under its beds for Copperheads and Knights of the Golden Circle, who were believed to be lurking everywhere. In actuality, there was very little overt or even covert opposition to the war in Iowa. Contemporary reporters and later historians have falsely inflated the activities of a few Peace Democrats such as Dean, Dennis Mahony of Dubuque, and John P. Irish, editor of the *Iowa City State Press* into a vast Copperhead conspiracy with secret lodges "organized in every township in the state." [11] Actually, the only incident of open defiance of governmental authority to occur in Iowa during the entire war was a minor fracas in Keokuk County to which history has attached the imposing name of "The Skunk River War." A young Baptist minister with the unlikely name of Cyphert Tally had become obsessed with the notion of the evil enormity of "Mr. Lincoln's War." Preaching fiery sermons in which he urged resistance to the state's military demand, Tally had attracted a small following, and this group, it was believed, intended to disrupt a Republican county convention which was to be held in South English on 1 August 1863. The delegates came to the convention well-armed, and when Tally and his followers, also armed, arrived on the main street of the small village, someone fired a shot. In the brief exchange of gunfire that followed, Tally, who had been exhorting his followers from the back of a wagon, was shot dead. His group scattered, only to reassemble in a camp outside of town.

11. Dan Elbert Clark, *Samuel Jordan Kirkwood* (Iowa City: State Historical Society of Iowa, 1917), p. 262. But see also Leland Sage's excellent refutation of Clark's charges, *History of Iowa*, p. 165.

. . .

Frantic messages to Des Moines brought Governor Kirkwood
and the state militia to the scene. The troops found the camp deserted, and thus ended Iowa's great Copperhead rebellion.
Hoxie and his superpatriots were not to let it be forgotten, however.

The Civil War had a great impact upon women as well as
men. Anticipating by some eighty years a time when women
would have a recognized place in the armed forces of the nation, a few young women actually managed to disguise themselves as teen-age boys and enlist in the infantry, to be found
out only when they were wounded or their bodies were being
prepared for burial. Many more, such as Lucinda Hay, the first
female student at Iowa College, joined Clara Barton on the bat-
tlefields, serving as nurses in field hospitals. Annie Wittenmyer,
a well-to-do widow living in Keokuk, had ample opportunity to
see the wounded soldiers who were brought to that city; she
saw, too, the great need for better and more immediate care for
the wounded at the scene of battle. She volunteered her services
to the Western Sanitary Commission and in 1862 was appointed
one of two sanitary agents in Iowa. She served on a hospital
ship stationed on the Mississippi to care for the wounded taken
from the battlefield at Shiloh, and she was one of the first to
enter Vicksburg after its fall, to establish hospitals for the
wounded of both armies. When a bitter dispute developed between her and Ann Harlan, the wife of Senator Harlan, over the
question of women going to the battlefield, Mrs. Harlan insisted
that it would be more proper to have the wounded soldiers trans-
ported home for nursing; Annie Wittenmyer stood her ground
and vindicated herself against false charges brought by the Har-
lans that she was misappropriating Sanitary Commission funds.
At a meeting of the Ladies State Sanitary Commission held in
Des Moines in November 1863, which was chaired by Senator
Harlan, Wittenmyer was stoutly defended by Mary Darwin,
who brought an essentially hostile convention to a standing ova-
tion when she said, "If a man . . . can gird on his sword and at
the call of his country rush to deadly combat, who shall forbid
that I, actuated by the same love of country, follow him, pick

him up wounded and dying from the gory field, and recall him
to life by my assiduous care? . . . We are glad that Iowa has
daughters as well as sons in this war." [12]

Wittenmyer's greatest contribution to the war, however, came
after she had left the Iowa State Sanitary Commission to join the
United States Christian Commission in 1864. With funds from
this organization she set up diet kitchens attached to military
hospitals throughout the country, where the wounded and dis-
eased soldiers could receive special diets, which often meant the
difference between life and death. For this distinguished service, she received national recognition and a public tribute from
President Lincoln.

For many hundreds of Iowa women, the war meant opportunities for education and employment that had heretofore been
closed to them. The University of Iowa, which had the distinction of becoming the first coeducational state university in the
nation, and several small private colleges, such as Grinnell,
Cornell, and Iowa Wesleyan, were happy to welcome female
students to their classrooms to replace the male students who
had gone off to war. Women moved into elementary teaching
and into clerical positions in such numbers as largely to pre-
empt those fields that had hitherto been male dominated. In
Chickasaw County in 1862, Emily Stebbins was appointed dep-
uty recorder and treasurer, the first woman to hold a county
courthouse job in Iowa.

For the great majority of women, the war meant sending
one's husband, son, or brother off to war and then assuming for
the first time the task of serving as the head of the family: planting and harvesting the crops, or carrying on the family business,
and being both father and mother to the younger children in the
family. The old, rigid Victorian patriarchal system had been
cracked.

When at last on 4 May 1865, fifteen thousand Iowa troops
marched in triumph with Sherman's army down Pennsylvania
Avenue to the White House, they looked "like the lords of the

---

12. Quoted in Louise R. Noun, *Strong Minded Women* (Ames: Iowa State University
Press, 1969), pp. 29–30.

world," as one observer commented, but it was as lords of a new world that they marched into a new era. They had fought for their land and they had won it, but neither they nor their land would ever be the same again.

In Iowa, the end of the Civil War meant victory for the Radical Republican cause. Before the last veteran had returned home, the Republican state convention, meeting in Des Moines on 14 June, passed a resolution urging the general assembly and the voters of Iowa to amend the state constitution by striking the word "white" from the clause on suffrage qualification. William Stone, who had succeeded Kirkwood as governor in 1863, gave his somewhat reluctant support to the proposal, and the general assembly, as required by the constitution, in 1866 and 1868 twice approved submitting the amendment to the voters. At that time only five states in the nation, all of them in New England, permitted male suffrage without regard to race. Although the conservative Republicans and the Democrats tried every possible ploy to defeat the amendment, including trying to tie it to a proposal for suffrage for women and restricting suffrage for blacks only to those who had served in the Union army, all such efforts failed. There was an attempt to rally the returning veterans, who had seen the Southern blacks in their most degraded state of slavery, to come out in opposition to the amendment, but this, too, had little success. In the general election of 1868, the voters of Iowa, by a substantial majority, approved of five amendments striking the word "white" from the suffrage, enumeration census, and militia clauses. Thus did Iowa join Minnesota as one of only two states in the 1860s to extend the suffrage to the blacks by state constitutional amendment prior to the passage of the Fifteenth Amendment to the United States Constitution.

The victory of the truly radical egalitarians was not complete, however. Blacks were still excluded from election to the general assembly and would be until the constitution was again amended in 1880. This amendment eliminated the last vestige of formal racial discrimination that had been written into our constitution. The Iowa Supreme Court, which as a popularly elected body could properly be considered as being represen-

tative of the wishes of the people, went even further than had
the constitutional amenders in establishing the principle of racial
equality within the state. In a series of decisions handed down
in 1868, 1873, and 1875, the court ruled that segregated schools
were unconstitutional in Iowa and that there could be no seg-
regation of passengers on Mississippi River steamboats while
in Iowa waters, which by implication applied to all common
carriers within the state. Thus twenty years before the United
States Supreme Court had even established the doctrine of "separate but equal," the Iowa Supreme Court had already rejected
it. In these remarkable decisions, Iowa was in advance by several years of nearly every other Northern state and eighty years
ahead of the landmark decision of Chief Justice Warren's Court
in *Brown* v. *Topeka Board of Education*. Iowa had earned the
encomium which Grant had given the state when during the
campaign of 1868 he had called Iowa the one "bright Radical
star." [13]

Legally, the black man in Iowa had achieved full equality
with the white man by 1880, but he was to learn within the next
century that the fight to end discrimination was far from over. It
took more than a state supreme court decision to establish equality of job opportunities, equality of pay in private industry,
unrestricted housing covenants, and, above all, full dignity as a
human being in all social relationships with a predominantly
white society. As late as our bicentennial year of 1976, the fight
for a genuine social reconstruction of society was still being
waged, and small battles were still being won, as, for instance,
when the Iowa chapters broke with their International Order of
Rainbow Girls by admitting black members into that hitherto
all-white organization.

For the women of Iowa, black and white, the Radical star of
Iowa did not shine quite so brightly in the immediate post-Civil
War years as it did for black men. Women suffragists, led by
Amelia Bloomer, Annie Savery, Jane Swisshelm, and Mary
Jane Coggeshall, among others, and aided by a few courageous
men such as Joseph Dugdale and John P. Irish, had high hopes

13. Paraphrase of Grant's words in a conversation with a prominent Iowa politician,
reported in *Des Moines Weekly Register*, 4 Nov. 1868, quoted in Dykstra, "Iowa:
'Bright Radical Star,' " p. 184.

in 1870 of tying women's political rights to the enfranchisement of black men. A proposal to submit to the people an amendment to the constitution which would delete the word "male" from the suffrage clause, quite surprisingly passed both houses of the Thirteenth General Assembly in March 1870. Two years later, when the motion for a required second approval came up for a vote in the Fourteenth General Assembly, it again passed the lower house, but was defeated in the senate by only two votes: ayes, 22; nays, 24; absent or not voting, 4. But the fight for the ballot in 1872 had not been in vain. The same Fourteenth General Assembly, meeting in special session the following January, eliminated the legal disabilities of women in its revision of the Iowa Code. The revised code for the first time provided that a wife could not be held liable for the debts of her husband; she could hold property and conduct a business on her own account; and she could sue and be sued without being joined by her husband. She could even sue her own husband for the protection of her property, and the law of inheritance for the spouse of one dying intestate now applied equally to both the husband and wife. Amelia Bloomer's husband, Dexter, wrote in an article published in the *Council Bluffs Republican:*

> Surely the women may justly claim Iowa as the most liberal and progressive of all States in its dealing with their property rights. But little remains to be conceded to them except the ballot, and it has been shrewdly said that it is because this has been refused, that our legislators have gone as far as they have in conceding property rights to women.[14]

The tireless suffragist Jane Swisshelm, although bitterly disappointed, tried to be understanding and hopeful. "Let us . . . learn to labor and to wait, knowing that the right will triumph in God's good time."[15] Not even she, who had the patience of Job, could have foreseen that God's, or at least man's, "good time" lay fifty years in the future. The women of Iowa would not obtain the ballot until given it in 1920 by a federal Constitutional amendment after another great war.

14. Quoted in Noun, *Strong Minded Women,* p. 222.
15. Quoted in Noun, *Strong Minded Women,* p. 220.

7

We Till the Land

$\mathcal{T}$HOMAS JEFFERSON, child of the Enlightenment, was devoted to order. He liked classical symmetry in his buildings, semantic precision in his laws, and geometric accuracy on his maps. It was this sense of order that inspired him to impose a giant checkerboard pattern upon the disorderly wilderness of trans-Appalachia which Britain had ceded to the United States in 1783. In response to a request from Congress to prepare a land ordinance for this territory, Jefferson complied with a proposal to divide the land up into hundreds, each consisting of ten units, ten miles square. The land would thus have the same decimal order as the new monetary system which he had also designed at Congress's request. His proposal also spelled out the manner in which the land would be settled. First, would come the army and the treaty makers to move the Indians out of the land. Then would come the surveyors to draw their straight lines, marking out the land units. Then would come the land-office agents to sell the land in square-mile sections of 640 acres. Finally, when the land offices were open and ready for business, then and only then would the settlers, in polite queues, enter to buy the sections and take possession of the land. Although Congress changed Jefferson's land ordinance by substituting a six-mile-square township for his hundreds-tens system, the procedures for settlement suggested by Jefferson were kept intact in the Land Ordinance of 1785. These eighteenth-century rationalists envisioned an America pushing westward with the regularity and order of counters in a game of draughts, moving inexorably toward the king's row.

Unfortunately for Jefferson's orderly design, men did not behave like checker pieces. They pushed and shoved; they did not wait for their turn to move; they came before the land was ready for them, forcing the harried army troops to hold them back until the Indians could be forced out.

The first two land offices in Iowa were not established by Congress until June 1838—one in Dubuque, for the sale of land in the Black Hawk Purchase lying north of a line running west from Davenport, and one in Burlington for all of the land lying south of that line. No one had legal title to land in Iowa until these land offices held their first public auctions. During the previous five years, however, twenty-three thousand settlers had pushed into the Iowa district and had staked out their own extra-legal claims to town lots and half-sections of farmland within the region which the Indians had ceded following the Black Hawk War. All of these people who made up the population of the newly established territory of Iowa were technically trespassers or, as they preferred to call themselves, squatters or preemptors. Only by emerging as the successful bidder at a public auction could the settler have his claim duly recorded and filed by the land-office registrar. The minimum bid which the land office would recognize at the public auction was $1.25 an acre, and, theoretically at least, anyone could appear at the auction, and by outbidding someone who might have been living on the land for the previous five years, could take claim.

To establish their extra-legal claims to land at the minimum price allowed at the auction sales, the squatters began to band together for their mutual protection. They would appear en masse at the auction when their particular township was put up for sale. Their collective presence served well as an effective deterrent to any further bids from outsiders above the $1.25 per-acre bid that the squatter would enter for the land he claimed. These early collective actions must have arisen quite spontaneously all over the Iowa territory open to sale, but in time many of these temporary groups became formalized and institutionalized into "claim clubs," with constitutions, officers, and prescribed rules stating qualifications for membership, the maximum amount of land the squatter could claim, and the annual improvements he must make upon his land to validate his claim.

The first formal claim club on record in Iowa was that of Keosauqua township in Van Buren County, which was organized in 1838. From there the organization spread to other counties throughout the state as new lands were ceded by the Indians and opened for settlement. Although the federal land laws never recognized their existence, the public did, and the clubs depended upon community pressure to back their authority—that and a stout hickory club, which, according to a Mahaska County report, "every man carried to defend himself and neighbors against over-bidders." If the federal government in Washington regarded such activities as being, in the words of Henry Clay, the work of "lawless intruders," the territorial government was much more tolerant. Governor Lucas in a public address stated that it "was necessary for them [the settlers] to enter into some agreement to secure their natural rights," and Chief Justice Mason in 1840 gave to the squatter the judicial recognition he had extended to blacks in the Case of Ralph the previous year. In *Enoch S. Hill* v. *John Smith, et. al.,* he rejected the plaintiff's argument that prior squatter claims were contrary to the laws of the United States. No federal land law, he asserted, could ever "disturb the peaceable and industrious husbandman whose labor was adding so much to the public wealth, changing the barren wilderness into fertile fields, and calling into almost magic existence whole states and territories, whose prosperity and power are constantly adding so much to the strength and glory of the nation." The fact that Chief Justice Mason, himself a large land claimant, was as much a squatter as John Smith et al., undoubtedly contributed to the vehemence with which he posed his highly rhetorical question: "Were we a community of trespassers, or were we to be regarded as occupying and improving the lands of the government by the invitation and for the benefit of the owner?" Mason was never to deviate from his initial opinion in upholding "squatter law." In a speech delivered twenty years later, before the Pioneer Association of Des Moines County, he insisted that the squatters, having no legal title to their lands, "became a law unto themselves, and I think I can safely state that I have never known justice to be meted out with more strict impartiality, or to be tempered with more genuine equity." [1]

Mason's judgment was accepted by later historians. Jesse Macy, Cyrenus Cole, and Irving Richman were to romanticize the claim clubs into an expression of grass-root democracy in its purest and noblest form, comparable to that practiced by the primitive Germanic tribes before they became corrupted by autocratic, centralized Roman law. Benjamin F. Shambaugh even included sample claim club bylaws in his book *The Constitutions of Iowa,* calling them the true "origin of laws and constitutional government" in Iowa, the laudatory work of "lawful men of the neighborhood, who from the beginning observed the usages and customs of the community." [2] The squatter was idealized into as heroic a historic figure for the farm belt as the cowboy was for the ranchlands of the Great Plains.

Recent historians, however, have taken a second and far less kindly look at these initial settlers and their claim clubs. Allan and Margaret Bogue, Robert Swierenga, and Leland Sage in their studies of the available data, have provided convincing evidence that many of these "plain, honest farmers," were in reality aggressive exploiters of the public domain, grabbing up illegally as much of the best timbered and watered lands as they could, far beyond the needs of a viable farm unit in Iowa in the mid-nineteenth century. Allan Bogue's summary judgment of the claim clubs was that while they undoubtedly

> "did protect many a deserving settler in the enjoyment of improvements and in the purchase of a home from the federal government, the clubs also shielded the activities of others whose motives and procedures were far less simple. The "actual settler" might be the victim as well as the beneficiary of the clubs. . . . Claim-club activity was often an effort to corner the wooded land of a new community.[3]

1. Quoted in Earle D. Ross, *Iowa Agriculture* (Iowa City: State Historical Society of Iowa, 1951), pp. 16; 14, 17–18; 19.

2. Shambaugh, *The Constitutions of Iowa,* pp. 27–49.

3. Allan G. Bogue, *From Prairie to Cornbelt* (Chicago: Quadrangle Books, 1968), pp. 38–39.

If recent studies have tarnished the haloes over the squatters' heads and have shown that claim clubs included organized bands of resident speculators, the historic importance of the clubs' activities should not be minimized. These clubs remain the first example of effective farm organization on the Iowa frontier, and they proved to the farmer in county after county that in collective organization, outside of the law, if necessary, there was strength. The historian interested in continuity can trace a consistent pattern of action from the "Constitution and Records of the Claim Association of Johnson County" of 1839, to the Granger co-operatives of the 1870s, the Farmers' Alliance Protective Association in its successful action against the barbed-wire trust in the 1880s, the Corn Belt Meat Producers' Association's forcing the railroads to give free passes to shippers in 1904, the Farm Holiday's efforts for a farmers' strike in the 1930s, and on up to the attempt of the National Farm Organization to achieve collective bargaining between producers and processors at the present time.

The claim clubs might effectively eliminate the outsider who came to the auction to overbid the squatter, but the individual squatter still had to come up with $200 in hard cash for the quarter-section of land to which he was laying claim. The land office accepted no checks, no IOUs, or paper currency from state banks. It wanted gold or silver notes only, and even the most successful farmers had difficulty accumulating that amount of acceptable specie. Out of necessity, the speculator entered the scene. If legend and history have made heroes of the squatters, they have in turn made villains out of the speculators and the money lenders, those "eastern dudes" who showed up at all public auctions with gold and silver notes in hand, ready to provide the necessary capital to the squatter—for a price, of course. The price exacted was not inconsiderable, interest rates often running as high as fifty to sixty percent a year for a loan of two hundred dollars to four hundred dollars. It is hardly surprising that the most popular melodramas written for rural America in the mid-nineteenth century all had slinking, black-caped villains who would appear in the first act demanding immediate payment for the money loaned to the honest farmer, only to be

"Curses, foiled again" in the final act to the tumultuous applause of the country audience. The only note in these dramas that probably did not ring quite true was that any one of these blood-sucking and sexless "loan sharks" would ever for a moment consider offering to give up the mortgage in exchange for the farmer's beautiful daughter.

More recent historians, however, present quite a different interpretation of the capitalist investor's role in settling the Iowa frontier. Robert Swierenga offers conclusive evidence to support his thesis that "despite some criticism by contemporaries and almost universal disparagement in subsequent historical literature, these entrepreneurs were as essential to the economic development of the West as were their clients, the frontier farmers." [4] They were indispensable in providing credit facilities in a state which until 1858 had no banks and where hard specie currency was always in short supply. Contrary to the popular notion that these speculators encouraged tenancy and withheld land from settlement, they actively sought immigrant buyers and "pressed sales at reasonable rates." Nor were the money lenders quick to foreclose on delinquent debtors. They sought their profits from the interest on their money, not in reclaiming mortgaged land. [5] In short, as Leland Sage points out, "while the speculators were not angels, they were law-abiding capitalists rather than blood-sucking absentee landlords or fly-by-night hucksters." [6] Exit the villain, stage right, from history.

Having secured his claim either by outright purchase or through credit extended to him, the next concern of the settler was to get as much land as possible into production for a cash crop. From the very first, the Iowa farmer was a commercial not a mere subsistence farmer, eager to turn his rich land into a production unit for the export of goods. Although he did not face the problems of the New England farmer who had to clear his land of rocks, or even the farmer of the Old Northwest,

4. Robert Swierenga, *Pioneers and Profits* (Ames: Iowa State University Press, 1968), p. 227.
5. Swierenga, *Pioneers,* p. 219.
6. Sage, *History of Iowa,* p. 69.

who had to gird and burn trees before the land was open to the plow, the Iowa farmer quickly discovered that every virgin land presents its own problem of preparation. In Iowa the problem was the high prairie grass with its thick, matted root system extending many inches below the surface. The small Eastern hand plow could not cut deep enough into this subterranean carpet to turn the soil over for planting. Many of the first settlers were thus forced to turn to the professional prairie-breaker, who would arrive in a small covered wagon which was his living quarters along with three to eight yoke of oxen and his breaking plow, a gigantic contraption mounted on wheels with a mold-board made of wood covered by sheet iron and a huge share, which could cut a furrow two feet wide. Two acres of prairie could be plowed in a day and the cost ranged from $2.50 to $4.00 an acre, another drain on the settler's limited cash reserves, for at a minimum it would cost him twice as much to prepare his land for its first planting as the land itself had cost him at the public auction. It is not surprising that it would often take a farmer six to eight years of successful farming on a few acres of his farm before he had sufficient capital to put the entire claim into production. Often it was cheaper for a farmer to buy land already improved from the original tenant at $10 an acre than to put in a claim for virgin land at $1.25 an acre.

Once the land was cleared, the farmer's concerns were the eternal problems of the tillers of the soil; weather, infestation of pests, plant disease, fencing, transportation of his crops to market, and current market prices. During much of the nineteenth century, the Iowa farmer was blessed with good weather conditions: adequate rainfall and long growing seasons. But with the turning of the first prairie sod, the ecological balance that nature had achieved in the grasslands after the retreat of the last glacial drift was forever disturbed. The prairie grasses, which over ten millennia of evolutionary development had grown resistant to plant diseases, were plowed under. The imported cultivated plants, wheat, oats, flax, and fruit trees, alien to the land, were only too vulnerable to disease. With thousands of acres under cultivation, the fungi of rust, scab, and orchard blight moved in on their rich feast. So also came the grasshoppers in 1873,

1874, and 1876, in great clouds like the Biblical plagues of Egypt, devouring all vegetation in their path. Some of the early pioneers had brought with them the barberry plant from New England, and in Iowa's rich soil it flourished like the proverbial green bay tree. But farmers soon discovered that one more disruptive element had been introduced into nature's delicate ecological order with disastrous results, for the barberry was a particularly inviting temporary host for rust fungi. Wherever it grew—and it grew everywhere—the neighboring wheat and oat plants grew black with rust. Only Indian maize or corn, perhaps because it had for so long been cultivated by the Indians, appeared resistant to the diseases that intensive cultivation in Iowa seemed to invite. By the 1880s the Iowa farmer had turned mainly to corn. Iowa had found its true destiny as corn raiser, hog producer, for the nation. In time, however, even corn under such heavy cultivation would invite its own particular infestations—smut, root rot, and more recently the European corn borer. The Iowa farmer, however suspicious he might have been at first of "book" farming, was forced to turn to the agricultural specialists at Iowa State College and to the county extension service for help. The long battle—one that will never end—had begun between science and nature for the control of Iowa's bountiful lands.

Even if a farmer was successful in getting a good crop planted and harvested, he still had to get his crop to market. Transportation was as critical a factor to the farmer as was the actual cultivation. Although both canals and plank roads were considered as possible means of improving Iowa's overland transportation, it was clear even to those who came to Iowa in the 1830s that the most viable solution was the railroad. The railroad was to be to the last half of the nineteenth century what the automobile has been to the twentieth. It not only provided the main vehicle for moving people and goods across a vast domain, but it was the chief stimulant to our basic industries, iron, steel, and coal. It dominated our politics for sixty years and, most important, it transformed our social structure by ending rural isolation.

Even without the Iowa farmer's desperate need for railroad

transportation, it was inevitable that Iowa, lying directly in the path of the most direct routes from Chicago to the Pacific coast, would become a thoroughfare for transcontinental railroads. Congress recognized this geographical fact in 1856 when it provided for four main arterial roads to cross Iowa by granting to the state out of the federal public domain four million acres of Iowa land (one-ninth of the total acreage of the state) to be used by the state as a financial inducement to bring the railroads in without delay. But the first railroad was already under construction in Iowa even before Congress had made its unnecessarily generous grant of land. This first Iowa railroad was the Mississippi and Missouri, which actually was an extension of the Chicago & Rock Island Railroad, to which it became united when the Mississippi was first bridged in 1856. The M. & M. reached Iowa City at midnight 31 December 1855, thus by one minute enabling it to collect the $50,000 reward that the citizens of Iowa's capital city had offered the railroad if it could arrive there before 1 January 1856. By the outbreak of the Civil War, the M. & M. had reached Grinnell, but it was to lose the race to the Missouri River at Council Bluffs to its rival, the Chicago, Iowa & Nebraska Railroad, later the Chicago & Northwestern, which, thanks to the driving efforts of its chief promoter, John Blair, successfully completed its trans-state road from Clinton through Cedar Rapids to Council Bluffs in January 1867, over two years ahead of the M. & M. The other two major roads to cross Iowa in that decade were the Chicago, Burlington & Quincy, initially backed by Governor Grimes, and the Illinois Central, whose route lay across northern Iowa from Dubuque to Sioux City. The president for the Iowa section of the Illinois Central was the president of the Pennsylvania Railroad, J. Edgar Thomson, who gave the contract to build a bridge across the Mississippi at Dubuque to his young Scottish friend and former employee, Andrew Carnegie. A fifth line, which eventually became known as the Chicago, Milwaukee, St. Paul & Pacific, crossed the northern tier of counties in the late 1870s, tying Iowa to both St. Paul to the north and to Canton in the Dakota Territory to the west.

By 1880, these five major lines plus many spur lines running north and south in the state gave Iowa one of the most complete railroad systems in the United States. With 5,235 miles of track, it ranked fifth among the states in railroad mileage, and no one living anywhere within the state was farther than 25 miles from a railroad station. The farmer's potential market was no longer thirty miles away, but global in dimensions. But the farmer again quickly learned, as he had when he plowed up the virgin grass, that each advance extorts its own price and penalty. The iron horse, which he had prayed for and paid for in land and taxes, continued to demand ever more feed. For the next forty years, the effort to tame and control the railroad would be the major item of business for the farmer in both his political and occupational organizations.

By 1880 also, due largely to the railroad, nearly all of Iowa's thirty-six million acres were under cultivation, and the frontier for Iowa was over. Iowa, containing one-quarter of all the grade-A land in the nation, had been disposed of in the following ways: 33.7 percent in cash sales; 39.7 in military bounty warrants; and 23.2 in state grants (including 11.7 percent to railroads, 5.6 percent in educational grants, and 6.6 percent for swampland and river improvements). Only 2.5 percent of the state or 902,000 acres was actually given free to homesteaders.[7] The Homestead Act of 1862 had come too late in the day to serve Iowa.

In the census of 1880, Iowa had a population of 1,625,000 and ranked tenth among the thirty-eight states in the Union. Of this population, 88 percent was recorded as being rural. Unfortunately, the federal census did not differentiate between farm and small-town populations until 1920, but it is safe to assume that at least two-thirds of all Iowans were living on farms in 1880. The Iowa farmer in his bib overalls, straw hat, and work boots, as immortalized by Iowa's most noted cartoonist, J.N. ("Ding") Darling, became the true symbol of the state and has remained so down to the present day, even though his numbers have shrunk to about twenty percent of Iowa's present population. The Iowa farmer has always been as glibly and easily char-

7. For a table on the disposal of Iowa lands, see Sage, *History of Iowa*, p. 70.

acterized as to personality and attitudes by historians and political commentators as he has been in dress by cartoonists. He has been portrayed as being basically conservative, isolationist, the last exponent of true laissez-faire in economics, and intolerant of alien peoples and new ideas. Much of this characterization is false, but not easy to refute, perhaps because the farmer has had more difficulty than anyone else in our society in establishing his own identity. He can identify with both management and labor in his aspirations and economic objectives. He is both producer and at the same time a heavy consumer of basic capital goods. Consequently, he was torn apart by the tariff issue. He is basically conservative and capitalistic in his political and social views, but at the same time he has repeatedly demonstrated the most overt and successful radical action throughout our history—far more than has labor. From Bacon's Rebellion in 1676 through the American Revolution, Shay's Rebellion, and the Civil War, down to the Populist revolt of the 1890s and the violence of the 1930s, it has been the embattled farmer who has been the most ready to take direct action to protect what he has. He is far more internationally minded than most Americans because he produces for a world market, and a war between Bismark and Louis Napoleon or a drought in Russia, he knows, will have a direct effect upon his pocketbook. Suspicious of the expert, he is at the same time more receptive to new ideas, new machinery, new products, and new methods than is either industrial management or labor. He is an individualist who enjoys working in the fields alone, but he also craves company. Most farm organizations from the National Grange to the Farm Bureau were initially inspired by the farmer's desire for some kind of social communication and an opportunity for an interchange of new ideas. The farmer is, in short, *sui generis,* a figure about whom one can make no easy generalizations or offer any pat characterizations.

Throughout the century and a half that Iowa's lands have been opened to white man's cultivation, there has been an ongoing agricultural revolution in technology, methods, and crop and livestock breeding that has been at least as dramatically radical as the continuing industrial revolution, although it has received far less attention. As Earle Ross has pointed out in his discussion of the farmer's willingness to adopt new machinery, "The record of the Middle West, with its unparalleled natural advantages and opportunities, was considerably in advance of the rest of the country. The prairie farmer was noted for getting his operations on wheels as quickly as possible—and preferably with a seat." Indeed so rapidly were the new machines of cultivating, planting, and harvesting standardized by the manufacturers and adopted by the Iowa farmer during the Civil War that "the only new principle to be added after this decade [of the 1860s] was that of artificial power." [8] First steam in the late nineteenth century and later gasoline and diesel engines in the early twentieth century would provide that power.

The scientific advancements in genetics and breeding were as impressive and revolutionary as the mechanical devices. The old livestock and poultry breeds of Europe were developed and modified to meet the changing tastes of the ever growing urban consumer society: more tender, corn-fed beef, bigger-breasted turkeys and chickens, hogs with less fat and more meat. The two greatest changes in crop production to affect the Iowa farmer in the twentieth century were, first, the introduction of the soybean from the Orient, and, second, the development of hybrid corn. The Iowa State Experiment Station began work on the soybean as early as 1910 by testing over three thousand varieties and strains brought in from China. At first used largely as a forage crop, the soybean came into its own during World War II as a source of oil and high-protein food. Ideally suited as rotation crop for corn, the soybean is today a major crop in Iowa, second only to corn in acreage and commercial value.

It was the development of hybrid corn, however, that had the greatest impact upon the Iowa farmer in the twentieth century and has enabled the state to become a granary for the nation and the world. Although the possibility of varietal hybridization of corn plants had been suggested as early as 1880, no serious experimentation was undertaken in this area until early in the twentieth century. Those farmers who wanted to do more to bet-

8. Ross, *Iowa Agriculture,* pp. 43, 55.

ter their corn yields than simply putting aside what looked like the best ears of their crop each year to use as seed for the following year were by 1900 involved in what was known as ear-to-row planting—that is they would choose a particularly fine ear of corn and instead of mixing its kernels indiscriminately in the seeder along with the rest of the seed, would carefully plant that ear, kernel by kernel, down one row. The results could then be judged at the fall harvest, and the best ears again be saved for the next year's planting. Corn shows were held throughout Iowa at which prizes were awarded for the best ears of corn. Individual ears that carried off top prizes would often sell at incredibly high prices—as much as $250 for the grand champion ear. But as all fields were open pollinated, there was no assurance that a champion ear would produce the same quality of corn the following year. The interest shown in ear-to-row planting was a clear indication that farmers were ready to consider innovations for the improvement of the corn plant. They found their teacher in Perry G. Holden, who came to Iowa State College in 1902 to head up the department of agronomy. The following year, at a meeting in Hull, Iowa, of the Sioux County Farmer's Institute, Holden proposed and won the approval of the farmers and the county board of supervisors for his idea of conducting area field demonstration tests on corn yields. Soon Holden was running Corn Gospel Trains, as he called them, throughout the state showing the farmers in each area what could be done through a careful selection of seed. In 1912 one of Holden's young disciples, Martin L. Mosher, went to Clinton County as Iowa's first county agent; there he conducted several corn variety tests.[9]

The work of Holden and Mosher, although diverting attention from the early experimentation in hybridization, actually helped set the stage for the ultimate triumph of hybrid corn not only in demonstrating to the farmer the practical benefits derived from carefully selected seed but also in persuading the farmer to turn to seed companies as a source of supply for scientifically devel-

9. See Martin L. Mosher, *Early Iowa Corn Yield Tests* (Ames: Iowa State University Press, 1962). Information also obtained in an interview with Mr. Mosher at the Mayflower Home, Grinnell, Iowa, 26 September 1976.

oped and tested seed. A potential market was being created for hybrid corn even before it had been developed.

The first steps in producing hybrid corn were taken in 1905 in New York by Dr. G.H. Shull with experiments in inbreeding, the pollination of the silk of the plant with pollen taken only from its own male component, the tassel. Shull discovered that in the first and second generations of inbreeding, there was a marked reduction in the vigor of the plant, but at the same time there was an increase in the uniformity of the plants. Furthermore, after two or three generations of inbreeding, the loss of vigor grew progressively less. Later two inbred plants were crossed to produce a single cross plant that inherited the characteristics of both parents. Uniformity of plants was maintained and yields were somewhat better, but still not great enough to be commercially attractive.

The next step necessary to make hybrid seed corn practical was not taken until 1917 in Illinois, when Donald Jones of Funk Seeds crossed two single cross plants, each the offspring of inbred parents, and thus produced the first modern hybrid seed corn. The Iowa Experiment Station in 1922 started its own program of developing hybrids following Jones's methods. The total process from the beginning of inbreeding until a tested hybrid is ready for the market takes about ten years. The first hybrids from Iowa State College went on the market in 1932. In the spring of 1933, at the bottom of the depression, a few Iowa farmers, adventurous enough to try anything to increase their income and with enough money in hand to buy the seed, put their fields into hybrid corn—seven-tenths of one percent of the corn acreage of Iowa, to be exact. These few farmers liked what they raised, and the word spread. The next year, two percent of the state's cornfields were planted in hybrid corn, and Iowa moved far ahead of all other states in the production of hybrid corn. In 1939, three-fourths of all Iowa's corn acreage was in hybrid corn, and by 1944, the triumph of hybrid corn was complete: 99.8 percent of all Iowa's cornfields were now hybrid as compared with 59 percent for the nation. Corn yields jumped from an average of 21.9 bushels per acre in the five-year period 1930–1934 to an average of 31.9 bushels per acre in the period

1940–1944. A farmer during the New Deal years could receive pay from the federal government for letting some of his fields lie fallow and still produce nearly as much hybrid corn on the remaining acres allotted him as he had previously when his entire acreage had been planted with open-pollinated corn.

Henry A. Wallace, editor of *Wallace's Farmer* and the son of Henry C. Wallace, Secretary of Agriculture under Harding and Coolidge, had been interested in genetic experimentation in plant breeding since he had been a student of George Washington Carver at Iowa State College in 1910. As editor of Iowa's leading farm journal, Wallace read the reports from Iowa State College of their experiments with hybrid corn in the 1920s with great interest—so great in fact, that he set up his own test plots on a farm outside Des Moines. He also became acquainted with Roswell Garst of Coon Rapids and, discovering in him the hard common sense of a practical farmer and the extraordinary talents of a super salesman, persuaded him to join in the creation of the appropriately named Pioneer Seed Corn Company, which moved hybrid corn into the commercial field. Other giant seed-corn drying and processing companies quickly provided competition to Pioneer: DeKalb, Cargill, Pfister, and Funk, as well as many smaller companies with their devoted regional followings. Soon all over the Middle West, motorists in the early summer could spot the commercial hybrid seed cornfields with their regular patterns of two "male rows" of one cross still proudly sporting their tassels, followed by their harems of six "female rows" of another cross which had been detasseled, but whose ears would produce the seed corn for next year's crop.

Because this detasseling operation of converting six out of every eight rows in the seed-corn plots from being hermaphrodite into being totally female had to be done by hand, hybrid corn not only changed the life of the farmer, but it also affected the lives of thousands of young people in small towns throughout Iowa. High school students from all over the state now had summer employment, and they came by the thousands out into the fields from mid-June until late in July to pull tassels under the hot sun. For many, it was their first introduction to farm life, and hybrid corn probably did as much to bring the

town youth to the country as consolidated schools and automobiles did to bring the country youth to the town.

The extraordinary high yield of hybrid corn which in forty
years was to raise Iowa's annual production of corn from 400
million bushels to over one billion bushels a year was due not
only to the quality of the seed itself but also to the changes in
the process of growing corn which the hybrid plant brought
about. The stronger, heavier stalks of uniform height made
practical the mechanical corn picker which ultimately developed
into the combination picker-sheller that could pick, husk, and
shell the corn directly from the stalk into the receiving wagon
right in the field. This operation not only speeded up the process
and greatly reduced the number of man-hours required to harvest the corn, but it meant an actual increase in production. A
farmer formerly might lose up to ten percent of his crop in corn
left in the field and in storage losses while waiting for the corn
to dry on the cob. The intensive cultivation of the stronger
hybrid plants drained the soil of its nitrogen much faster than
the open-pollinated corn, forcing the farmer to apply artificial
fertilizers to his fields. He used such generous amounts of fertil-
izer that corn growth was further stimulated, and frequent rotation of crops became unnecessary. There could now be an almost continuous cropping of corn. The density of the plant
stands also made cultivation of the rows difficult, so the chemist
once again came to the rescue with new herbicides as well as
pesticides to eradicate weeds and pest infestations which the intensity of cultivation encouraged. These increased chemical
costs were more than offset by the greater yields and the savings
in labor costs. As Jill Rendleman, a student of agricultural history, has pointed out, there has been during the past three decades a successful integration of many separate aspects of corn
production—hybridization, fertilization, technological improvements, and farm management practices—which can largely be
attributed to the introduction of hybrid corn.[10] The farmer was
no longer the simple tiller of the soil; he had become a remark-

10. Jill Rendleman, "The Development and Effects of Hybrid Corn in Iowa and the
Corn Belt," unpublished seminar paper, Grinnell College, 1976.

able hybrid himself—part geneticist, part chemist, part mechanic, part processor. Agri-culture had, in short, become agribusiness.

Yet in spite of the revolutionary changes that have occurred in agriculture during the last century and a half and in spite of the technological changes outside of agriculture that have completely transformed the farmer's style of life, the farmer himself has remained a remarkably consistent figure in our society. This consistency is vividly illustrated in the collection of letters by two Iowa farm families, the Ephraim Fairchilds of Jones County and the John Kenyons of Delaware County written in the late 1850s, and the diary of Elmer G. Powers of Boone County, covering the years 1931–1936, recently published under the title *Years of Struggle.*[11] Living in primitive isolation on the edge of the frontier, tilling the soil with the same kind of primitive tools that their great-grandparents had used, too poor even to own a horse and so having to depend upon the muscles of their own arms and backs as their only source of power, the Kenyons and Fairchilds could not in their wildest dreams have ever imagined the world of Elmer Powers with its automobiles, trucks, and tractors, its unlimited source of power in electricity; its governmental agencies that paid Powers *not* to grow corn and sent out FERA (Federal Emergency Relief Act) workers to build him a new privy; its movies with their Bank Nights, and the chain stores with their packaged goods in multiple profusion (how Sarah Kenyon had longed for just a little white sugar when there was none to be had in the whole county). And yet, curiously enough, in spite of the great environmental chasm which eighty years had dug between the generations, these three families could have reached out and touched each other through their writings, for their concerns, their hopes and fears, their accomplishments and failures, were essentially the same. Both generations knew what depression was, both knew what it meant to live on the brink of failure, not sure you could pay your taxes or rent and stay on the land. Fairchild in 1858 was

11. "Iowa Farm Letters, 1856–1865," edited by Mildred Throne, *IJH* 58 (1960): 37–88; Elmer G. Powers, *Years of Struggle,* edited by H. Roger Grant and L. Edward Purcell (Ames: Iowa State University Press, 1976).

hoping the legislature would authorize banks for the state so his county would get a bank and he would have access to credit. Powers in 1933 was hoping that his bank would manage to stay open. Both generations were concerned with the market, frequently ending their letters and diary entries with the current prices for wheat, corn, and hogs. The prices that Fairchild quoted were those he obtained every month or so from the local trading centers, prices that probably bore little relationship to actual prices prevailing in the urban centers. Powers got his market quotations daily over the radio, directly from Chicago, Omaha, and Kansas City. Kenyon dreamed of the day when he could move his produce to a market more distant than twenty miles away; Powers had a market that was global, but he was painfully aware of the fact that this universality of transportation was a two-way road, and he cursed the importation of foreign food products that reduced his prices. Both generations were highly suspicious of town folk with their superior ways, their lack of understanding of the farmer's problems. And both knew well that ultimately they were at the mercy of the weather. All of the mechanical wonders of Powers's world had not been able to tame the vagaries of nature, and in 1936 Powers had to endure the worst weather in the history of Iowa—first, a winter of such intense cold and of so many raging blizzards that for weeks he and his family were as isolated from their neighbors and town as the Fairchilds and Kenyons had ever been—this followed by a summer of such heat and drought that the corn shriveled and burned in the fields, and the pastures in mid-July were as brown as they usually were in late October after the first killing frost. In spite of trucks and tractors, electricity and experimental stations, nature was still supreme, and the farmer was never allowed to forget it.

Above all, the link that tied the two generations together was a love for the land that was almost religious in its intensity. Powers on 1 January 1932 recorded in his diary:

> Today is the beginning of a new year. I believe everyone is speculating more than usual as to what the New Year will bring.
> . . . Personally I still think the farm is by far the best place of all. The future may not look so good from a financial standpoint.

However, for many folks the farm is more than a business and a place to try to accumulate wealth. It is life itself. First of all, the soil, the feel of the earth. The respect they have for it. The fields. The weather and the changing seasons. All life itself comes from these several things. Then there is the plant life. The crops. The trees. The livestock and poultry and all of their young things to be cared for. The responsibility of growing the food and flesh for a distant and often unappreciative city. Just to be close to and work with nature is one of life's greatest opportunities.[12]

Sarah and John Kenyon and Ephraim Fairchild, if they could have read that, would have known exactly what Elmer Powers was attempting to convey, far better than Powers's own contemporaries in Boone or Des Moines ever could. And today's farmer, riding in his enclosed tractor cab equipped with air-conditioning and a tape cassette recorder, although almost as far removed in technological space from Powers as Powers was from Fairchild, would still know what Powers meant about farming being "life itself."

12. Powers, *Years of Struggle*, pp. 11–12.

8

We Build Our Towns
on the Land

*F*EW of the first immigrants who rushed into the Black Hawk Purchase in the 1830s came with the intention of being townspeople in this new land. These early settlers had been farmers back East, and in moving west, they wanted to continue doing the only things they had ever known, tilling the soil and raising livestock for market. But of necessity towns had to be built to provide marketplaces and the basic minimal services for the farmers. As the first farmers settled as near as possible to the great river which was their highway to the outside world, so the first towns in Iowa were the Mississippi River towns: Dubuque, Burlington, Keokuk, Fort Madison, Davenport, and Bellevue. The river was to mold them and to give them a character unlike that of other towns in Iowa. Most of these river towns looked out and down the Mississippi to St. Louis, Memphis, and New Orleans. The river culture, an amalgam of north and south, east and west, was their culture, distinct from and often antagonistic to the culture of their own state.

Of the river towns, only Dubuque, with its lead mines, had a reason for existence other than the river. Consequently, by attracting among its first wave of settlers recent Irish immigrants, poor enough and hungry enough to go down into the mines, Dubuque was always to be a city apart, different not only from the rest of the state but also from the other river towns of Iowa with which it competed. It would be a Democratic stronghold in a state predominantly Republican. It was the first Catholic archdiocese in Iowa, and with its cathedral and its colleges of Loras and Clarke it would remain the center of Catholic culture in a Protestant state.

Very quickly the river lands were taken up and as the line of settlement moved farther to the west, new towns had to be built in the interior. The townspeople competed with the farmers for the land, as they both sought the same sites, navigable streams with wooded areas close by to provide lumber for construction. Only a few of these early town builders dared to plat their town lots on the open prairie as did J. B. Grinnell and Henry Scholte in founding their towns of Grinnell and Pella some miles distant from any streams or groves. When county lines were drawn, the center of the county became another choice spot for a town site, for these town builders knew that to have the county seat would be one means of insuring the prosperity and longevity of the town. Fierce contests frequently developed between two small towns within a county, both vying for the courthouse. In Webster County, the contest between Fort Dodge and Homer for the county seat was settled by a wrestling match, each town choosing its most muscular gladiator to go to the mat for the future of his community. When J. F. Duncombe pinned his opponent, Fort Dodge got the courthouse, Duncombe won the political honors he sought, and defeated Homer nodded away into oblivion. In some counties the struggle was not determined in such a straightforward, classical manner. After Primghar was designated the county seat of O'Brien County, the irate citizens of nearby Sanborn went over in the dead of night and stole the records from the courthouse. But sober second thoughts as well as Primghar's threat of a lawsuit induced Sanborn to surrender the records and Primghar kept the county seat.

While the land was first being settled, the practical distance for a farmer to travel to bring his produce to market and to buy his supplies was no more that three or four miles, so little towns were built, eight to ten miles apart across the state as the settlers moved westward. They existed because of and for the farmer— a mill, a general store that sold everything from food staples to hardware supplies and dry goods, a post office, which might be located in the general store, a blacksmith shop, perhaps a church and a schoolhouse and a few houses for the families of the merchants and clerks. That was the extent of many of these interior towns, little more than inconspicuous breaks in the cultivated countryside around them, and yet from the first, there was a sharp line of distinction between town people and farmers that both sides were acutely conscious of.

To this land the first settlers had to give names—to the streams, the woods and hills, and especially to the political and social units, counties, townships, and towns. For the hundreds of Iowa towns, the names ranged from the poetically imaginative, such as Steamboat Rock, Strawberry Point, and What Cheer, to the many pedestrian "villes" and "burgs," prefixed by the names of their founders. Some town fathers remembered their old homes in the east or farther away in Europe: Lehigh, Shenandoah, New Providence; or Berwick, Calmar, and the all-inclusive Norway.

For some, the naming of a town was a serious business that the inhabitants agonized over for months, perhaps changing their minds three or four times before they were finally satisfied. For others it was but a frivolous game, a whim of the moment. Ladora got its name from a music teacher in the area who suggested that the town be named for three musical syllables. The town of Indianola owes its name to a newspaper story telling of a robbery in Indianola, Mississippi. The word "Indianola" was euphonious enough to appeal to one of the founding fathers who read the newspaper the day the town was named. Primghar and Le Mars are both manufactured acronyms; the first being a word designed from the first letter of each of the eight surnames of the men who platted the town, while the name Le Mars was due to the sudden inspiration of one of the several Cedar Rapids women who, with their husbands, accompanied John Blair, the great railroad builder of Iowa, on a special excursion trip along his Illinois Central line. When the party reached the terminal point of construction in the middle of Plymouth County and Blair asked what name should be given to the station he planned to build there, each woman had a different suggestion. The issue was finally resolved when one of the guests proposed that they take the first letter of the first name of each of the ladies present and make a word. The first acronym formed was Selmar, but this was quickly dropped in favor of Le Mars, which sounded more elegant to the ladies.[1]

The greatest single source of names for Iowa towns, as the Le Mars story illustrates, was the railroad builders and their associates. Blair himself gave his name and those of his children to half a dozen towns in Iowa. Another railroad owner, Charles Whitehead, who was an avid hunter, named three towns on his Des Moines & Fort Dodge Railway for three of his favorite prey: Mallard, Plover, and Curlew. A brakeman on the Milwaukee Line was to be immortalized by having his name, Britt, adopted for a town in Hancock County. Ironically, Britt would eventually become the hobo capital of the United States. There each year since 1900, hundreds of these "knights of the open road," who have always been the bane of the brakeman's existence, gather to eat the gallons of mulligan stew the town provides and to elect the King of the Hoboes for the coming year.

So, in one way or another, the towns of the land got their names, and were duly noted on the maps and the post office lists for the state. But a town needs more than a name in order to survive. It needs an economic base to support its social and political structure. Except for the river towns, which were in fact busy ports of entry and exit, few of the early towns of Iowa had any basis of economic support other than the farming communities that surrounded them. The blacksmith shop and gristmill were usually the only two manufacturing establishments in the town, and they, like the retail stores, existed to serve the farmer. According to the federal census of 1840, taken two years after Iowa became a territory, the largest single industrial unit in Iowa was the lead smelter in Dubuque, which produced 500,000 pounds of lead per year and had a capital investment of $38,500, representing 20 percent of the total $199,000 of capital invested in manufacturing in the state—this at a time when

1. See H., K.A., and L. J. Dilts, *From Ackley to Zwingle* (Ames: Carter Press, 1975), for a brief account of how the 99 counties and many of the towns of Iowa received their names.

Iowa was already producing 1.5 million bushels of corn and over 150,000 bushels of wheat a year.

When the railroads first came into Iowa in the 1850s and 1860s, existing towns vied with each other in offering financial inducements to the railroads to extend lines through their communities. Limited by the state's constitution from becoming indebted for more than five percent of the value of the taxable property within the municipal corporation, towns could and often did evade this restriction by raising money not through taxation but through popular subscription in order to lure the railroads in their direction. The town merchants knew that with the coming of the railroad, the days of the captive farm market were limited. Farmers would take their produce to the grain elevators and livestock yards at the nearest railroad station and, while there, would do their marketing and purchase that town's services. It was far more important to get a railroad station than it was to have a courthouse. One reason why J. B. Grinnell founded his town on the open prairie where he did was that he had advance information that the Mississippi & Missouri railroad would pass that spot and would be interested in building a station there. Let Montezuma have the county seat if Grinnell could get a depot on the main trans-state line to serve his community and college. The railroad saved some communities, destroyed others, and built many of its own towns that would not otherwise have existed.

The extension of railroads across Iowa as well as the rapid development of a statewide banking system to provide the needed capital meant that industry in Iowa no longer had to be concentrated on the Mississippi River. The processing of farm produce and the manufacturing of farm implements and other agriculture-related products quickly dominated and have maintained their pre-eminence on Iowa's list of manufactured goods. Other than adequate railway facilities, the determining factor in the location of these industries such as meat packing and grain processing was the ambitious and zealous effort of a few men in a given community and the receptiveness of the community. Waterloo became a major center for the meat-packing industry, but any other railroad town would have served as well had it had a John Rath to start and successfully push the business. Similarly, men with capital in Sioux City took full advantage of their railroads, river traffic, and the town's location as the center of a tristate cattle-feeding and hog-raising area to make Sioux City in the early decades of this century second only to Chicago as the largest meat-packing city in the United States.

Occasionally a local, home-developed industry would prove successful enough to attract a much larger out-of-state company, which would move in and convert that industry into a subsidiary plant. Such was the case in Waterloo, where the Waterloo Gasoline Traction Engine Company, founded in 1892, produced an engine known as the "Waterloo Boy." The engine won such favor with the farmers of the region that the powerful John Deere Company of Moline, Illinois, bought out this potentially strong rival and made Waterloo a center for its production of tractors.

Many of Iowa's industries, particularly those unrelated to agriculture, owed their location and development to the inventive genius and promotional talents of a single individual within the community. A jeweler in Fort Madison, Walter Sheaffer, tinkering in the back room of his shop in 1912, came up with an idea for a fountain pen that could be filled by a simple lever-and-bar device instead of the inefficient and messy medicine dropper then in use. A farm-implement dealer in Newton, Fred Maytag, became interested in the possibility of improving and providing power for the few crude, hand-turned washing machines then on the market. By equipping his washers with either electric motors or small gasoline engines, he liberated both the city and farm housewife from the scrub-board and the washtub, and he made Newton the washing-machine capital of the United States. A young pharmacy student, Carl Weeks, had the happy idea of adding cold cream to face powder. With a fancy French name of Armand, the product achieved instant popularity, and—unlikely as it might seem—Des Moines became a major contributor to the cosmetic industry.

The success of one industry frequently attracted competing firms to the same community. At one time, for example, there were five rival washing machine companies in Newton, but

Maytag was so far ahead in the field that only it has been able to survive in national competition with the great diversified electrical-equipment companies of General Electric and Westinghouse. But competition among rival companies within the same community can also be a goad to success for all concerned. This has been most notably true with the insurance business in Des Moines. The first life insurance company was not established in Iowa until 1867 when the Equitable Life of Iowa was founded with an announced capital of $100,000. Backed by some of the most powerful and wealthy landowning men in Des Moines, Wesley Redhead, B. F. Allen, and, most notably, Frederick M. Hubbell, Equitable Life was successful from the start, but it soon attracted competitors. In 1879 the Bankers Life Association was organized by Edward Temple, formerly of Chariton, and a group of Des Moines businessmen. Friendly rivals from the start, Equitable and Bankers Life have over the years frequently exchanged personnel and have worked closely together in both professional and civic matters. These two companies along with eleven other Des Moines-based insurance companies had in 1976 a billion and a quarter dollars in total premiums, and have made Des Moines the insurance center of the Midwest.

Occasionally a small town in Iowa has not waited for the serendipitous discovery of a single genius to bring to it economic health. It has, as a community, deliberately planned, organized, and supported an industrial venture. Such was the case in Forest City, which by the early 1950s, with the decline of the railroads and the easy access of the farming community to nearby Mason City, found itself in serious economic difficulties. The local businessmen formed a development commission to consider the possibility of a new industry for the town. One of the commission's members, John Hanson, a local furniture dealer, had recently visited California. He returned with a strong conviction that the old restless pioneer mobility had by no means ended with the passing of the frontier. Americans, as Ben Franklin realized when he invented the rocking chair, liked to be in motion even when sitting still. Hanson's bright vision for Forest City was the motor home, a single unit that included car and living quarters. So was born the Winnebago, and in the happy, cheap-energy days of the 1960s, Forest City, population 2,930, became the motor-home capital of the United States. Anyone investing $10,000 in the company in 1966, two years later found himself in possession of stock worth $1,864,000. Forest City in 1968 had more millionaires per capita than any other town in the Middle West.

Many Iowa communities have had their economic destinies determined for them by the peculiar circumstances of their environment. Muscatine, for example, had an unusually rich supply of river clam shells close at hand, and this unclaimed natural resource led to the development of a thriving pearl-button industry. Some of the richest gypsum deposits in the United States lie in the immediate vicinity of Fort Dodge. They were first exploited, not by manufacturers of plasterboard, but by two con men, who, in 1858, cut a huge slab of gypsum from a ledge near the town, shipped it to Chicago where it was carved into a human figure, ten feet long, and then buried it on a farm near Cardiff, New York. A year later it was "discovered" and pronounced a petrified prehistoric man. The two hucksters sold their Cardiff Giant to P. T. Barnum, and it became the star attraction of his show. James Hall, a distinguished geologist, called this "the most remarkable archeological discovery ever made in this country," and the sculptor Hiram Powers solemnly proclaimed, "No chisel could carve such a perfect man." [2] It was not until thousands of Barnum's suckers had paid to see the petrified wonder of the age that the giant was finally exposed as a fake. Fortunately for Fort Dodge, the gypsum deposits had by then been found to have greater value than to provide a sideshow attraction for P. T. Barnum. Its gypsum production by the 1930s ranked second in value in the United States.

Iowa's greatest natural resource, aside from its rich soil, lay in its extensive coalfields, extending through twenty-one counties in the south-central section of the state. Albert Lea, in his survey of the state in 1835, had first come upon the coal de-

2. Quoted in *Iowa: A Guide to the Hawkeye State,* Federal Writers' Project, WPA, (New York: Viking Press, 1938), p. 261.

posits in eastern Iowa, and the first mine was opened five years later in Jefferson County, near Fairfield. Production was limited, however, until the railroads provided adequate transportation and became themselves major customers for Iowa's soft bituminous coal deposits. The area around Oskaloosa in Mahaska County was the first major center, and as these mines were exhausted, operations on an even larger scale developed in Monroe and Appanoose as well as in Polk, Jasper, and Wayne counties. Welsh coal miners came in large numbers, and small villages like What Cheer, Colfax, and Centerville became prosperous towns as new fields were opened up. Whole new communities came into existence, one of the most interesting being the town of Buxton in Monroe County, founded in 1900 by the Chicago Northwestern Railway, which owned 30,000 acres of coalfields. Unable to get an adequate supply of labor at prices it was willing to pay, the railway imported hundreds of blacks from Kentucky and Alabama. Within a year Buxton became a city of 6,000 people, of whom 5,500 were black, the only town in Iowa in which the whites were ever in a distinctly minority position. Eager to keep its imported labor happy at low wages, the railroad owners set up a model company town with the largest exclusively black Y.M.C.A. in the country and an auditorium that featured concerts of Southern blues and Dixieland music. Adequate housing was provided along with medical and legal services, staffed with black professionals. It was the most notable example of a black company town in the country. By 1915 the mines of Buxton began to give out. Following a strike in 1918, the last mine was closed, and the population began to drift away. Today, nothing remains of Buxton but some still visible scars in the open fields. For many decades after the mines had closed, however, hundreds of the former black residents of Buxton would return each year to the empty land for an annual picnic, to meet old friends and to remember the days when they had heard W. C. Handy play "The Memphis Blues" and Booker T. Washington laud them for having made into a reality his educational philosophy.

The high point of Iowa's coal production came in the war years of 1917 and 1918 when nearly nine million tons of coal were mined annually. After that, there was a slow decline until, by the 1940s, Iowa's coal production was but a minor factor in its economy. Many of the towns that had come into being, like Buxton, because of the mines simply vanished with hardly a trace of their existence. Other small towns tried to develop new industries as What Cheer did with its clay deposits, or quietly declined to small farm trading centers. Much coal still lies under the surface soil of Iowa, and it is possible that as the world energy crisis becomes more acute, new Buxtons may arise out of the cornfields.

Iowa alone of all the midwestern states east of the Missouri River has no central metropolitan area, no Chicago, Detroit, St. Louis, Minneapolis, Milwaukee, or Indianapolis to dominate the state's social, economic, and political structure. Its largest city, Des Moines, with only slightly over 200,000 people does not rank in population among the top one hundred cities of the nation, and its next largest city, Cedar Rapids, is only half the size of Des Moines. Although in 1960 Iowa's urban population did for the first time surpass its rural population, Iowa has remained a state of small towns and the state with the largest number of farm residents, both in percentage and in absolute numbers, of any state in the Union. Much of Iowa's industrial production is directly related to agriculture and consequently has no natural center for concentration. Meat can be packed in Sioux City, Waterloo, and Ottumwa, each city drawing from the vast agricultural region that surrounds it. Farm implements are manufactured in many towns throughout the state. The John Deere Company, which, with 20,000 employees, is the largest employer of labor in Iowa, has scattered its production centers in the state among four different communities. The largest concentration of labor within a single Iowa community by one company in 1970 was the Collins Radio Company of Cedar Rapids with 11,500 employees.

There was for Iowa no single dominant port of entry, such as New York, Philadelphia, Chicago, or Cleveland, where wealth became so concentrated as to dominate the economic life of the state. Nor was there any concentration of natural resources such as the coalfields of western Pennsylvania which created Pittsburgh or the oil fields of east Texas that built Dallas and Houston. Iowa's coal lands were widely spread across a quarter of the state and its agricultural lands were everywhere.

Iowa businessmen failed to take advantage of the state's very early pioneering efforts in the automobile and aviation fields. The first successful "horseless carriage" to be built and demonstrated in the United States was William Morrison's electric car, which appeared on the streets of Des Moines on 4 September 1890 much to the amazement of the inhabitants. Morrison had begun his experiments in 1887 at the same time as Daimler and Benz in Europe, but he chose to develop a battery-powered car rather than a gasoline-fueled internal-combustion engine. The Morrison Electric could seat twelve persons and attain the speed of 20 miles an hour. Shown at the Columbian Exposition in Chicago in 1893, Morrison's car helped to stimulate the interest of other young mechanics in Iowa and elsewhere in building horseless carriages. The first gasoline-fueled car built in Iowa was the Mason Car of 1902, which later became the Mason-Maytag Car with an assembly plant in Waterloo. Other mechanics and buggy makers entered the field, most notable, H. W. Spaulding, a successful manufacturer of buggies in Grinnell and the two Duesenburg brothers, Frederic and August. Many antique-car buffs still regard the Duesenburg as the greatest car ever built in America.

Similarly Iowa took an early lead in aviation. A young Grinnell farm boy, Billy Robinson, in a monoplane he had designed and built, established a new flight record on 17 October 1914 when he flew 390 miles from Iowa to Indiana at an average speed of 80 miles an hour. Robinson was called to Washington in 1916 to discuss the building of airplanes as part of the nation's defense preparedness. Before any concrete plans to establish an airplane factory in Iowa were developed, however, Robinson plummeted to his death in a cornfield near Grinnell while trying to break the altitude record of 17,000 feet. Waterloo, Grinnell, and Des Moines were not destined to become the Detroit or Wichita of the American automobile and aviation industries.

The diversity and decentralization of Iowa's industries have had social and political consequences as profound as the economic ones. Although a leader among the states in enacting safety regulations for mines and later for railroads, thanks largely to the efforts of Lorenzo Coffin of Webster County, who first got the state and then the federal government to require automatic couplers on all railroad cars, Iowa's record in enacting progressive labor legislation is hardly a distinguished one. Except for the coal miners, labor was generally not concentrated enough in any one place to organize effectively. By 1885, the Knights of Labor had only 25,000 members in the state, and most of these were miners. Other than the Des Moines Cigar Makers' Union, which was organized in 1867 and the Typographical Union, organized in 1868, few industrial workers in Iowa, except miners and skilled railroad men, were organized in the nineteenth century. Iowa did not even give formal legal recognition to unions until 1886.

At the height of the red scare in 1918, the Iowa legislature passed one of the most stringent criminal syndicalist laws in the nation. This law provided for a twenty-year jail sentence for the conviction of any person "who by word of mouth or writing advocates . . . crime sabotage, violence, in accomplishing industrial or political reform." [3] With language as vague as this, the law could be used against any labor organizer in the state. Fortunately only a few union leaders have ever been charged with violating this law, most notably in the case of William Sentner during the Maytag strike of 1938, and the convictions that resulted were invariably reversed by a higher court. Nevertheless, the law itself remained as a potential threat not only to labor unions but to the civil liberties of all Iowans until it was finally eliminated from the Iowa Code in 1977.

In 1935, largely in protest against Iowa's criminal syndicalist law, the Iowa Civil Liberties Union was formed by a small group of civil libertarians who took quite seriously the state's motto, "Our Liberties We Prize and Our Rights we will maintain." Over the past forty years, the ICLU has been engaged in many court cases and in much legislative lobbying in defense of

3. *Iowa Code,* Sec. 689.10–13. See Edward S. Allen, *Freedom in Iowa: The Role of the Iowa Civil Liberties Union* (Ames: Iowa State University Press, 1977) for a full discussion of the criminal syndicalist law in Iowa.

those "liberties we prize." But perhaps its greatest service has been in educating the people to know what those rights are which should be maintained.

Another piece of antiunion legislation that organized labor was unable to block was a "right to work" law. Iowa was one of the first states to take advantage of the Taft Hartley Act of 1947, which allowed states to outlaw the closed shop. Although bitterly attacked by organized labor, the law still remains firmly entrenched in the Iowa statute books with little prospect for its repeal in the foreseeable future.

It has been said that the reason organized labor was weak in Iowa and quite ineffective—at least prior to the New Deal—in getting favorable state legislation was that most Iowans, farmers and factory workers alike, were rugged individualists who resented outside dictation either from government or unions. Yet in a survey by the commissioner of labor statistics for the State of Iowa in 1894 taken among 19,000 wage earners at a time when very few Iowa workers were organized, a clear majority of those responding, both union and nonunion workers alike, thought that labor unions were beneficial.[4] Nor does it seem correct to accuse farmers of being the major source of opposition to the collective action of labor. Farm organizations, beginning with the Grangers, who worked for the unionization of railroad workers, through the Populists of the 1890s, down to the Farmers' Union and the National Farmers Organization have supported labor unions along with their own collective-action efforts for economic betterment.

The major force within the state opposing unions and prolabor legislation has not been the farmer or the wage earner, but has come from the small towns of Iowa. Here doctrines of laissez-faire and the free-enterprise system are most fervently and sincerely believed in. The one great advantage that many towns in Iowa could offer to prospective industrial developers was that they could furnish nonunionized labor. This attraction has been an important factor in the decentralization of industry in Iowa.

4. See Bernard Mergen, "A Quantitative Study of Wage Workers in Iowa, 1894," *Annals of Iowa*, 3rd Series, 41 (1972): 1114–1127, for an analysis of this survey.

The small towns in Iowa have had an impact upon the state in many areas other than labor-management relations. Lewis Atherton, one of the few historians who have given serious attention to the small town, has attempted to dispel some of the myths about small-town life, but even he fails to give full credit to the impact the small town has had upon America's social, political, and cultural life.[5] Certainly in Iowa, where there is no large metropolitan center and where all of our cities are in reality small towns grown somewhat larger, an understanding of the small town is critical to an understanding of the state. Almost from the beginning, the townspeople have exerted an influence far beyond that which their numbers would suggest. They have dominated the state legislature, and their values—both social and political—have been taken as the state's values. The farmer may be the state's standard symbol, but it has been the influential people in Iowa's small towns who have molded the state in their own image. Many of the characterizations made of the Iowa farmer are in reality those of the town merchant, banker, lawyer, and physician. It is the latter group, far more than the farmer, which has maintained its unswerving loyalty to the Republican party and which in the past has been far more isolationist in its foreign policy views.

The many paradoxes that exist in small-town life have led to what Atherton has called the two extremes in fictional interpretation, that of adulation and of condemnation, depending upon whether one was a Sinclair Lewis or an Octave Thanet. The small-town merchant fears bigness: big government, big unions, even big business, yet at the same time he exhibits a "boosterism" that would put Madison Avenue to shame in his efforts to make his little town bigger. Every small town in Iowa greets the passing motorist with its Chamber of Commerce siren call: "Welcome Stranger to Friendly Granger"; "Blairsburg, Some Towns Are Bigger, None Better"; "Rockwell City, The Golden Buckle on the Corn Belt"; and "Jewel, A Gem in a Friendly Setting." New industries are courted with the same zeal that the

5. See Lewis E. Atherton, "The Midwestern Country Town—Myth and Reality," *Agricultural History* 26 (1952): 73–80.

railroads once were. The small-town merchant roundly condemns compulsory associations and bureaucratic regulations; he sings the praises of voluntary associations and individual action—right-to-work laws and freedom of association, yet woe betide the hardware-store owner who does not belong to the Chamber of Commerce and one of the service clubs in town, Rotary, Kiwanis, or Lions.

The small town is generally regarded by its inhabitants as the last bastion of pure, simple democracy in the United States, but neither in the large cities nor certainly on the farms are class lines so rigidly drawn or so permanently part of one's inheritance as in the small towns. Mobility upward, or even downward, is very difficult—the only real chance for mobility is out. In most small towns, residential sections are carefully delineated according to class structure. If the town predates the railroad, it may be a river or a main highway that serves as the dividing line, but for most Iowa towns it is the railroad, and the phrase, "on the wrong side of the tracks," is as meaningful in Iowa as ever the phrase "to the manner born" was in feudal Europe.

There is a mutual dependency between the small town and the farming community which both recognize, and yet this long association has not inspired mutual trust. The farmer suspects the merchant of trying to fleece him, and the townsman sees the farmer as a constant malcontent who is never satisfied with anything—weather, crops, or progress.

The small towns have been pictured in novels and songs as social deserts in which a Carol Kennicott is left stranded to gasp out her life in utter boredom. Yet a social life in a small town can be intense and demanding. The hundreds of women's clubs that exist in small towns throughout Iowa bringing women together in each other's homes twice a month to read and discuss the latest books of history, biography, and fiction have no counterpart in the cities of America. It is easy for a Norman Lear to parody these efforts at "cultural uplift," but in the women's conscious endeavor for enlightenment, these clubs make a significant contribution to continuing adult education that has too often been overlooked. Small-town politicians have frequently blocked needed social and economic legislation in the state legislature, but much of the social progress that has been made in Iowa has been due to the voluntary, unpaid, and largely unsung services of small-town housewives who know how to organize. The League of Women Voters, one of the most effective study and action groups in America for the past fifty years, has been dependent upon the small town for much of its membership and its success.

There is a smugness of attitude within the small town that is a constant source of exasperation to the farmer and of bemused wonder to the city dweller. When the editor of the *Atlantic News-Telegraph* could with all seriousness write in an article for one of Iowa's historical journals, "The great literary works of past ages were none of them produced in the rush and roar of a metropolis," [6] and thus cavalierly dismiss Shakespeare and Dickens, Dostoevski and Balzac, it is not surprising that Sinclair Lewis's novels would find an appreciative audience in New York among the many who had fled from their own hometown Babbitts.

Yet, curiously, the seventies have seen a new social trend that the demographers had not expected—the flight of young people from the city, which they had found stifling, back to rural America. In 1976, the *Des Moines Register* repeatedly hailed this boom in Iowa's small-town population, and Governor Robert Ray proudly proclaimed, "When I came into office, we were losing highly educated and talented young people. Now more and more people are seeing the benefits of Iowa." [7] This expression of the booster spirit has impressive figures to support it. For the first time in this century, Iowa's predominantly rural counties have shown an increase in population—almost 10,000 people since 1970, after having lost 28,000 people in the previous decade. But Governor Ray cannot claim this as an exclusively Iowa phenomenon. Nationwide, more people have left the metropolitan areas than have moved in—a million and a half people since 1970—and they are moving beyond suburbia to the small towns. In Europe there is evidence that much the same

6. Edwin P. Chase, "Forty Years of Main Street," *IJH* 34 (1936): 229.

7. Quoted in Eileen Ogintz, "A Rediscovery of Roots," *Des Moines Sunday Register,* 19 December 1976.

population shift is under way. It may be possible that the small town has had good reason all along for its complacency. As a woman in McGregor, who with her husband recently left the city to open up a shop in that small river town, told a *Des Moines Register* reporter, "We are happier than we have ever been. I wish we had done this years ago." [8] The ghost of Edgar Lee Masters, that caustic critic of the small town in the 1920s, must now be as tormented as he once thought all small-town people were, for today Spoon River is filling up with willing exiles from his beloved city.

8. Quoted in Ogintz, "A Rediscovery of Roots."

9

We Politick for the Land

BY the outbreak of the Civil War Iowa had become a
predominantly Republican state; by the close of the Civil War it
had become a one-party state. In 1849 it had elected a Democrat, Stephen Hempstead, to the governorship. He would be the
last Democratic governor until 1889, and of the twenty-one
chief executives in the twentieth century, only four have been
Democrats. In 1852, Iowa gave its electoral votes for the presidency to the Democratic candidate, Franklin Pierce, but it
would be another sixty years before Iowa again cast its electoral
votes for a Democratic candidate. Since Woodrow Wilson carried the state in 1912, through the election of 1976, a majority
of Iowans had voted Democratic in only four presidential contests, for Franklin Roosevelt in 1932 and 1936, for Harry Truman in 1948, and for Lyndon Johnson in 1964. In the 120 years
since the formation of the Republican party in Iowa, that party
has controlled both houses of the state legislature for all but
twelve years. The GOP record for representing Iowa in Congress, both in the Senate and the House, has been almost as
consistently successful, as well as for holding a majority of the
elective state and county offices.

Although the Democratic party remained a more conspicuous
and vocal minority in Iowa than did the Republican party after
Reconstruction in the Deep South, the effect of being a one-
party state has been for Iowa not dissimilar to that experienced

by Mississippi or Alabama. Whenever one party is so firmly entrenched within a state as to make the outcome of the canvass of votes a near certainty, one consequence has been that the leaders of the dominant party of that state will generally have little chance to be selected for the national ticket or to secure a high-level presidential appointment. Only one native Iowan has been elected President of the United States, and Herbert Hoover left the state at such an early age that Iowa's claim on him is about as strong as Texas's claim to Eisenhower. With the exception of Senator William Allison in 1888, no resident of Iowa has even been a serious contender for the presidential nomination of the Republican party. The state has been equally unsuccessful in obtaining the second position on the national ticket. Only one Iowan, Henry A. Wallace, has been elected Vice-President, and he was a Democrat. Quite naturally it has been the doubtful states with large electoral votes, New York and Ohio, who were to become the most prolific mothers of Presidents, and Indiana, the mother of Vice-Presidents.

As for high-level presidential appointments, only twelve Iowans have served in the cabinets of Republican Presidents. Only two Iowans have been appointed to the United States Supreme Court: Samuel F. Miller, nominated by Lincoln in 1862, and Wiley B. Rutledge, by Franklin Roosevelt in 1943. Clearly a wheel that rolls as smoothly down the Republican track as has Iowa receives very little of the high-grade patronage oil.

Another obvious effect of Iowa's having been a one-party state during the past century has been the factionalization of the majority party almost from the moment it became dominant. There is, of course, a strong tendency for internal friction within both major parties in America, given our two-party, nonideological political structure. When a party becomes as strong as the Republican party has been in Iowa, it can afford the luxury of intramural divisions to a far greater extent than can the minority party, whose only hope for success lies in maintaining its unity. Basically, the many small divisions that have existed within the Republican party can be clustered around one of two poles—either conservative or liberal. Although these two terms have had different meanings at various times in our history, there remains a clearly identifiable continuum of thought related to the ultimate goal of those bearing each of these labels. One can draw a clear line of relationship that must be called "liberal" which ties the governorship of James Grimes to those of several of his Republican successors: Cyrus Carpenter (1872–1876), William Larrabee (1886–1890), Albert B. Cummins (1902–1908), Dan Turner (1931–1933) down to Robert Ray, who, in standing up to the large trucking interests, responded in a way that would be quite understandable to Larrabee, who pushed vigorously for railroad regulation, or to Cummins, who battled out-of-state corporate interests. All of these men represent a continuing liberal tradition within the Republican party, no matter how different the circumstances or in what guise the opposing faction may appear.

Similarly, there has been a strong conservative philosophy within the state Republican organization almost from the beginning that has been quite consistent, even though conservatives might label themselves Radical, as they did during Reconstruction; Standpatters, as they did from 1875 through the Progressive era; or "real Republicans," as they have done more recently. Unlike their liberal opponents, they have seen corporate power not as a threat to the welfare of the people, but as a source of immediate benefit to themselves and their party and ultimately, through a "trickle down" process, of benefit to the economic prosperity of the people. Most of them sincerely believed that "what is good for General Motors is good for the country" long before Charles Wilson enunciated his famous epigram.

In Iowa, the conservative faction within the Republican party has had the distinct advantage throughout most of the party's history of a better organized and more persistent leadership. It found its first effective leader in Senator James Harlan of Fairfield. When Harlan was joined by his fellow Republican and former governor of Iowa James Grimes in 1859, the two Iowa senators presented a united front of extreme Radical republicanism to the nation. Yet there were points of difference between the two men indicative of the divisions within the Republican party. Superficially these differences might be seen as nothing more fundamental than a clash between two strong personalities, each ambitious to control the party within his state. Even though voting together on most issues, Harlan and Grimes never cared for each other personally and both were active in Iowa in building their own fences and corralling their own separate groups of friends. But the differences between the two men were deeper than the personal desire of each man for party control.

Grimes, unlike Harlan, saw the necessity for some kind of regulation of the corporate interests, particularly the railroads, which he and Harlan had both so assiduously promoted; Grimes raised embarrassing questions about the continuing necessity of a high tariff to protect industries that were no longer infant; and finally, Grimes risked his political future by providing the necessary vote in Andrew Johnson's impeachment trial to save the President from conviction. Excoriated by his own party for his "not guilty" vote for Johnson, Grimes still might have survived this storm and have remained a leader of the liberal faction within his party had not ill health forced him to resign from the Senate in 1869, thus leaving the field to Harlan.

Harlan's control of the Republican party in Iowa and in particular of its conservative faction, was to be short-lived, however. Having resigned from the Senate in 1865 to serve as Secretary of the Interior in Johnson's cabinet, a Lincoln appointment which Johnson honored, Harlan soon broke with his chief, and demanded back "his" seat, still vacant in the Senate. Ruthlessly pushing aside the claim of Iowa's popular war governor, Samuel Kirkwood, for that seat, Harlan used his machine to good effect in getting the Iowa legislature to elect him for a new term. The disgruntled Kirkwood and other friends of Grimes, such as James F. Wilson, took their liberal following straight into the waiting arms of an anti-Harlan conservative faction led by the railroad builder and Civil War hero, Grenville Dodge, and his ambitious young political protégé, Congressman William Boyd Allison. The Harlan machine was still powerful enough in 1869 to defeat Allison's first bid for the Senate to fill the unexpired term of Grimes by electing one of Harlan's friends, Judge George Wright. But it was Harlan's last political victory. Harlan would have been well advised to have let Dodge and what remained of the Grimes machine have Grimes's seat, for, frustrated in that effort, Dodge and Allison decided to take on Harlan himself. For two years they worked incessantly and efficiently to build up enough votes in the Iowa legislature to defeat Harlan when he would come up for re-election in 1872. Their campaign paid off, and in early January 1872, Allison won the endorsement of the Republican caucus in the Iowa legislature by a single vote. The fight was over and Harlan had lost his seat in the Senate and his control of the Republican party in Iowa.

Allison's struggle for power with Harlan had not been a contest between conservatives and liberals, for both men essentially represented the conservative faction of the party. The railroads would not be the losers no matter which man won, but with Allison's victory, the conservative economic and political interests both within and outside the state had an able young machine politician, who would, for a whole generation, be generally successful in keeping the party in line at the county, state, or national level. For over a third of a century, Allison was to be the dominant voice of Iowa Republicanism. Ironically, Allison came from Dubuque, the most solid bastion of Democratic strength in the state, but in reality, the entire state was his home, which he ruled from his throne of power in Washington.

Courtly and gracious, soft-spoken and polite, Allison never conformed to the stereotype of a party boss. Yet Allison held on to power with the iron-gripped clasp of New York's Roscoe Conkling or Ohio's Mark Hanna, and his party machinations, like theirs, reached down to the lowest precinct level.

Allison was ably assisted in his rise to power and in his holding on to that power by James S. ("Ret") Clarkson, the able publisher of the *Iowa Register* (which later became the *Des Moines Register*). Clarkson, whose career as editor-publisher spanned much of Allison's own career in the Senate, was a member of a distinguished family of journalists in Iowa. His father, Coker F. Clarkson, had built the *Iowa Register* into a leading Republican paper in the state soon after the capital was moved to Des Moines. "Father" Clarkson was a close and devoted friend of Harlan, and when the struggle for power between Harlan and Allison reached its climax in 1871, the elder Clarkson found himself in opposition to his children, who were supporting Allison. Acknowledging the rise of a new generation more graciously than did Harlan, "Father" Clarkson stepped aside, turning the paper over to his two sons, James and Richard. The *Iowa Register* began its long association with Allison, which paid off handsomely for both sides. As Allison's influence grew, so did the *Iowa Register*'s until it became the dominant newspaper of the entire state.

Although basically a conservative, Allison was never an ideologue. He was no Grover Cleveland or Herbert Hoover, who would go down to defeat rather than compromise a principle. Allison was interested in power more than philosophy and could, when expedient, compromise his belief in sound money by adding his name to a modified silver purchase bill, or he could give tacit approval to moderate railroad regulation when absolutely necessary. His caution in taking a firm public position on any issue was legendary in Iowa, and many apocryphal stories were circulated about his refusal to commit himself in advance to anything, even to the sun's rising in the east on the following morning. Yet he could deliver the votes and always managed to find a compromise that would be acceptable to those who really counted in the power structure of both Des Moines and Washington. While the people of Iowa laughed good-naturedly over his cautious hesitancy to make a public commitment, the industrial leaders of the nation smiled contentedly over his private commitment to their best interests.

Full credit must be given to the senator from Iowa for building and maintaining his power structure until his death in 1908, for Allison lived in difficult times when depression and farm protests could have easily destroyed anyone less astute than he. The Democrats rarely posed any threat, but the dissident factions within his own party were always there, always a danger to conservative rule.

Allison came into the Senate just as the country was plunged into the worst depression it had known. But the farmers of the

Midwest had already been in serious economic trouble since 1870, when farm prices began their precipitous decline. With that decline in income, the farmers began to organize more effectively for economic and political action than they ever had before, using the National Grange as their vehicle for organization. The Grange, which had been founded by Oliver Kelley, a government clerk in Washington, as a secret society to promote cultural, social, and intellectual interests for the isolated midwestern farmer, established its first Iowa unit in Newton in April 1868. Its growth in the state was slow at first, but with hard times, the farmer became interested in the opportunities the local Grange presented for getting together with his fellow farmers to discuss mutual problems. Vigorously promoted by William Duane Wilson, the editor of the *Iowa Homestead,* the state's leading farm journal, and by "Father" Clarkson, who was still writing an agricultural column for the *Iowa Register,* the Grange in Iowa grew rapidly. By November 1873, there were 1,823 Granges in Iowa, with every county but four having at least one local Grange. Although forbidden by national charter from political partisan activity, the local Granges did not hesitate to speak out on the political and economic issues of the day. When 1,200 delegates representing 50,000 Iowa Grangers met in Des Moines in January 1873, demanding regulatory railroad legislation, the incumbent politicians and the railroads knew they were in trouble. Out of that meeting came the formation of the Anti-Monopoly party, a third party to which disgruntled Republicans who would never vote Democratic might resort and to which the Grange could give its tacit, if unofficial, approval. In the state elections that fall, the Anti-Monopoly party achieved a stunning victory, winning eight of the twenty-two senate seats up for election, and a majority of one in the house. Only the great popularity of Governor Cyrus Carpenter, himself a sharp critic of the railroads, saved the Republicans from a more disastrous defeat.

The legislature, which convened in 1874, could no longer avoid passing some kind of remedial regulatory legislation. The bill that it passed, Iowa's version of the so-called Granger Laws, although allowing the legislature to set maximum freight and passenger rates, satisfied no one. The Grange was unhappy because it had wanted a commission to set the rates. Nor did the bill satisfy the river towns, for it failed to prevent railroads from lowering their rates on through-traffic to Chicago, thus further hurting Dubuque and Burlington as terminal points in competition with Chicago. It did not satisfy the western areas of the state, which were still trying to encourage railroad construction to meet the needs of their growing population, and it did not satisfy the unhappy farmers in the rest of the state because it did not provide for adequate funds and machinery for enforcement.

Certainly it did not satisfy the outraged railroad managers, who had been caught by surprise with this sudden uprising of a populist revolt. The Burlington Railroad, in particular, headed by the astute and intransigent Charles Eliot Perkins, announced its intention of not complying with the law until it could be tested in the federal courts. In the meantime, Perkins made plans for a political campaign to get the hated law repealed. Using the immense resources at their command, both financial and political, Perkins and his cohorts Joseph Blythe and John Runnels, through a judicious use of railroad passes and other equally unsubtle methods of bribery and political blackmail, attacked the law in the columns of the small-town newspapers and in the cloakrooms of the legislature with great effect.

The railroad managers had good reason to hope that the United States Supreme Court would come to its rescue by declaring Iowa's law void along with similar laws passed in Wisconsin, Minnesota, and Illinois, even before the necessary spade work had been accomplished to get the legislature to repeal the law. They remembered well how the United States Supreme Court in the case of *Gelpcke* v. *the City of Dubuque* in 1862 had stepped in to protect the holders of Dubuque city bonds, issued to subsidize the railroads, after the Iowa Supreme Court had declared those bonds invalid by ruling that the Iowa legislature had had no right to delegate its powers of taxation to a municipality so that it could tax the people for a public improvement, such as railroads. Although largely forgotten by history, this was an important case, for it set a precedent of the United States Supreme Court's overruling a state supreme court in its interpretation of its own state constitution. Moreover, for the first time, the clause in the United States Constitution forbidding states to impair contracts, which since Marshall's time had been used with such telling effect to protect private property interests, had been used not against state legislative action, but against state judicial action. Over the vigorous dissent of Justice Miller, the only Iowan on the Court, a nearly unanimous Supreme Court had flexed its muscles in an unprecedented way in order to protect out-of-state interests.

Unfortunately for Perkins and company, however, the Gelpcke case could not be used as a precedent in striking down the Granger legislation, for the time-honored impairment-of-contract clause did not apply in this instance. Iowa, along with all of the other midwestern states, had carefully included in its grants to the railroads clauses which acknowledged the right of the state to regulate all railroads to which state grants of land had been given. The Granger laws were thus not an impairment of contract. A new clause in the Constitution would have to be found to protect railroads against state regulatory laws, and as the Court revealed in a series of cases upholding the Granger laws in 1877, including the case of *Chicago, Burlington and Quincy Railroad* v. *Iowa,* it was not quite yet ready to make use of the due-process clause in the Fourteenth Amendment in a substantive way to protect private property against restrictive state legislation.

That sort of interpretation would come later, but in the meantime Iowa's law remained on the book. Failing in the courts, President Perkins and his allies proceeded to force through a repeal of the 1874 regulatory law. This was accomplished at the next session of the Iowa legislature. But it is not accurate to say simply that Iowa's Granger law was repealed. Instead, it was replaced by a law creating a state railroad commission with power to investigate and report to the state legislature on unfair practices and exorbitant rates, for possible remedial action. If there had to be some kind of regulation, the railroads certainly preferred a commission, particularly a commission appointed by the governor and paid for by funds supplied by the railroad, as the Iowa law of 1878 provided. Here was a commission that the railroads could easily control, and so there was celebration in the railroad executive offices in Burlington and Dubuque and Chicago in the spring of 1878. The celebrants should have tempered their joy with the realization that the principle of regulation had been maintained. Given the wrong kind of governor and too independently minded a commission, the railroads could still be in trouble.

By the late 1870s, however, both business and the conservative faction of the Republican party breathed easier. They seemed to have survived the farm protest relatively unscathed. Farm prices were going up, and the farmers were far less militant. The Granges, after unsuccessful experiments in co-operative economic enterprises, especially their disastrous attempt to manufacture farm implements, which resulted in the bankruptcy of the Iowa State Grange, were declining precipitously in numbers, and the Iowa farmer was once again going his old independent way.

A new storm swept the corn belt in the next decades, however, which again threatened the political stability of the state. Allison's adroitness was once more to be fully tested. The decade of the 1880s saw the rise of the Farmers' Alliance, more overtly political, although less well organized than the Grange had been. The Greenback party selected an Iowa maverick Republican, James B. Weaver, as its candidate for President in 1880, and he received over 300,000 votes, nearly enough to give the election to the Democratic candidate. In Iowa, Weaver received over ten percent of the vote. Four years later a Democrat, Grover Cleveland, was elected President, and although Iowa remained in the Republican column, the Democrats received a larger percentage of the vote than at any time since 1852. Moreover, there were new demands for effective railroad legislation, and this time the farmers were joined in their protest by the editors of many small-town newspapers, heretofore the staunchest allies of Iowa conservatism.

As if this were not enough, the Republican party was also being torn apart by the prohibition issue. Absolute prohibition of all intoxicating beverages, including wine and beer, became for the 1880s the kind of issue that the abolition of slavery had been in the 1850s in arousing passionate controversy, and the temperance adherents in Iowa were far more numerous and vocal than the abolitionists had been. This issue cut across conservative and liberal lines, dividing former political allies and creating new coalitions in ways that were most disturbing to the party professionals. Old party stalwarts like former Governor Samuel Kirkwood, an outspoken opponent of prohibition, openly advocated ticket-splitting to punish the dominant prohibitionist element within the Grand Old Party, while a few Republicans such as the distinguished Waterloo attorney Horace Boies took the extreme action of leaving the party and becoming Democrats. The Democrats, quite naturally, enjoyed this division within the ranks of the enemy. They remained united in their advocacy of a county option and a statewide licensing plan, and they were more than willing to welcome any wandering Republicans into their fold.

Throughout all of this turmoil, Allison remained as inconspicuous as possible, thankful that as a United States senator he did not have to take a public stand on what was purely a state issue. A master of double talk, he was able to issue vague statements that could be interpreted as being favorable to both the friends and foes of prohibition. Even so, he must have experienced considerable discomfort as he saw the political order he had created over the past decade threatened by the kind of ideological fanaticism he detested. Nor were his old allies entirely dependable in dealing with this intramural quarrel. Clarkson was much too openly allied to the prohibitionists to be of any help in keeping the antiprohibitionists in line, and there was some indication that Allison's railroad friends were actually engaged in stirring up the prohibition issue in order to keep the public and the state legislature so preoccupied that they would not have time to deal with more dangerous topics like railroad rates and corporation taxes. An interesting letter from one of Perkins's most active henchmen, J. Sterling Morton of Nebraska, the future Secretary of Agriculture under Harrison, hinted at this. Morton wrote boastingly to Perkins that he (Morton) was becoming quite a religious writer and included a collection of news stories he had ghostwritten for publication in southwestern Iowa newspapers supporting the old-time religion and attacking demon rum.[1]

If the railroad politicans were indeed hopeful that the emotional fervor of the 1880s could be channeled into the prohibition controversy, they were to be disappointed. All that this intraparty tempest succeeded in doing was first to add a prohibition amendment to the Iowa constitution in 1882, which the Iowa Supreme Court on a technicality promptly ruled unconstitutional; then to get that recent convert to the Democratic party, Horace Boies, elected governor in 1889; and finally to place on the Iowa statute books the Mulct Law of 1894, one of the most inane laws ever passed by the Iowa legislature. Under the provisions of this law, there was to be statewide prohibition, but in any town with a population over 5,000, a majority of the voters could approve an option by which the law would not be enforced against any saloon keeper who paid a tax of $600 a year. Rarely has a law so openly provided for a legal means of bribery for its nonenforcement! It was enough to drive the most ardent prohibitionist to drink.

Worst of all for the conservatives, all of this commotion over prohibition did not keep more serious economic issues off of the legislative calendar. It only distracted the usually perceptive Allison into making the serious error of embracing a political maverick as one of his own, and both he and his railroad friends were to pay for this error. The man he promoted to the governorship in 1886, William Larrabee, had all of the right credentials: He was a wealthy mill owner and landholder from Clermont in Fayette County, one who had worked early and hard to get railroads into Allison's section of the state, a party regular in the state senate who had voted against the Granger law of 1874, a man whom Allison had not known well but had always liked. In this case, however, Allison simply had not done his homework carefully enough. Had he done so, he might have discovered that Larrabee had some rather peculiar ideas. Larrabee had

1. See J. Sterling Morton to Charles E. Perkins, 1 December 1878, in the Burlington Archives, Newberry Library, Chicago, and quoted in Mark Genereux's unpublished paper, "Iowa Legislative Politics in the 1870s: The Burlington Takes Hold," Grinnell College.

voted against the Granger law not because he opposed regulation but because this law was too rigid and was not, in Larrabee's opinion, an effective regulatory tool. Larrabee was a
small-town businessman, who resented big business even more
than he feared big government. Larrabee was also deceptive in
manner. He seemed to be quite colorless in personality and a
most ineffectual public speaker. One could not imagine his
being able to set off an explosion even in a gunpowder factory.

Larrabee in office proved to be something quite different. His
public speaking did not improve, but his actions spoke far
louder than his words ever could. Angered over the discovery
that the Burlington was overcharging the state in shipping coal
to the state institution for the mentally retarded in Glenwood
and unable to get the satisfaction he had expected from his
friend Charles Perkins, Larrabee had his suspicions aroused.
Further investigation showed that in the eight years of its existence, the railroad commission had been totally subservient to
the railroad interests and had done nothing to fulfill its mandate.
Abruptly, in his second inaugural address, Governor Larrabee
declared war on the railroads and on his own railroad commission. Never has an Iowa governor acted with greater vigor to
achieve a major legislative reform. He went across the state
speaking for effective regulation. He mumbled his words, but
the farmers and small-town merchants sat on the edge of their
chairs to catch every syllable. He brushed aside the traditional
niceties of the separation-of-powers doctrine and appeared in
person at legislative hearings and party caucuses to testify for
and cajole hesitant legislators into voting for a new railroad act.
The result was the first really effective and enforceable regula-
tive act for railroads in the state's history. Although the act, as
finally developed and as passed unanimously in both houses in
April 1888 did not deal with passenger rates, it did strike down
the worst abuses of the railroads in handling freight—special
rates, rebates, higher charges for shorter hauls than for long
hauls, and railroad pooling arrangements. Most important, it
created a new commission with real powers to fix rates, which
were to be held in all court suits as *prima facie* reasonable maximum rates. In other words, the burden would now be on the

railroads to prove to the court that the rates were unreasonable. A supplementary bill provided that the commissioners hereafter were to be elected by the people and paid out of general taxes, not from a fund provided by the railroads. Governor Larrabee spent the remainder of his second term defending his law in the courts and getting the railroads to comply with its terms. Having won both battles, he refused to consider a nomination for a third term. He turned the office over to his Democratic successor and retired to his beautiful home, Montauk, near Clermont. He carried with him the gratitude of the Iowa farmers for what he had done, and the gratitude of the railroads that he was at last out of office.

To the credit of Allison, it must be said that he never publicly repudiated Larrabee in spite of the anguished cries from Joe Blythe, from Nathaniel Hubbard of the Chicago, Northwestern, or from his other railroad allies. Allison was not one to denounce a friend—or to admit that he had made a mistake. But this friendship may have cost Allison the presidency in 1888, for there is strong evidence that Allison failed to get the crucial votes of New York and Pennsylvania at the Republican convention that year because of the radical Iowa railroad legislation with which Allison, through Larrabee, was tainted.[2]

Although repeatedly refusing all offers for political office, Larrabee out of office remained more than an unpleasant memory to the conservatives. He continued to encourage, through his writings and personal contacts, liberalism within the party, and to the degree that anyone could influence the ambitious young politician Albert B. Cummins, with whom Larrabee was first allied in the legislative battle for the railroad act, it was the Sage of Montauk. It is not an overstatement to say that with Larrabee, whom history has so curiously neglected, Iowa progressivism had its real beginnings.

The railroads did not go into mourning because the conservative Democrat Boies had replaced Larrabee in the governor's chair, but for Allison, the years 1888–1890 marked the low

---

2. See Leland Sage, *William Boyd Allison* (Iowa City: Iowa State Historical Society, 1976), pp. 223–224.

point in his political influence within the state. Not only had he missed his one big chance to become President in 1888, but Iowa now had a Democratic governor, and in the congressional elections of 1890 the state sent six Democrats out of its eleven representatives to Washington. Even more alarming was Allison's own very narrow victory for re-election to the United States Senate. There was even talk in Washington circles that Iowa, the GOP's most loyal child in the Midwest, had become "a doubtful state."

Yet curiously enough during the tumultuous 1890s, when so much of the prairie lands blazed with Populist fire, Iowa retreated into conservative Republicanism, apparently little affected politically by the depression of 1893, little moved by Kelly's army of desperate have-nots which moved across the state to join Coxey's army in its march on Washington, little aroused by another bid of its native son James Weaver for the presidency as head of the new People's party in 1892. Horace Boies was defeated in his try for a third term as governor by a lackluster Republican, Frank Jackson, proving conclusively that Iowa was again back in the Republican fold, where any Republican, no matter how inept, could defeat any Democrat, no matter how able. Weaver as the Populist candidate in 1892, although increasing his national vote three times over that which he had received in 1880 as the Greenback candidate, and winning twenty-two electoral votes, got only half the vote in Iowa that he had received in his previous bid. And as the Populist silver-money craze reached its climax in the election of 1896, William Jennings Bryan's percentage of Iowa's popular vote was lower than any Democratic presidential candidate's since Hancock in 1880. It was as if Iowa had exhausted all of its political fury in the 1880s, or perhaps it was saving its energies for the new Progressive revolt that lay ahead. In any event, by 1896, while Republican leaders in other midwestern states were wringing their hands in despair over the divisions within their party and the possibility that that madman Bryan might become President, Allison again was quite relaxed. He easily won a fifth term to the Senate from a party more united than it had been in fifteen years.

Prosperity has its own perils, however, and as the Allison machine guided the state into what promised to be a prosperous new century, trouble once again broke out among the ranks of the faithful. Allison in Washington and his Iowa "Regency," consisting of Blythe, Perkins, and Hubbard, who controlled the state machine for him, had little difficulty in pinpointing the trouble. The liberal dissidents, young and old, who had been quiet but not necessarily happy during the 1890s, were beginning to stir and move again. There was Larrabee, of course, along with such influential newspaper editors as A. B. Funk of the *Spirit Lake Beacon,* John Hartman of the *Waterloo Courier,* Emory English of the *Mason City Daily Times,* and George Roberts of the *Fort Dodge Messenger.* Even more alarming to the old order, these dissidents were attracting men of property who should have been quite content to keep things the way they were: Fred Maytag of Newton, Warren Garst, banker of Coon Rapids, Thomas Way of Mason City, one of the largest landholders in the state, and most distressing of all, Frederick Hubbell of Des Moines, the wealthiest man in the state. All of these men were making tracks down a trail that led straight to one man—Albert B. Cummins.

That Cummins had long been a friend of Larrabee was well known, but he had also performed faithful service for Allison and the machine. Even Joe Blythe had at first liked him. But as Leland Sage points out, Cummins was "a young man in a hurry, consumed by ambition." [3] After one term in the Iowa House of Representatives, Cummins had hoped for the nomination for governor in 1891, only to be told it wasn't yet his time. He was even more disappointed when he was passed over for the junior United States senatorial seat in 1894 in favor of Blythe's father-in-law, John Gear, a former governor of Iowa. The final blow to his ego came when the machine insisted that Gear should run for a second term in 1900. The old man was so decrepit that he could barely walk, but run he did, and Cummins finally got the message. Someone up there didn't like him, and it was now time for him to strike out on his own. He waited

3. Sage, *History of Iowa,* p. 226.

in the Allison camp only long enough to see whom the machine would appoint to the Senate to replace Gear, who had conveniently died two months after his second election. That appointment went to Congressman Jonathan Dolliver of Fort Dodge. Without further ado, Cummins gathered his friends about him and prepared to do battle.

It is difficult now to understand why Allison and the Regency so deliberately drove Cummins away. It was one thing to push Weaver out into the political wilderness in 1877; it was quite another matter in 1900 to give the Progressive dissidents within their own party the strong leader they desperately needed. Cummins was no more an ideologue than was Allison. He had made no demands on the party platform—he had only wanted office. Dolliver, whom the machine did bless with the senatorial appointment, was at least as liberal as Cummins, but Dolliver had won Allison's friendship and trust as Cummins had not. Without Allison's support, Cummins had no chance for preferment from Governor Leslie Shaw, who was part of the Regency.

Cummins conducted a brilliant campaign to wrest the Republican convention's nomination for governor away from the machine. That he could do so as easily as he did showed clearly that the Regency's hold on the state was slipping and that the party was looking for new leadership for the new century. In the ensuing campaign, Cummins stole much of his democratic opponents' ammunition by emphasizing the Republican party's new tariff plank, which his friend George Roberts had written. This plank, which called for flexible tariff schedules in order to check monopolies, was not a particularly original idea as Roberts was the first to admit. But powerful speaker that he was, Cummins sold it to the state and eventually to the nation as the Iowa Idea, a nice, alliterative slogan that caught attention and focused the spotlight of progressivism on Iowa.

In this campaign and in his three terms as governor, Cummins was aided immensely by a dramatic change in the *Des Moines Register*'s editorial policy as a result of the Clarksons selling the paper in 1902 to a group of Cummins's friends, including George Roberts, A. B. Funk, Fred Maytag, and the liberal editor from Algona, Harvey Ingham. A year later, this group sold out to an Algona banker, Gardner Cowles. Ingham remained as editor, and under Cowles and Ingham, the *Des Moines Register* became the dominant voice of Progressive Republicanism in Iowa. Because of the paper's influence throughout the state, it has been in the twentieth century a major factor in explaining the vitality of liberalism within the state, not only with respect to economic and political issues, but also in the area of civil liberties.

As governor, Cummins gave Iowa the kind of leadership for Progressive reform that was surpassed only by La Follette in Wisconsin. Cummins may not have been an ideologue, but he was an activist, and all of the action in these years was in the Progressive camp. Supported by a few wealthy friends, influential newspaper editors, and the rising new urban middle class interested in consumer protection and greater participation of the people in the political process, Cummins pushed through the legislature a remarkable series of regulatory and democratic participatory measures. A railroad tax bill in which taxes would be assessed on published reports of earnings, an insurance bill that gave the state the power to license and examine insurance companies, a pure food and a pure drug bill, a bill outlawing free passes, thus eliminating the railroads' most effective device to "win friends and influence people," and what Cummins regarded as his greatest triumph—a direct-primary law.

The Progressive spirit, so dramatically promoted by the governor in state government, was also in evidence at the local level in Cummins's home town. In 1907, Des Moines scrapped its old, corruption-ridden, city-ward government and replaced it with the commissioner form of government. Five commissioners were elected at large and each commissioner was responsible for and accountable to the public in the conduct of his own specific department. The so-called "Des Moines Plan" was praised by Progressives throughout the country and was adopted by several other cities.

During these six years of action on the state front, however, Cummins still had his eye on that long-coveted Senate seat. When in 1907 it was evident that the aged and ailing Allison had no intention of retiring, Cummins decided to meet the issue head on and declared his intention to run against the old man. This was an act of lese majesty that neither the party leaders nor the people, voting for the first time in a preferential primary, could countenance. Allison won both the party's endorsement and the people's primary. It was his last hurrah. Two months after the primary, he came home to die, and by his death, Allison gave to Cummins what he had so long denied him while alive. In November, in a special primary, Cummins won his party's endorsement for a full term and also was elected by the legislature to fill out the remaining three months of Allison's term. Cummins left immediately for Washington to be sworn in as senator.

Although Senator Dolliver had remained loyal to Allison to the end, serving as his most effective campaigner for the preferential primary, he welcomed Cummins to the Senate as a much needed recruit to the Progressive cause. Together the two men in a manner reminiscent of Harlan and Grimes in the 1850s presented a united front against the forces of reaction within the Senate. Together they won victories for conservation and a more effective national regulation of railroads, and together they went down to defeat on tariff reform. Once again, Iowa was the "bright Radical star" of the nation.

Iowa progressivism glittered far more brightly on the national scene than it did at home. Cummins had no well organized Regency as Allison had had to manage the state in his absence, and the Standpatters quickly moved in to fill the vacuum. Although the conservatives were unable to block the election of a Progressive, William Kenyon, to the Senate in 1911, to fill the vacancy caused by the sudden death of Dolliver, worn out by his Senate battle for tariff reform, within the state they once again gained control. It was commonly said that Iowa exported its Progressives to Washington and kept its conservatives at home, as one Standpat governor followed another in the years after Cummins left Des Moines. The bottom of the conservative barrel seemed to have been reached, however, with the governorship of William L. Harding during World War I. Harding was not only a Standpatter somewhat to the right of Blythe, but he was also a superpatriot. By executive fiat, he decreed that hereafter only English could be spoken in private as well as in public schools and in all conversations on trains, over telephones, and in all public places including church services. When five respectable German-American farm wives were arrested for talking German to each other on their rural party line, Iowa and its governor became the laughingstock of the nation even in that war-hysterical time.

The postwar decade of the 1920s was a period of political confusion for Iowa on both the national and local scene. Progressivism was kept alive in Washington, not by Cummins, who, once he appeared to be firmly entrenched in his Senate seat by his re-election in 1914, grew increasingly conservative, but by Senator Kenyon, once moderate but now one of the most liberal leaders of the farm bloc in Congress, and by Warren G. Harding's Secretary of Agriculture, Henry C. Wallace. Wallace was the third of four Secretaries of Agriculture whom Iowa has given to the nation: first, James ("Tama Jim") Wilson, who had a longer tenure of office than any Secretary of Agriculture in history, serving from 1897 to 1913 under Presidents McKinley, Theodore Roosevelt, and Taft; second, E. T. Meredith, publisher of *Successful Farmer* and *Better Homes and Gardens,* who had a brief tenure of one year under Wilson; third, Henry C. Wallace, publisher of *Wallace's Farmer,* who served under Harding and Coolidge from 1921 until his death in 1924; and fourth, his son, Henry A. Wallace, Secretary of Agriculture under Franklin Roosevelt from 1933 until Roosevelt chose him as his running mate in 1940. All four men served with distinction, but it was the two Wallaces, father and son, who most vigorously fought the farmers' battles during two of the most difficult periods for the farmers in our history. It was Henry C. in the early twenties who worked closely with the farm bloc in Congress to find some solution to depressed farm prices due to overproduction. This meant doing battle with his fellow native Iowan in Harding's cabinet, the Secretary of Commerce, Herbert Hoover, who regarded himself as Harding's prime minister, with authority to override the programs and proposals of other department heads. Hoover's solution to the farm problem was for the farmers to form co-operatives, not for the federal government to intervene in the workings of a free market. His dispute with Wallace was the beginning of an alienation between Hoover and his native state that would reach its climax in 1932.

President Harding's lure of a federal judgeship to get the dangerous Kenyon out of the Senate in 1922 and the sudden death of Henry C. Wallace in 1924, which his son would always blame on the nervous tensions and frustrations caused by Hoover's interference, lost for the Progressives and the farmers of Iowa their two strongest allies in Washington at a time when they were most needed. For there was little of the Coolidge prosperity evident in Iowa. Farm prices plummeted in 1921–1922. Many small-town banks that had overextended their resources in loans to farmers during the peak war years went bankrupt, wiping out the savings of thousands of small investors in Iowa. The rural Midwest was a rudderless boat floundering in a trough of depression on the high seas of American prosperity.

The politics of Washington under Coolidge and Hoover offered no help, nor did the politics of Iowa under Governor Nathan Kendall and John Hammill. The one man who burst forth like a flame on the Iowa political scene at this time and who seemed to know the needs of the farmer was a well-to-do attorney and landowner from Washington, Iowa, Smith W. Brookhart. (The middle initial—quite appropriately, most Republicans thought—was for Wildman). Brookhart, in spite of his wealth and small-town background, was a genuine Progressive, an early supporter of Cummins, who felt betrayed by Cummins's growing conservatism. In 1920 Brookhart challenged his former hero in the Republican primary for his Senate seat, and as might be expected, was badly defeated, carrying only twenty-eight of the ninety-nine counties, but Brookhart's name became known, and one of the counties he carried was Polk, Cummins's own home ground. In 1922 Brookhart ran for the unexpired term of Senator Kenyon, and this time he won the Republican primary handily against a field of five. He was the nominee of a party whose leaders detested him, but by now Brookhart had won the affections of the Iowa farmer, and he won by a landslide. It was only a two-year term, however, and in 1924 he had to run again. This time both Cummins and the Standpatters worked aggressively for the Democratic candidate, Daniel Steck, but Brookhart, according to the official certified returns, won by 800 votes. The returns were challenged by Steck, with the connivance of Cummins, and the United States Senate, by a vote of forty-five to forty-one, in a gross violation of the democratic process, declared Steck the winner. Iowa had its first Democratic senator since George Jones in 1858, but it was a victory the Democrats could take little pride in.

Having waged five campaigns in four years (three primary and two general) the indomitable Brookhart, bloodied by the stabs in the back by his own party but unbowed, was ready for another round. He set to work to defeat Cummins in the latter's bid for re-election in 1926. It was the old story in Iowa senatorial politics, which should have had a familiar ring to Cummins: young Allison taking on the old Harlan in 1872, young Cummins's taking on the old Allison in 1908, now it was old Cummins's turn to meet the challenge of a young buck. The people, angered over the Senate's having denied them the man whom they had elected in 1924, turned out by the thousands to vote. Hoist by his own petard, Cummins crashed to the ground. Brookhart had a majority of over 70,000 votes and carried eighty-five counties. Cummins, like Allison, died within two months after the primary, but unlike Allison, he died a defeated and bitter man.

So in the midst of Coolidge conservatism, Iowa elected the most radical senator in its history, a man who had denounced his own party leadership and had refused to support Coolidge in 1924, a man who openly advocated public ownership of railroads and utilities, direct federal aid to farmers, and the unionization of labor. He had remained a Republican and had worked within its system because he felt he had to have a political base to win and to have some effect in the Senate. But for all the help he got from his party, he might as well have run as an independent. Along with La Follette, he was denied committee assignments in the Senate. His rumpled suits were the cartoonists' delight and in the *New York Times,* he was depicted as some kind of freak which Iowa, as a bad joke, had turned loose on the nation. Isolated as he was, he could accomplish little in the Senate.

With the collapse of the stock market eight months after Hoover's inauguration in 1929, the Coolidge good times were over. The whole nation was plunged into a depression that the farmers had been suffering for the past decade. Misery may love company, but in this case, the sudden misery of the rest of the nation only made the farmers' plight far worse, as banks and insurance companies foreclosed mortgages in a desperate effort to keep their own institutions afloat, and farm prices fell to all-time lows, corn at ten cents a bushel, pork at three cents a pound and beef at five cents a pound. The farmer of 1857 got better prices than these. If the Old Guard within the Republican party, remembering 1893, thought it could ride out this depression with the same ease as it had the Populist revolt, it was to be severely disappointed.

The more radical farmers, tired of looking to either Washington or Des Moines for help, turned to one of their own farm organizations, the Farmers' Union, for ideas and action. The Farmers' Union, which had its origins in the south in 1902, had gradually spread north and west until by 1929 its major base of strength lay in the corn and wheat regions of the country. Iowa had not organized its first union until 1917, but during the depressed 1920s, the growth of the Farmers' Union had been impressive, a strong competitor to the more conservative Farm Bureau, with its ties to the state and federal government. By 1927 the Iowa Farmers' Union had found a dynamic and impulsive president in an old-time Populist and Campbellite preacher, Milo Reno, whose farm program was simply stated: cost of production plus a reasonable profit for the farmer. Now with prices far below the cost of production, farmers were ready to listen, some were even ready to revolt. It remained to be seen whether or not this revolution could be contained within the existing political system.

The first acts of violence occurred in the summer and fall of 1931 when the farmers of Cedar and Muscatine counties took direct action to prevent the further testing of their cattle for bovine tuberculosis in what came to be known as the Cow War. There had been a tuberculin testing program in Iowa since 1919 on a voluntary basis, but in 1929 it became compulsory. It was curious that it was against this law that desperate farmers took their first violent action of the depression, for the Iowa farmers had always supported high standards of grading and testing for their grain and livestock products. They had believed in and been greatly aided by scientific experimentation, and usually the veterinarian was the farmer's close ally and friend, someone whom the farmer often trusted more than he did his family doctor. But the state, perhaps unwisely, had hired a special force of state veterinarians, outsiders who came into a county to eradicate all tubercular cattle and who would then move on to another county. All cattle reacting to the test would be removed from the herd and destroyed, the farmer receiving compensation from the state after the infected cattle's value had been appraised. By 1931, many farmers argued that they were not receiving adequate compensation from the state's limited funds. They were also not convinced that the test was reliable, a suspicion which Reno and especially a Muscatine radio promoter of a quack cancer cure, Norman Baker, fostered. There happened to be a high incidence of bovine tuberculosis in the area around Tipton and Muscatine, and when one farmer after another began to lose an entire herd, the farmers armed themselves and blocked the entry of the state veterinarians to their farms.

Governor Dan Turner, who had taken office only in January of that year, was himself a farmer from Corning. An old-time Progressive liberal whom the Republican party had turned to in deperation in order to win the election, Turner was probably the most sympathetic friend the farmers had ever had as governor of the state. But Turner was determined to enforce a law that he thoroughly believed in. In September he sent troops into five counties in southeast Iowa, and the testing continued under armed guard. Later when the Democrats took office in 1933, the force of state veterinarians was greatly reduced, so that one state veterinarian in each congressional district supervised, but the actual testing was carried out by local veterinarians whom the farmers trusted. After that, there were no further incidents, and within fifteen years bovine tuberculosis, the scourge of young children, had been entirely eliminated from the state.

In Cedar and Muscatine counties, however, the spark of the

farmers' revolt had been struck. Fanned by Reno, the fire quickly spread north and west across the state. Following the Cow War, Reno laid plans for a statewide farmers' strike. A Farmers Holiday Association was formed in Des Moines in May 1932, and plans were made for a general strike. Reno sincerely believed that if all agricultural products could be held off the market for just one week, the farmers would win their battle to achieve "cost of production plus." What would happen to prices when after a week all the farmers dumped their produce on the market, Reno did not say. The strike got under way on 11 August; the roads leading into Sioux City were picketed, and violence flared when trucks carrying produce to market were turned back. Near Sioux City, one fatality occurred when a young man, driving a truck loaded with milk cans, failed to halt when ordered to do so. One of the picketers fired a gun, intending only to frighten the driver, but the shot went through the windshield. As one of the observers of the incident later recalled, "It was a freak shot, but the kid was just as dead anyway. Well, a bunch of picketers leaped up on the back of the truck to empty the milk cans. And what do you suppose they found in the cans—not milk but bootleg whiskey! The damned-fool kid, if he'd only stopped and told them that he had whiskey not milk in those cans, they'd have let him through." [4]

Frightened by the violence, which he had not anticipated, and lacking funds to sustain a strike, Reno called off the strike on 1 September, thus ending the first phase of the Farmers Holiday movement. The strike had been a failure. Only a small percentage of the farmers of the state had signed up, and many of them, by knowing in advance what roads were going to be picketed, violated their own pledges by running their produce to market.

The second phase of the Holiday occurred during the long, terrible interregnum between the defeat of Hoover in November 1932 and the inauguration of Franklin Roosevelt in March 1933. This phase was concerned with forcing a holiday on farm foreclosures. It was to be a moratorium on domestic debts compara-

4. Interview with Ed Clafkey, Ford auto dealer in Akron, Iowa, July 1957.

ble to the moratorium Hoover had declared on the European war debts. This movement had far greater support than had the marketing strike, not only among the farmers but also from the general public, who could identify its own debt problems with that of the farmer. By a variety of means, including amicable agreements between the parties concerned or by so-called dollar sales, when farms up for auction would bring only a one-dollar bid, or by threats of force, the Holiday Association was successful in postponing or thwarting foreclosure sales until the new administration in Washington could take action. This phase also ended in violence. A group of farmers near Le Mars, after failing to get Judge Charles Bradley to halt foreclosure proceedings, took the judge from his courtroom out into the country and threatened to lynch him. Although the farmers finally left him physically unharmed, the sheriff of Plymouth County called for state troops, and the newly inaugurated Governor Clyde Herring declared martial law and sent in the militia. Thus twice within eighteen months armed might of the state was used against its own citizens—conservative Republican farmers who were now in revolt against the system.

The great majority of farmers, however, was still willing to give the system one more try, by turning the rascals out in the hope of voting saviors in. In November 1932 Iowa went overwhelmingly Democratic at the county, state, and national level. Roosevelt carried the state and the nation by almost precisely the same margin that Hoover had defeated Al Smith four years before—58 percent to 40 percent. Unfortunately, some good friends of the farmer were also turned out, victims of the economic disaster they had long warned the country about and had worked hard to prevent. Governor Dan Turner, Senator Smith Brookhart—who finally ran as an independent in 1932, and Congressman Gilbert Haugen, coauthor of the McNary-Haugen bill, all deserved better fortunes than the accident of history had given them.

The New Deal that the Roosevelt administration gave to Iowa agriculture is a familiar story. Of all the segments of our population, the farmers, not only of Iowa but of the entire nation, probably received the most direct and long-lasting benefits from the New Deal. Much of the credit for this success should be given to Roosevelt's Secretary of Agriculture Henry A. Wallace, who now had the opportunity to put into action many of the imaginative proposals he had had ample time to consider during the long years of living out the Coolidge and Hoover administrations. Although Milo Reno and some of his more dissident followers quickly became disenchanted with the Roosevelt-Wallace farm policies and drifted away to Senator William Lemke of North Dakota and his strange far left–far right coalition of Dr. Francis Townsend, Father Coughlin, and Gerald L. K. Smith, most Iowa farmers gave their enthusiastic endorsement to such measures as the Agricultural Adjustment Act (AAA) and the Farm Credit Act, which brought immediate relief, and to the Rural Electrification Administration (REA) and the soil conservation programs which had profound, long-range impact upon their life-style and methods of farming.

Iowans played a notably large role in shaping and directing the New Deal. Henry Wallace brought his Iowa friends into Washington: Chester Davis as head of the AAA and Paul Appleby as Undersecretary of Agriculture. The former Iowan, Harry Hopkins, head of the Works Progress Administration (WPA) and eventually Roosevelt's closest advisor, remembered his classmates at Grinnell College and made Florence Kerr director of the Women's division of the WPA and Hallie Ferguson Flanagan director of the Federal Theatre Project. Indeed, a study of the top 236 administrators under Roosevelt showed that in their educational background, Grinnell College ranked thirteenth, the only small liberal arts, nonuniversity institution among the sixteen schools these administrators attended.[5]

Although the Democrats in Iowa won by landslide margins in the elections of 1934 and 1936, the farmer by 1938 was relatively prosperous, and Iowa ended its brief marriage with the Democratic party. The governorship and the state legislature as well as most of the county offices were returned to the Republicans. Except for Harry Truman's surprising victory in Iowa in

---

5. See Kathryn Jagow Mohrman, "The Educational Backgrounds of New Deal Administrators," unpublished M. A. thesis, University of Wisconsin, 1969.

1948, the state throughout the 1940s and 1950s was nearly as Republican as it had been in Allison's time, and without the sharp internal dissensions between Wets and Drys, Standpatters and Progressives, that had so distressed him. A Democrat, Herschel Loveless, did manage to get elected governor in 1957, and re-elected in 1959, thus proving that if farm prices dropped, the farmers were still movable, but generally the postwar Eisenhower years showed Iowa, like Mississippi, still holding true to a political tradition that had been born in the Civil War a century before.

In the 1960s, however, for the first time in Iowa's history there began a political shift between the two parties, unrelated to a great moral issue, such as slavery or prohibition, or to economic depression. Undoubtedly there were many underlying causes for Iowa's slow movement away from its traditional allegiance to the Republican party: a growing urban population, better organized and more politically conscious labor, perhaps sheer boredom with the long line of Republican governors—good, grey eminences all, who got elected in these years. The Republican party desperately needed a Larrabee, Cummins, or Brookhart to shake it and the voters out of their lethargy.

At the same time the Democratic party was beginning to change. It had always been, in Iowa, basically conservative—frequently more so than the Republican party. Not even the New Deal had shaken the state organization out of its basic complacency in being a minority party controlled by a few ethnic groups, the Irish and German Catholics in Dubuque and Carroll counties and the Danes in Shelby County. But now new groups were pushing their way into the party: labor leaders in Des Moines, Cedar Rapids, and Newton; college people in Iowa City, Grinnell, Cedar Falls, and Ames; and women everywhere who were at last beginning to use their political power forty years after getting the vote.

In 1962 the Democrats found a new leader in Harold Hughes, a former truck driver, reformed alcoholic, and apostate Republican who was elected governor in 1962 and gave the state its most exciting and progressive administration since Cummins. It was Hughes who modernized the Democratic party in Iowa and, for the first time since Augustus Dodge, made the party more than simply an ineffectual third party in a state that had no second party. After three successful terms as governor, Hughes moved on to the Senate, but he left behind a strong organization that was winning elections at every level of government. He was greatly aided, of course, by outside events: the Goldwater candidacy of 1964, which Iowa, disliking extremists in either direction, rejected as emphatically as it had rejected Bryan in 1896; by the rising political activism of the youth; and finally by the Vietnam War. It took some time for the people of Iowa to get the message about the war. It took all of Hughes's own political prestige, which he laid on the line in opposing the war; it took student protest meetings on the steps of the Old Stone Capitol in Iowa City, where a century before equally idealistic youth had held rallies in support of a war; it took the courage of one farm wife, Peg Mullen of La Porte City, who singlehandedly took on the Pentagon and showed that its casualty figures were false; it took editorials in the *Des Moines Register* and countless evenings of television news, which brought the horrors of the war into every living room in America—but finally the message got across. Both political parties were shaken and torn by that war, both parties had played a part in prolonging it, but in Iowa, as elsewhere, it was the Democratic party that more vigorously opposed it and ultimately benefited politically from that opposition.

When Hughes left for the Senate in 1969, the Republicans recaptured the governorship. Robert Ray, a liberal Republican was elected governor four times, a feat unprecedented in Iowa history. A change in the Iowa constitution increased the term of office for state officials from two to four years, with the result that, upon finishing his fourth term, Ray would have been governor for ten years, almost twice as long as any other governor in our history. His liberal stands won him the support of many Democrats, and it was his personal popularity that kept the Republicans from losing the state offices in the 1970s when in that post-Vietnam–post-Watergate period they lost both Senate seats, all but one of the congressional seats, and both houses of the Iowa legislature.

Elections in the mid 1970s indicated that the most hopeful statement the Republicans could make was that "Iowa is now a doubtful state." But Iowa was called doubtful in 1888 and Democratic in 1934, only to revert back to its traditional Republican loyalty. Whether the Civil War was now finally over and the new political alignments were creating a new political history for the state remained to be seen. The patterns of history seem to repeat themselves. A century ago Ulysses S. Grant called Iowa "the bright, Radical star" of the nation. In the year of our bicentennial the liberal Americans for Democratic Action were, in effect, to rate Iowa the most liberal state in the Union, basing its judgment on the voting records of Iowa's two Democratic senators, Dick Clark and John Culver. The patterns of history may be repetitious, but as they always reappear in quite different contexts, we continue to be surprised, not bored, by their reoccurrences. And it will continue to be some individual, a Grimes or Savery, Allison or Larrabee, Cummins or Hughes, who will impose his or her own unique personality on those patterns—to the amazement of the public and to the delight of the historian.

10

We Enhance the Land with Learning and Art

$\mathcal{A}$MERICA, product of the Enlightenment, has always made its obeisance to formal education. The Ordinance of 1787, in its rules of governance for the newly acquired Northwest Territory, paid its respects with succinctness and clarity: "Religion, morality, and knowledge being necessary to good government and the happiness of mankind, schools and the means of education shall forever be encouraged." And the Land Ordinance two years earlier had already given concrete reality to this noble sentiment by providing, "There shall be reserved the lot No. 16 of every township, for the maintenance of public schools within the said township." [1] Obeisance does not always mean commitment, however, and specific regulations do not necessarily mean immediate compliance. The 640 acres reserved for educational purposes within each township should have provided more than an adequate fund to set up a system of public education throughout that vast domain, but in most instances the land was disposed of too quickly, and the funds were swallowed up in the general operating expenses of the territory.

Consequently the first schools in Iowa, the Berryman Jennings school in the Half-Breed tract near Nashville in 1830,

1. Text of ordinances in Henry Steele Commager, *Documents of American History*, 2 vols. (New York: Appleton Century-Crofts, 1973), 1: 131, 124.

Mrs. Rebecca Parmer's school in Fort Madison in 1834, and the several subsequent schools prior to 1838 were all private schools. Governor Lucas, when he arrived on the scene, was dismayed to find the lack of public schools in the territory. He promptly sent a message to the territorial legislature demanding action. "We must show to our friends east that we mean to have schools," he told his secretary.[2]

Lucas was only the first of a long line of governors to discover that it was far easier to send strong messages on behalf of public education to the legislature than it was to get any action from the legislature. Throughout the state's history, it has been the executives who have pushed for adequate educational support, and it has been the legislature that has pulled back. Only a few exceptionally strong governors such as Grimes, Larrabee, Cummins, and Shaw were able to translate the glittering promises of their inaugural addresses into the reality of educational bills passed by both houses of the legislature. Public education, except in a few of the larger river towns, did not effectively begin in Iowa until Governor Grimes asked Horace Mann, the distinguished Massachusetts educator, to head up a commission in 1856 to study and report on Iowa's educational needs. Much of the Mann report, calling for a central Board of Education with "full power to legislate and make all needful rules and regulations in relation to Common Schools" was embodied in the new state constitution of 1857 and in the general school law of 1858, but with the several strings attached: that the actions of the board, and indeed the existence of the board, could at any time "be altered, amended or repealed by the General Assembly." Few of the legislators had the vision of Grimes when he said in his inaugural address, "The safety and perpetuity of our republican institutions depend upon the diffusion of intelligence among the masses of the people" and "the prevention of the evils of poverty and crime is much less expensive than the relief of one or the punishment of the other." [3]

2. Quoted in T. S. Parvin, "Early School Legislation in Iowa," *Annals of Iowa*, 2nd Series, 3 (1884): 37.

3. Quoted in Irving H. Hart, "The Governors of Iowa as Educational Leaders, 1838 to 1949," *IJH* 54 (1956): 236.

One of the many difficulties in a rural state such as Iowa, where the population was spread thinly over a large area, was that the very limited educational resources were also spread, equally thinly, over the state. The one-room rural schoolhouses, usually painted white, not red, became the standard of public education in Iowa. They have been romanticized in song and story into the very essence of our democracy, and some progressive educators of today even insist that they were educationally sound in their ungraded structure, with children of different age groups mingling together and learning from each other. But for those graduates of the one-room schoolhouse who had the ambition and the means to go on to higher education only to discover how poorly prepared they were, Hamlin Garland presented a more realistic appraisal when he wrote in *Boy's Life on the Prairie:* "The school-house stood a mile away on the prairie with not even a fence to shield it from the blast . . . painted a glaring white on the outside and a drab within . . . this bare building on the naked prairie seemed a poor place indeed." [4]

Indeed, it was a poor place, yet it provided the only education that hundreds of thousands of Iowans were ever to receive. Dependent almost entirely upon local property-tax levies for support, the rural school districts had only the barest of sustenance, hardly enough to put up adequate buildings, provide the minimum furnishings, and to hire as teachers young girls who themselves had only an eighth-grade education, for whatever each individual teacher was able to collect from the parents of her pupils. As late as 1896, the average length of attendance for the country school pupil was a little less than two months per year, and in 1910, at least ten country schools had only one pupil per school while 3,018 country schools, about one-quarter of the total, had less than ten students per school. In many of these small, independent rural districts, which the Iowa legislature had authorized, there were more school officers administering the school system than there were teachers and pupils in the school. Within a single township there might be from 35 to 45

4. Hamlin Garland, *Boy's Life on the Prairie* (Boston: Allyn & Bacon, 1926) quoted in George S. May, "Iowa's Consolidated Schools," *Palimpsest* 37 (1956): 1.

school board members administering eight or nine schools for thirty to forty pupils. The one advantage the single-student school had was in the handling of discipline. As *Midland Schools* pointed out in 1906, "When the whole school gets down behind its lone geography book, the teacher knows there is something doing and she investigates." [5]

The answer quite obviously lay in a unified township school district, a solution which the Land Ordinance of 1785 had anticipated and which one governor after another from Grimes to Cummins had urged on the state legislature. The great problem, of course, lay in transporting students several miles each day to a central school, but that was not an impossibility even in that time of bad roads and with only horse-drawn vehicles for transportation, as Massachusetts had demonstrated as early as 1869. The state, however, had to be willing to furnish funds for transportation. Much of the difficulty lay in what people meant when they said the magic word "education," which no one, quite naturally, was opposed to in principle. For many, education meant simply the basic Three Rs. If a student got "a little readin', a little ritin', and a little 'rithmetic," that was enough. His education was complete. One of the most devastating blows that educational reformers in Iowa were ever dealt was the revelation in the 1880 census that Iowa had the lowest rate of illiteracy. For the next sixty years Iowa school boards and state legislatures were to remain smugly content with the fact, impervious to the observation of Amos Currier, dean of the State University of Iowa's School of Education, that "ability to read and write *was* a high personal distinction 1,000 years ago, but greater things are needed to justify boasting at the close of the nineteenth century." [6] It was not until 1902 that the general assembly finally made school attendance compulsory between the ages of seven and sixteen, but even then it set up no real standards as to what kind of school the child would be attending.

Much credit must be given to Buffalo Township in far north central Winnebago County for establishing the first consolidated

5. Quoted in May, "Iowa's Consolidated Schools," p. 6, taken from *Midland Schools* (Des Moines, Iowa) 16 (1906).

6. Quoted in May, "Iowa's Consolidated Schools," p. 3.

township school in the small town of Buffalo Center in 1897. Taking immediate advantage of an Iowa law of that year which authorized consolidation "when there will be a saving of expense, and the children will also thereby secure increased advantages," (note the order of priorities here) the township school board began closing the subdistrict rural schoolhouses, and transporting the children to the new central school in town in six horse-drawn hacks. This bold pioneering step was emulated in a few other districts, mainly in northern Iowa, in the first decade of the twentieth century, but it was not until the general assembly authorized $500 in state aid annually for the transportation of students to each school district that would consolidate, that the movement finally began to accelerate. Thanks to this rather small carrot and to the tireless efforts of State Superintendent of Public Instruction Albert Deyoe, who with his assistant James Woodruff traveled the state persuading local independent districts to consolidate, there were 439 consolidated school districts in Iowa by 1921. Then for the next twenty-five years, due to depressions and war, the consolidated movement came to an almost complete halt. It did not begin again until the legislature in 1945 appropriated $2 million for transportation costs and at the same time passed the Agriculture Land Tax Credit Act, which had the effect of shifting much of the tax burden for education from the farmers' local property taxes to the state's general tax fund. In 1955 the old 1897 law on consolidation was replaced by the Community School District Act, and as of 1 July 1966, all county schools in the state were closed. Every farm child now has available the same education from kindergarten through twelfth grade as the town child, and the bright-yellow school bus for the last twenty years has been the most conspicuous vehicle on Iowa country roads. The weeping that Governor George Wallace did so publicly over "the busing of poor little children" has struck most rural Iowans as being more ludicrous than genuinely lachrymose. Iowa farm and small-town children have been bused for years, as indeed they have been in rural Alabama, to their own considerable advantage.

The history of higher education in Iowa is not dissimilar to that of primary and secondary education: the conflicting demands of economy in government and priorities given to the tax dollar, with the need to provide adequate educational facilities and resources for an ever more complex and advanced agrarian and industrial society. As with primary education, the first colleges in Iowa were private schools, most of them little more than academies, founded and poorly supported by various church denominations: Loras, Iowa Wesleyan, Clarke, Grinnell, Coe, and Cornell were among the first, each with a fixed, classical curriculum and with more attention given to rigid social regulations than to free academic inquiry. During the post-Civil War period, scores of additional private colleges were founded in small towns across the state, many of them mercifully of short duration, but all of them with a visionary purpose, and, with very little support, carrying the major burden of providing higher education for the state. Twenty-three of these private colleges have survived to the present time, most of them offering an adequate program of instruction and a few of them achieving deserved national recognition as outstanding liberal arts colleges.

The state tended to be as parsimonious in its support of public higher education as it was in the support of the common school. Although one of the first acts of the general assembly after Iowa became a state was to charter a "State University of Iowa," it was not until March 1855, that the university, having been granted two townships of land by Congress, opened its first classes with a faculty of two members. One of the early and continuing controversies concerning the university has been the question of location. Even before the first classes got under way, there were proposals in the legislature to establish five branches of the nonexistent university, but all such attempts were vigorously resisted by Governor Grimes. The constitution of 1857 apparently settled the question for all time by permanently fixing the location in Iowa City, but as late as the 1960s, there was still serious consideration being given to building another state university in the western part of the state, which always felt itself deprived of easy access to public higher education. Given the limited resources, it is fortunate that Iowa has resisted the temptation to which many states succumbed of creating numerous university branches. There are those who have argued that the university might have done better to have moved along with the capital to Des Moines. Certainly the Universities of Minnesota and Wisconsin have done better than Iowa financially over the years, due in part perhaps to their being located adjacent to the seat of government. On the other hand, it can be argued that a university which is within walking distance of the capitol pays a high price in having more regular legislative interference in the academic affairs of the school.

For the first several decades of the university's existence it was little more than a university in name only and was frequently referred to contemptuously as the "Johnson County High School," even by those whose educational standards were not very demanding. It was not until the regents selected George Shaeffer of Cornell University to be president in 1887 that the university began to fulfill the hopes of its founders. During his tenure, and particularly during the long tenures of Presidents Walter Jessup and Virgil Hancher, the university won academic distinction throughout the Middle West. Its medical school under Dean Ewen MacEwen and its law school under the deanships of Wiley Rutledge and Mason Ladd were particularly strong among the state universities of the region.

The second state institution of higher education to be established in Iowa was the Iowa State Agricultural College and Model Farm, which, although founded in Ames in 1858, did not begin to function until the Morrill Land Grant College Act provided funds adequate to build a campus, hire a faculty, and attract able administrators. With a grant of over 200,000 acres of land, four-and-a-half-times the amount which the University of Iowa had received as an initial endowment, Iowa State College had few of the early growing pains of its older sister institution. And the college—now Iowa State University—with its various colleges and departments of agriculture, engineering, applied sciences, home economics, and veterinary medicine, and with its many county extension services and experimental stations of immediate benefit to Iowa agriculture and industry, has usually found a more receptive audience among the Iowa legislature and the Board of Regents than has the University of Iowa.

The third and final state college to be established in Iowa was Iowa State Teachers College, which eventually achieved university status as the University of Northern Iowa. Founded in 1876, it initially took over the abandoned buildings of a Civil War Orphans Home in Cedar Falls. Many of its faculty and administrators feel that this was an appropriate place for their school to have had its beginnings, for it has always been something of an orphan when the legislative patrimony was being distributed. But none of the Iowa public universities has been exactly pampered by an overgenerous legislature. In a study made by the Carnegie Foundation on state funds for higher education, Iowa in 1975 ranked twenty-sixth among the states in the percentage of appropriations allotted to higher education from the state's general revenue, while its neighboring state South Dakota ranked first. Yet in terms of fiscal ability to pay, based upon income per capita, unused tax capacity, and the existing unemployment rate, Iowa should rank sixteenth and South Dakota should be in twenty-eighth place. It is a matter of priorities.

In the golden decade of educational prosperity during the 1960s state appropriations for higher education in Iowa were greatly increased, but much of this increased allotment went into the creation of a much-needed sixteen-area, post-secondary educational system to provide vocational and technical training, adult education, and community services as well as two years of pre-professional liberal arts education. Previously existing municipal junior colleges and secondary vocational schools were merged into this system. These area colleges with their sub-branches now provide across the state the kind of educational opportunity which had hitherto been offered only in some of the larger towns. This is a commendable achievement, but it represents a further demand upon the limited educational dollar.

In one notable respect, Iowa has from the first been a true pioneer in making available what the Ordinance of 1787 called ''the means of education'' to all persons, regardless of sex or race. The University of Iowa in 1857 was the first state university in the country to open its doors to women, and not only was Iowa College (now Grinnell College) one of the first coeducational private schools in the country, but among the first women it admitted in 1860 was a young black woman. Because this was such a daring innovation, the faculty polled the trustees for their opinion before admitting such an unusual applicant. To the eternal credit of the Trustees of Iowa College, their nearly unanimous vote was a resound affirmation for admitting her. Only one trustee replied, "No, let Oberlin do it."

These important precedents established early in the history of Iowa have had an immeasurable impact both on the individuals involved and upon the culture of the state and the nation. The great botanist George Washington Carver, a former slave from Missouri, began his college education at Simpson in Indianola, and completed it at Iowa State College. Another black, Alexander Clarke of Muscatine, who had organized and conducted the famous Colored Convention in Des Moines in 1868 to push for the amendment to the Iowa constitution to extend the suffrage to blacks, at the age of fifty-seven began his law studies at the University of Iowa and became the first black to argue cases before the Iowa Supreme Court. An Iowa woman, Arabella Babb Mansfield, a graduate of Iowa Wesleyan, in 1869 was the first woman in the United States to be admitted to the bar for the practice of law, and women were admitted to the first class of the University of Iowa Medical College. Writing in the *Annals of Iowa,* Jennie McCowen, M.D., could state with some satisfaction:

> The medical profession of Iowa, as a body, is noted for its justice, courtesy and liberality towards women practitioners. . . . Not only are they [women] freely admitted to all medical societies . . . [but] this year two ladies were given credentials to represent the State Society in the American Medical Association, the highest body in the profession.

Dr. McCowen had to admit, however, that full equality had not as yet been achieved. "The Iowa Equal Suffrage Society has adopted the motto of the State with the change of a single word, thus: 'Our liberties we prize, our rights we will *secure.*' " [7] But she was confident, with the large number of educated women in Iowa, that these rights would soon be theirs to maintain. She

7. Jennie McCowen, "Women in Iowa," *Annals of Iowa,* 2nd Series, 3 (1884): 107, 111.

would have found it hard to believe that it would take another Iowa woman, Carrie Chapman Catt, thirty-six more years of unstinting effort before the Constitution of the United States would become as liberal as the A.M.A. was in 1884.

Fortunately, not all the "means of education" urged by our founding fathers for the new territory of the west were to be limited to formal education for youth in the classroom. In that large and much neglected area of informal adult education, the newspaper has played a significant role. Many an illiterate adult has used the local newspaper as his first reading primer, laboriously sounding out each word, often with the aid of his own third-grade child, until slowly the magic of the printed word became instantly familiar. Iowa was fortunate from its earliest territorial days in having a lively press whose impact upon the cultural and political education of its readers cannot be overestimated. The first newspaper in Iowa, the *Du Buque Visitor,* published by John King, was established in 1836, while Iowa was still a part of Wisconsin Territory. It lasted only a year, but it soon had numerous successors: the *Fort Madison Patriot,* the first Whig newspaper in the state; the *Burlington Territorial Gazette,* which later became the *Burlington Hawkeye-Gazette,* the oldest newspaper in the state today, and, under the editorship of John McCormally, still one of the liveliest and youngest in spirit; the *Iowa Sun and Davenport News;* and then with the establishment of each new town, at least one and frequently two or three newspapers expressing various shades of political opinion and each hoping to survive from the patronage of advertisers and subscribers who shared the paper's own political views. By 1861, according to Daniel J. Kenny's *American Newspaper Directory* published in that year, there were in Iowa one hundred and fifty-eight newspapers, most of them weeklies, and about equally divided politically between a Democratic and a Republican editorial policy.[8] From the Civil War to the present time, the press of Iowa has been as predominantly Republican as the state itself, although small-town newspapers fre-

8. Cited in Douglas C. McMurtrie, "Directories of Iowa Newspapers, 1850–1869," *Annals of Iowa,* 3rd Series, 20 (1935): 14–17.

quently grew increasingly cautious in expressing bold political
opinions for fear of offending potential advertisers or subscribers. The outstanding newspaper editors of the state in the late
nineteenth century, with but a few notable exceptions, were all
Standpat Republicans, beginning with James Clarkson of the
Iowa Register, and including such stalwarts of the party as
David Brant of the *Cedar Rapids Gazette,* Samuel Mercer Clark
of the *Keokuk Gate City* and George Douglas Perkins of the
Sioux City Journal, who was as conservative in his politics as
he was radically innovative in journalism. Under his editorship,
the *Journal* was the first paper in the state to have the linotype,
a photoengraving plant, a perfecting press, and the first to em-
ploy a cartoonist on a regular basis. One of the few notable
Democratic editors of the post-Civil War period was John P.
Irish, who in the editorial columns of his *Iowa City State Press*
campaigned vigorously not only for the Democratic party, an
activity considered to be eccentric enough, but for causes even
more lost, such as woman suffrage in 1872. Later in the century
and in the early decade of the twentieth century, the Republican
press demonstrated the same internal divisions as the party itself. As noted elsewhere, an important element of the press of
Iowa, led by the *Des Moines Register* under the Cowles-Ingham
management, spearheaded the Progressive movement in Iowa
and contributed greatly to the political success of Cummins,
Dolliver, and Kenyon. In 1976, the *Des Moines Register and
Tribune* continued to dominate the state with a circulation of
over a half-million, nearly one-fifth of the total population of
the state. Local papers outside of Des Moines, both dailies and
weeklies, have managed to survive this competition by consoli-
dating rival newspapers in the same town and by giving a heavy
emphasis to local news and local advertising.

Another agency of great importance in providing a means of
education to the people has been the free public library. The
first territorial assembly in 1839 passed a law authorizing the in-
corporation of public libraries, but apparently what was meant
by a public library was one supported by individual subscription, not by public taxation, and it was not until 1870 that the
Iowa legislature first authorized city councils to establish a free

public library and to levy an annual tax to maintain it, provided a suitable lot and building should first be donated to the city for a library. Consequently the first libraries in Iowa, beginning with Fairfield in 1853, were subscription libraries, open to anyone who could buy a share and pay the small assessment, usually one to three dollars. The first free public library supported by taxes was opened in Independence in 1873, followed by that in Osage in 1875, but the subscription library continued to prevail until at the turn of the century Andrew Carnegie moved in with his millions to stimulate the free public library movement throughout the nation. Many professional librarians would later criticize his having given too many libraries to towns too small to provide adequate support. Like the rural schools, these libraries were unable to provide effective professional service.[9] But to many youths and lonely old people in little towns like Humboldt, Montezuma, or Alden in that pre-radio–pre-television era, the words cut in stone over the door "Let There Be Light," which Carnegie asked to have placed on all his libraries, were the warm invitation to enter the magic world of learning that Carnegie had hoped they would be.

The hunger for enlightenment, for some contact, no matter how vicarious, with a more urbane world, which lay behind the free library movement, also inspired the development of the Lyceum in the nineteenth century. One must admire the high sense of Transcendental mission that would bring Ralph Waldo Emerson and Bronson Alcott in their old age to the Iowa frontier for lectures in Davenport, Cedar Falls, and Webster City. But come they did, enduring the hazards and discomforts of railway and stagecoach travel, and poor accommodations for the very small remuneration that was offered. And one must also admire those frontier townspeople who paid out their precious fifty-cent pieces to hear Emerson lecture badly on "Man of the World," or Theodore Tilton pontificate on "The Art of Using the Mind." In the 1866–1867 season, the Cedar Falls Lecture Association brought—among others—P. T. Barnum, the inde-

9. See Ralph Munn, "Hindsight on the Gifts of Carnegie," *Library Journal* 76 (1951): 1968.

fatigable Tilton, who appears to have come every year the lecture series was in existence, Emerson, and Wendell Phillips. Barnum was the star attraction, grossing $234.50 for the association, while Emerson brought in only $62.85.[10]

The public lecture movement under one auspice or another continued strong in the Midwest until the late nineteenth century. One of Max Beerbohm's most endearing cartoons is of Oscar Wilde, standing in a pose which only Zero Mostel could duplicate, lecturing to a group of Iowa farmers on the beauty of the lily that Wilde holds in his hand. Both Wilde and his audience were longsuffering martyrs for the cause of culture.

It was Chautauqua in the early twentieth century that filled the cultural gap left by the demise of the Lyceum. Anyone who lived in a small Iowa town during the first decades of this century can remember the thrill of seeing the great canvas tent that had magically appeared overnight in the city park. And for the next three wonderful days the whole town would wallow in a vast sea of culture: Swiss bell ringers and earnest young sopranos and tenors in duets from *Carmen* and *La Traviata* in the afternoon; at night, genuine three-act plays "straight from Broadway"; and always William Jennings Bryan, lecturing on "The Prince of Peace." Bryan in the early 1920s finally won the ovations from the small towns of Iowa that he had sought in vain through three presidential campaigns. But Henry Ford's flivver and the new radio stations, WOI in Ames, WSUI in Iowa City, and WHO-WOC in Des Moines and Davenport, slowly strangled Chautauqua in its tent, and by 1930 it was as dead as Emerson's Lyceum.

Library books, public lectures, and visiting actors and musicians may fulfill a basic human need for entertainment and enlightenment, but ultimately, no region can survive parasitically on an imported culture. It must interpret itself to itself and to others. It must enhance itself with story and song, must paint and carve its own portrait for the world to see. It takes the creative urge of the single individual, unsatisfied with being the passive spectator of another culture, to effect this interpretation:

10. See Luella M. Wright, "Culture Through Lectures," *IJH* 38 (1940): 115–162.

a Susan Glaspell in Davenport and a Hallie Ferguson in Grinnell to push the American stage out beyond the old traditional proscenium arch into the new arena of a people's theater; a young horn player in Davenport, Bix Beiderbecke, to catch the syncopated sounds of the river traffic coming up from New Orleans and to add his own special blue note to American jazz; and a band conductor in Fort Dodge, Karl King, his head filled with the sounds of political rallies, steam calliopes, and Iowa high school football stands on a Saturday afternoon, to blend all these sounds together into hundreds of new marches to rival those of his master, John Philip Sousa.

It takes a free-lance writer, Hamlin Garland, from his exile in New York to remember the "middle border," and a young schoolteacher in Grundy Center, Herbert Quick, to tell of the stark barrenness and sheer beauty of the Iowa farm. Above all, it takes one Cedar Rapids artist, Grant Wood, to paint Iowa's portrait: its farm couples standing in Gothic angularity; its small towns peopled with Daughters of the American Revolution; and the land itself, not flat, but softly round and fecund—all permanently delineated, so that the New York motorist speeding across Iowa on Interstate 80 will glance out his window and say, "Why it looks just like a Grant Wood painting," surprised to discover that nature frequently follows art.

Iowa has always been too sensitive about the artists and writers it has lost to other states and countries, due in part to the state's having no metropolitan cultural center—no Chicago for a school, no Harlem for a renaissance. The nearest approach to a cultural center the state had in the late nineteenth century was Davenport, and this was due not only to its river location but also to the remarkable influence of one woman, Alice French, whose own novels written under the name of Octave Thanet are largely forgotten today, but whose personal impact upon the culture of her time far exceeded in importance her own skill as a creative writer. It was she who gave early encouragement to many young writers such as Susan Glaspell and her husband George Cram Cook, Floyd Dell, and the poet Arthur Davison Ficke. As with Mabel Dodge Luhan on a much grander scale, French did not often understand or even sympathize with the art and life-styles of her young protégés, but she was committed to the creative spirit, and with her wealth and position, that was important.

It was Iowa City in the early twentieth century that was to assume for itself the cultural capital of Iowa and even to dream ambitiously of the more grandiloquent claim to being the Athens of the Middle West. With Grant Wood and later James Lechay and the master print maker Mauricio Lasansky as teachers, the university had a fine-arts department of great distinction, but it was in the promotion of creative writing that the school acquired national renown. Beginning in 1915 with the efforts of John T. Frederick, who was himself a novelist and poet of great talent, to encourage young writers through his literary magazine, *The Midland,* and continuing with Norman Foerster's School of Letters in the 1920s, the university established itself as one of the few important academic centers for creative writing in the country, a graduate school that would accept novels, plays, poetry, and short stories in lieu of masters' theses or doctoral dissertations and whose standards were high enough to warrant the granting of these advanced degrees. In the mid-century, under the direction of Paul Engle, who proved himself as skilled an entrepreneur as a practitioner of creative writing, the highly acclaimed Writers' Workshop and the later International Writers' Workshop attracted to the university campus important writers to do a stint of a year or two. For some like Philip Roth, the open spaces of rural Iowa proved to be a cultural shock so traumatic as to send them scurrying in haste back to the warren-hutch security of Manhattan or Brooklyn; for others, like Vance Bourjaily, so attractive that they stayed on permanently. But however helpful these distinguished visiting artists might be in showing by example what good writing is and in giving fame to their host institution, they could not themselves teach how to create an Iowa literature. Nor was the academic scene necessarily the best milieu for the creative artist, particularly the writer. Without a major metropolitan center in which artists could congregate and find stimulation in that companionship, Iowa's art like so many other aspects of its culture has remained remarkably diffuse and decentralized. The novelist, the painter, and the

poet have looked to the small town and to the farm for their subject matter, and to society at large for whatever patronage and
recognition they may receive.

It has been the land and the people of Iowa that have produced the strong note of realism which has always been dominant in Iowa literature from Hamlin Garland to the present.
Even the "pretty writers" of the Iowa scene, Bess Streeter
Aldrich, Margaret Wilson, and Octave Thanet, on occasions
conveyed a real sense of what it is like to contend with nature
on the farm or with society in a small town. Iowa realism at its
best, as in Ruth Suckow's *The Folks* and Curtis Harnack's *We
Have All Gone Away,* in the poetry of Paul Engle and James
Hearst, in MacKinlay Kantor's fictional history of *Spirit Lake,*
is harsh and honest. It transcends the narrow limits of regional-
ism, but remains rooted in the Iowa soil.

Paul Engle, in his poem "For the Iowa Dead," eulogizes the
Iowa farm boys falling and dying in Asia with the words:

> Most of their life was simply, to make life:
> The clover planted and the cattle bred.[11]

The artist's life is also dedicated to making life. Between him
and the farmer there can be then a familiarity born of natural understanding. The artist does not stand with Ruth "in tears amid
the alien corn."

---

11. Reprinted in Gary and Judith Gildner, eds., *Out of This World: Poems from the
Hawkeye State* (Ames: Iowa State Univ. Press, 1975), p. 54.

An Epilogue

The Land Still Unpossessed

S̄O, Robert Frost, we have done that which you said must be done. We have cultivated our fields, built our towns, our churches, our schools, and factories. We have fought for the land, politicked for it, drawn its portrait, and enhanced it with story and song. We have become possessed by the land you said we already possessed. In so doing, we have surrendered ourselves to it.

And that, according to Frost, should be the end of the story. But the haunting suspicion remains that perhaps Robert Frost started with the wrong premise in saying the land was ours before we were the land's. We can and, indeed, have become possessed by the land, but is the land, after all, ours to possess? The final words to this story more properly should be given not by a New England poet but by Iowa's first author, Chief Black Hawk. In dictating his autobiography following his defeat and capture at Bad Axe, he spoke to those who came to claim possession:

> My reason teaches me that land cannot be sold. The Great Spirit gave it to his children to live upon, and cultivate as far as it is necessary for their subsistence. . . . Nothing can be sold but such things as can be carried away.[1]

1. Chief Black Hawk, *Life of Ma-Ka-Tai-Me-She-Kia-Kiak or Black Hawk*, (1834; reprinted Iowa City: State Historical Society of Iowa, 1932), p. 88.

Black Hawk, like most of his people, knew that stewardship did not mean possession. He intuitively understood this simple truth which the later white settlers only partially and belatedly have come to accept.

Black Hawk knew what it meant to be possessed by the beauty of the rich land which one could never possess but only use in trust. On the Fourth of July, 1838, at a great celebration in Fort Madison to celebrate Iowa's new territorial status, he made his valedictory speech to the triumphant new owners:

> The earth is our mother; we are now on it with the Great Spirit above us. It is good . . . I loved my towns, my cornfields and the home of my people. I fought for it. It is now yours; keep it as we did; it will produce you good crops.[2]

And so it has. We have grown rich from the good crops of this land. But our pride in holding this land is not due solely to the material benefits we have reaped from our temporary stewardship. Increasingly, in an urban society, we grow more appreciative of what it means to be possessed by the pastoral. Black Hawk's full truth, given in pride, of belonging to this land is becoming more meaningful to many Iowans today than is Ruth Suckow's half-truth, given in humility, of being so dully rural. In this age of extremes, we can now boast proudly of the golden mean that is Iowa.

2. Quoted in Cyrenus Cole, *I Am a Man: The Indian Black Hawk,* (Iowa City: State Historical Society of Iowa, 1938), p. 269.

Suggestions for Further Reading

The first comprehensive history of Iowa was Benjamin F. Gue's four-volume *History of Iowa* (New York: Century History Company, 1903). Abolitionist, editor, farmer, educational leader, and politician, Lieutenant-Governor Gue may have been something of a Renaissance man, but unfortunately that versatility of talents did not include literary style. He was no Thomas Hutchinson or Jeremy Belknap, chronicling the history of a state in which he played a major role. Only the most determined student of Iowa history would today be persistent enough to read through this multivolume work to find the useful information that is there. The most recent and by far the best general history of Iowa is Leland Sage's *A History of Iowa* (Ames: Iowa State University Press, 1974). It is highly recommended to anyone interested in reading a short, well-written history of the state, although, as with Gue, the emphasis here is on political rather than on economic or social history.

Some of the early travel books and guidebooks to the state provide fascinating reading. They present a picture of the open prairie land as it must have appeared to the first immigrants. The best of these are Albert M. Lea, *Notes on the Wisconsin Territory* (Philadelphia: H. S. Tanner, 1836); J. B. Newhall, *A Glimpse of Iowa in 1846* (Burlington: W. D. Skillman, 1846); and John Plumbe, *Sketches of Iowa and Wisconsin* (St. Louis: Chambers, Harris and Knapp, 1839). Fortunately, all of these rare volumes have been reprinted by the State Historical Society of Iowa, Iowa City (hereafter referred to as SHSI), and are readily available in most libraries.

SHSI has also over the past fifty years published its Biographical Series, with the major attention given to Iowa politicians. Although uneven in quality, this series contains some fine biographical studies. Particularly notable are Leland Sage's *William Boyd Allison* (1956) and Mildred Throne's *Cyrus Clay Carpenter,* published posthumously in 1974.

Agriculture has from the beginning been the dominant economic and social interest of the state. Earle D. Ross's *Iowa Agriculture* (Iowa City: SHSI, 1951) is indispensable for anyone who would understand Iowa. The more recent studies of Allan G. Bogue, *From Prairie to Cornbelt* (Chicago: University of Chicago Press, 1963) and Robert P. Swierenga, *Pioneers and Profits* (Ames: Iowa State University Press, 1968) add important data to but in no way replace Ross's study. For an understanding of what it has meant to be a farmer in Iowa during good times and bad, *Years of Struggle: The Farm Diary of Elmer G. Powers, 1931–1936,* edited by H. Roger Grant and L. Edward Purcell (Ames: Iowa State University Press, 1976) and Carl Hamilton's *In No Time At All* (Ames: Iowa State University Press, 1974) are both richly informative in content and delightfully personal in style.

Anyone with the time and patience to go laboriously through the back files of Iowa's three major historical journals, *The Palimpsest* and *The Iowa Journal of History and Politics* (which unfortunately ceased publication in 1961) published by the SHSI in Iowa City and the *Annals of Iowa,* published by the Iowa State Historical Department in Des Moines, will be amply rewarded by the many excellent and highly readable articles on Iowa history. A more convenient collection of short monographs on various aspects of Iowa history is available in *Patterns and Perspectives in Iowa History,* edited by Dorothy Schwieder (Ames: Iowa State University Press, 1973).

These few brief suggestions for further reading are quite obviously not intended to serve as a general bibliography. Those who are interested in pursuing particular topics related to the state's history and culture should consult the *Iowa History Reference Guide,* edited by William J. Petersen (Iowa City: SHSI, 1952). Every conceivable subject from Animals and Birds of Iowa to the Weather and Winnebago Indians has its own bibliographic section. This guide, now twenty-five years old, is sorely in need of being brought up to date. The guide would be more useful if, in the revision, it could be carefully annotated.

Index